"The teachings of the Buddha a ... ...ipaksa
has a canny way of making them so for us. He teaches here the best
prescription I know for true happiness. What could be more basic,
and totally transformative, than conscious breathing, mindful sitting
and walking, and opening the heart? *Wildmind* brings us directly to
that awakened wisdom of our true nature. Taste and see!"
—Gary Gach, author of *The Complete Idiot's Guide to Buddhism*

"Of great help to people interested in meditation and an inspiring
reminder to those on the path."
—Joseph Goldstein, co-founder of the Insight Meditation Society and
author of *One Dharma: The Emerging Western Buddhism*

"Bodhipaksa has written a beautiful and very accessible introduction
to meditation. He guides us through all the basics of mindfulness and
also loving-kindness meditations with the voice of a wise, kind, and
patient friend."
—Dr. Lorne Ladner, author of *The Lost Art of Compassion*

"Bodhipaksa is a meditation teacher of years and it shows. Filled
with case studies, practical advice, and uplifting quotes, *Wildmind* is
one of the most comprehensive and accessible books on the subject
– covering everything from preparation for meditation and the
meditation process, to the many practical benefits of meditation in
everyday life."
—Maggie Hamilton, *MindBodySpirit* Magazine

"I am warmly grateful for all your inspired work, wisdom, and
profoundly human compassion."
—Caroline

"I feel the most valuable thing I will be taking away from this class is
that I can change almost any situation and my feelings about how I
react. I find myself being so much more understanding in almost every
life situation."
—Ginny

Wildmind

A step-by-step guide to meditation

Bodhipaksa

Windhorse Publications

Published by
Windhorse Publications
169 Mill Road
Cambridge
CB1 3AN
UK
info@windhorsepublications.com
www.windhorsepublications.com

Cover design by Stefanie Ine Grewe
Printed by Bell & Bain Ltd., Glasgow

Illustrations by Jacob Corn www.jacobcorn.co.uk
Photographs on pages 1, 19, 47, 83, 183, 217 and 309
by Amoghavira www.amoghavira.com
Gatha on page 210 from *The Blooming of the Lotus* by Thich Nhat Hanh, © 1993 Thich Nhat Hanh,
reprinted by kind permission of Beacon Press, Boston.

British Library Cataloguing in Publication Data:
A catalogue record for this book is available from the British Library.

ISBN: 9781 899579 91 4

As this work is not of a scholarly nature, Pali and Sanskrit words have been transliterated
without their diacritical marks.

Contents

3

Mind like the clear blue sky: breathing with awareness

4

In beauty may I walk: walking meditation

5

Heart like the sun: cultivating loving-kindness

6

Metta in daily life

About the author

Bodhipaksa was born Graeme Stephen in Dundee, Scotland, in 1961. He has been practising Buddhist meditation for twenty years, and became a member of the Triratna Buddhist Order in 1993. He has been teaching meditation for more than ten years, including two years in the University of Montana's religious studies program. While at the University of Montana, he developed approaches to teaching meditation online using the multimedia capabilities of the Internet, and he now runs a thriving online meditation teaching service called Wildmind at www.wildmind.org.

Previous publications include *Vegetarianism* (Windhorse Publications, 1999), an account of the relationship between Buddhism and vegetarianism, and 'Reinventing the Wheel' – a chapter in *Spiritual Goods: Faith Traditions and the Practice of Business* (Philosophy Documentation Center, Virginia 2001), an overview of Buddhist business ethics. Bodhipaksa holds an interdisciplinary Master's degree in Buddhism and business studies.

He is currently working on another meditation book, also based on the material he has written for Wildmind. He is married and lives with his partner, Shrijñana, and Yoda their pet iguana, in New Hampshire, USA.

Acknowledgements

I would have nothing to offer if it were not for what has been passed on to me by others. I would like first to thank Urgyen Sangharakshita, whose spiritual teachings introduced me to Buddhism and gave my life new meaning and direction. May he have long life and continued happiness.

I am also indebted in particular to several members of the Triratna Buddhist Order who have been a source of instruction on meditation. The most notable of these teachers have been Vajradaka, Tejananda, and Kamalashila, whose book, *Meditation: The Buddhist Way of Tranquillity and Insight*, I would highly recommend, and which has been a source of advice and inspiration.

In addition there have been many other meditation teachers whose ideas, imagery, and practices have found their way by a process of osmosis into my own teaching and into this book. I thank you all, although you are too numerous to mention by name.

I'd also like to thank all of my students over the years. You have stimulated me, forced me to clarify my thinking, and on many occasions shamed and inspired me into taking my own practice more seriously. Without you I could never have written this book, and I owe you a debt of gratitude for sharing in the process of learning with me.

Particular thanks go to Tejananda, Henry Harlow, and Gillian Golding, who read this book in manuscript form and gave me valuable feedback.

Lastly, I'd like to thank all of my friends in the Dharma who have supported me, challenged me, tested me, encouraged me, shown me patience and kindness, and been incredibly generous in many ways, small and large. Again you are too numerous to mention. You are all greatly appreciated.

introduction

---

why wildmind?

Wildmind versus 'wild mind'

Wildmind might seem an odd name for a book on meditation. Isn't meditation about calming down and relaxing? Isn't it about 'taming your mind' rather than letting it run wild? Yes and no.

There are two kinds of wild mind. The first is what you might expect. Most of us, when we first learn to meditate, are shocked to discover how unruly our minds are. Thoughts come and go at bewildering speed, seemingly unconnected to one another. The wild mind (the normal state of mind for many of us) is said to be like an excited monkey in a fruit tree, discarding one half-eaten fruit in favour of the next temptation. Our minds can seem like butterflies, flitting from one flower to another, never settling. Our minds can seem overwhelmed by a chaotic flood of images, memories, and imaginings. Our thoughts can seem like leaves swirling in an autumn gale. Our emotions can seem like a storm at sea. And although our mind is wonderfully alive, this unruly experience is shallow and unsatisfactory, at worst deeply unpleasant, disturbing, even destructive. It's this kind of wildness – even craziness – that we rightly want to get away from.

But there is another kind of wildness that we can experience. If we patiently work at calming those unruly forces, we find that rather than our mind becoming less alive, it becomes more vital and energetic. We can cultivate a mind that's as spacious as a clear blue sky, as still as a lake at dawn, as stable as a mountain, and as full of subtle currents of energy as a forest is full of wild creatures.

The second kind of wild mind has the grandeur and beauty of true wilderness, and is a source of richness and fulfilment. It's a place we can spend the rest of our lives exploring. For the sake of clarity, I'll call this our Wildmind (one word, with a capital W), in contrast to the chaotic kind of wildness, which I'll call our wild mind (two words, no capitals). Our wild mind has a kind of beauty to it as well, but the attraction is of superficial excitement. When a lake is whipped up by the restless wind, it's not possible to see into the depths. Similarly, when our mind is disturbed by chaotic and seemingly untameable energies, we live out of touch with our depths. When our mind is full of 'sound and fury', we cannot hear the subtler and intuitive voices within that can guide us wisely through life, for that sound and fury does indeed often signify nothing.

Of course, our wild mind and our Wildmind aren't really two separate minds. These are descriptions of two ways in which our mind can function. If the waves on the ocean are our wild mind, then the Wildmind is the ocean itself. The waves are not separate from the ocean, just the most superficial manifestation of it. Our Wildmind reaches down into the depths beneath our wild mind, just as the deeps of the ocean are untouched by storms above. With patience, you can learn to tap into those depths, and live with more calmness, focus, and energy. You can learn to be more alive, more loving, more purposeful, more creative.

> **"We can cultivate a mind that's as spacious as a clear blue sky, as still as a lake at dawn."**

You can learn to be as patient as sky that allows clouds to pass through without obstruction. You can learn to be as steady as a mountain. You can learn to have the persistent energy of a stream that wears away granite rocks over countless millennia. You can learn to see into your depths and discover inner riches that you never suspected. That is what this book aims to help you to do.

Our limited wild minds can never help us to live a truly meaningful life. Much of the frantic running around of our minds represents a preoccupation with the trivial – worries about status and image and the possession of ephemeral objects. We can get caught up in sidestepping the deeper existential issues of our lives, pretending that our pain – and even impermanence itself – can be avoided if we just refuse to slow down. The Wildmind, on the other hand, is not afraid to look suffering in the face. It sees pain as an opportunity to learn, not a sign of failure. It embraces impermanence because in a fixed universe there would be no freedom.

A meaningful, satisfying, and fulfilling life is not a life that is free from suffering; it is a life in which we face suffering with mindful dignity, learn what we can, and thus progress. Much of the modern anguish we experience is actually caused by our inability mindfully to experience simpler forms of pain. With the spaciousness and freedom that comes with the experience of the Wildmind, we are better able to understand, forgive, let go, and move on. This does lead to greater happiness as well as to a sense of a life well lived, but it does not imply a shallow lack of pain. A life without challenges and stresses is hardly worth living.

"You can learn to see into your depths and discover inner riches that you never suspected.""

How is your wild mind connected to your Wildmind? There is no magic wand you can wave to change your heart and mind. We live in a world where we want quick fixes, some new tool that will change us now, as quickly as a new hairstyle can change our appearance. But in learning to change deep-rooted patterns of thought and emotion, there are no quick solutions. These things take time and, like some of the best things in life, this kind of change requires patience and application. This book won't totally transform you overnight, so if you're looking for a quick fix, you can do one of two things: you can return this book to the bookshop (I'm sure they'll understand) or you can take the first step in developing patience and commitment to personal change by beginning to entertain the insight that good things take time.

The concept of Wildmind is becoming something of a tradition in Western Buddhism. Natalie Goldberg is the Buddhist author of a book on creative writing called *Wild Mind*. She teaches how to get past the superficial inner critic that can inhibit our creativity and learn to free our creative energies by tapping into deeper and more creative levels of our experience.

All too often we stifle our creativity with relatively superficial worries. Many writers have experienced the sheer terror of the blank page, which looks so daunting in its perfection. A thought for a first line arises, and the hand makes a movement, but the inner critic thinks, 'No, that's not good enough.' The critic is worried about what your mother would think, what your children would think, what someone who will never meet you might think. I don't mean to be disrespectful to our inner critics; after all, we need a sense of discrimination, but we often end up failing to take the risk of being creative – in life as well as in writing – in case we fail.

Goldberg teaches us how to set the critic to one side so that we can freely create. Keep your hand moving, lose control, don't think, don't worry about punctuation and spelling. Once you've created, then is the time for your critic to be brought out to tidy things up, to reshuffle text and delete unnecessary words. The source of your creative power is 'raw, full of energy, alive, and hungry', and Goldberg's book is a very nearly indispensable guide to learning to tap into that level of your mind so that you can write more freely. I found it invaluable when I first started writing.

The Buddhist teacher and environmentalist Gary Snyder also uses this term. He points to the wilderness as our teacher, and says, 'The lessons we learn from the wild become the etiquette of freedom.'[1] He suggests that we need to get below the superficial 'civilized' level of our consciousness. 'The depths of mind, the unconscious, are our inner wilderness areas,' he tells us, and we have to experience ourselves more deeply in order to learn from them.[2]

Snyder points out that no one regulates a wilderness, and yet it's not chaotic. Wilderness is self-organizing and balanced. Dictionaries talk about the wild in terms of what it is not (at least in human terms): the wild is 'not tame', 'not cultivated', 'unruly'. Snyder prefers to see it on its own terms. Wild animals are 'free agents, each with its own endowments'. Wild plants are 'self-propagating, self-maintaining, flourishing in accord with innate qualities'. Wild behaviour is 'artless, free, spontaneous, unconditioned … expressive, physical, openly sexual, ecstatic'.

While the dictionary sees things from the point of view of the superficial critic, Snyder looks at wilderness as an insider – as part of the creative force of the wilderness itself. He sees his positive and appreciative definitions of wildness as very close to how the Chinese define the term *dao*, the way of nature. He also points out that the dao is 'not far from the Buddhist term *Dharma* with its original senses of forming and firming'.[3]

We all have our inner wilderness (even if it has been kept in check so long that we've forgotten about it). Snyder calls this inner wilderness area 'the wild mind' (what I've called the Wildmind), and suggests that we need to learn to trust in the self-disciplined elegance of the Wildmind. Our inner wilderness areas are, like the wild, not chaotic, excessive, or crazy, but free and spontaneous, and abundantly creative.

I agree, and this book is largely a tribute to the work of Gary Snyder and Natalie Goldberg. This is a guidebook to the inner wilderness. It's a guide to discovering, or rediscovering, our innate exuberance, emotional self-reliance, and spontaneity, free from the restrictive conditions of habit and fear.

The unexamined life ...

The unexamined life is not worth living. (Socrates)

According to Buddhist teachings, our minds are inherently pure and luminous. Sometimes, when we're struggling with the stress of uncooperative children, or feeling frazzled trying to keep up with the unrealistic expectations of our employers, this can be hard to believe. But the same teachings go on to say that our inherently pure and luminous minds are contaminated with 'defilements' – those very states of stress, anger, and self-doubt that plague our lives. Perhaps this is more familiar territory.

The aim of Buddhist meditation is to clear away the 'defilements' so that we can experience ourselves – more deeply and more truly – in our primordial purity, clarity, and freedom of mind. Meditation helps us to cut through the agonizing clutter of superficial mental turmoil and allows us to experience more spacious and joyful states of mind. It is this pure and luminous state that I call your Wildmind.

You have almost certainly had experiences that are close to the stillness, joy, and expansiveness that are the nature of your Wildmind. You may have experienced your Wildmind while in nature, for example. Your Wildmind is the mind that resonates with nature. It is the part of you that experiences awe and reverence in the face of whatever is greater than you. It is the childlike part of you that experiences a profound wonder at the mystery that anything is, and – even more mysteriously – that you can be aware of it.

A friend of mine once said that the reason he loved being in nature was that he could look at the vastness and power of the natural world and know that there was no way you could – in any meaningful way – own or possess it. Nature is far bigger than we are, and will outlast every one of us. It can't be owned, but it can be emulated. It is possible to look at the vastness and power of the natural world and seek to pattern ourselves after it. Although nature cannot be our possession, it can be our mentor.

You can strive to have a mind as spacious and pure as the vast dome of the heavens. You can strive to have a mind as clear and still as a lake at dawn, which reflects the world undistorted. You can cultivate a heart that radiates love and compassion as the sun shines its life-giving warmth and light to all, without discrimination.

"Your Wildmind is the mind that resonates with nature."

Your Wildmind is the mind that resonates with the elements and nature, but it is also your 'natural mind' in the sense that it is your own truer nature. It is the state of pure awareness inherent in all of us, which lies in the depths, waiting to be revealed through patient purification of the mind. In the Nyingma Tibetan tradition, they call the Wildmind *rigpa* – the state of primordial radiant awareness. (Other Tibetan schools use the term *mahamudra*.) *Rigpa*, or Wildmind, is contrasted with *sems*, which is the superficial, turbulent aspect of our mind in which too many of us are caught up. The wild mind, or *sems*, is like waves on the surface of water. When water is disturbed, it is impossible to see into its depths; the surface is chopped into ever-changing patterns that prevent clear vision. But when the surface waters are stilled, the depths – which have always been still – are accessible. The object of Buddhist practice is freedom from the disturbed mental states on the surface, so that we may live from the spontaneous, profoundly intuitive, lucid depths.

We do not enter our inner wilderness areas all at once. We cannot get to know the wilderness on a day-trip. As we begin to practise we may at first simply enjoy a peaceful respite from our tendencies to create suffering for ourselves. We may notice a little more calmness in our lives. We may notice that we lose our tempers less often. We may start to notice that someone we used to regard as being decidedly irritable is now behaving more decently towards us.

Later, we might begin to have important insights into our lives. It's as if we've been climbing a steep path, seeing little but the ground in front of us, and then we turn round and find ourselves awestruck by the new perspectives open to us. When we have such insights we find that we change quite rapidly, and old and restrictive habits may start to drop away without apparent effort.

About the same time, we may find that we enter states of mind previously unknown to us. One day, while sitting meditating, we find we've slipped into a state of quiet bliss in which there is a complete absence of inner tension, and where our minds have mysteriously stopped chasing after things that were obsessively compelling just a few moments ago. There's a feeling of lightness and clarity, and rightness — as if we've come home.

"We cannot get to know the wilderness on a day-trip."

Eventually, so the sages tell us, we'll learn to be comfortable with discomfort, we'll be able to accept the uncertain nature of the universe as a gift, we'll have explored the fiercest and most frightening aspects of our inner wilderness and discovered that there never was anything to fear. We'll rejoice in the openness of existence and feel an overwhelming sense of compassion for those who run around like rats in a maze. We'll be living completely and congruently from the depth of our insight, and helping others will be our play.

In this way we'll come, stage by stage, exploration by exploration, to know ourselves completely.

Seeking the beauty within

Every aspect of ourselves other than the Wildmind is relatively shallow, trivial, and unsatisfactory. When we are at our most inspired and creative – those are the times when the surface has stilled and the Wildmind is becoming manifest.

It can be a source of tremendous self-confidence to know that there is a part of you untouched by anything you have ever done, no matter how deluded and harmful it might have been. When I was younger, and had been trying to practise meditation and Buddhism for a little over a year, I went on a four-week intensive meditation retreat, on which we spent about seven hours a day meditating. I say I had been trying to practise meditation and Buddhism, but it would be truer to say that to a large extent I had been trying to convince others (and perhaps even myself) that I was practising Buddhism and my practice was very superficial.

At that time I felt very unsure of myself, very insecure, and I tried to compensate by adopting a persona, which literally means 'mask', of course. This persona consisted of trying to appear very knowledgeable about Buddhism, and trying to impress people with my intelligence. I suppose what I wanted was for people to be impressed and therefore to like me. Of course what actually happened was that I was a royal pain in the butt, throwing my arrogant opinions around and being critical of everyone (especially those who were far wiser than me), and finding fault in everything. My strategy for being liked and admired was – as is so often the case – profoundly counter-productive.

Things happen when you meditate for seven hours a day, day after day. You are forced to face up to who you really are. You try to run and hide from your own experience through falling asleep and becoming distracted in fantasy, but ultimately there is no avoiding that person with whom, above all others, you feel uncomfortable – your own self. And I did not like my self – with a vengeance. Eventually something had to give. Towards the end of the retreat I had a powerful experience in which I was stewing in my own negativity, running over the details of a conflict I had stirred up with another person, trying to justify myself, trying to look at it from every angle but straight on, convinced there was a way that I could be the one who was in the right. I must have invested a huge amount of energy in keeping the truth at bay – the simple and unavoidable truth that I had been arrogant and insensitive to another person.

Eventually, I ran out of energy with which to fight the truth, and ran out of places to hide, and the truth came crashing through my defensive systems and swamped me. I felt awful. I felt myself to be completely worthless. I felt utterly lonely and desolate. I felt an unbearable weight of suffering descend upon me. To be honest, I had never felt so low. Tears streamed down my face as I sat in a row of silently meditating figures in a long, low candlelit shrine-room. Some of the others were smiling blissfully. Their meditation was going well and they were in their own private heavens. On the shrine, the Buddha statue sat serenely, surrounded by flowers and bathed in fragrant incense. In my small corner of the shrine-room I was in a very different realm. I had constructed for myself a very potent and virulent hell.

Yet there was a sense of something else as well. There was a faint, almost imperceptible, feeling of relief. It was the relief, I now think, of having let go the tremendous effort it had taken to blind myself to the truth of how badly I had behaved.

Then an extraordinary thing happened. I was sitting there, wrapped in my blanket against the chill air, the smell of incense in my nostrils, tears wetting my cheeks, and I had a sort of vision. I say it was a 'sort of' vision because it was an internal rather than external experience, but it hit me just as strongly as any external vision would have.

What I saw was this: my true nature was a flawless, multifaceted jewel, hanging in the soft velvet darkness of space. The jewel was incomparably lovely, and it was the most essential thing about me, at the core of my being. But it was soiled, somewhat stained and dusty. These dust marks were the normal faults and foibles that I, as a normal human being, had. But for some reason – perhaps due to some quirk of my conditioning – I could not accept these faults. I desperately wanted to be pure and flawless and I was not. I was ashamed of my faults. I felt I couldn't live with them.

The most sensible thing to do, of course, would have been to get rid of those faults – to work at polishing the jewel – but I was so ashamed of having faults that I tried to deny they were there, and if they weren't there, how could I work to get rid of them? My alternative strategy – the one that got me into my own private hell – was to try to 'mask' these faults with my persona. I tried to pretend that I had no faults, I tried to convince myself that I knew everything, I tried to rationalize away my anger, I tried to convince myself and others that I was a serious seeker after truth. And that was the biggest irony of all, because the truth was something I did not want to face. In this vision I realized that what I had been doing was trying to hide the dirt on the jewel by applying cosmetics, and what I had created was a ludicrous ball of muck. I had been getting further and further from my own true nature by pretending to be someone I was not.

❝Once you realize your normal states of mind are just the superficial dust and grime covering the essentially spotless diamond of your being – there is no turning back. There is no other way to live.❞

It then became obvious to me that what I had to do was reverse the process that I had put so much energy into. I had to stop trying to conceal my own imperfections, and instead strip them away to reveal the inherent purity that had always been there. That is the task I have been engaged in, falteringly, in the years since: polishing the jewel of my own being to allow its natural radiance and beauty to shine through. And it is no false modesty to say that there is a long way to go before all the grime is gone.

All any of us has to do is face up to the task of working patiently and with compassionate determination to polish the jewel of our being, clearing away the dust and grime and letting the pure light of our own nature shine through. This is a task that requires a degree of heroism.

Sometimes it seems that it would be easier just to give up, but once a certain degree of awareness has been gained – once you realize your normal states of mind are just the superficial dust and grime covering the essentially spotless diamond of your being – there is no turning back. There is no other way to live. As the Dutch philosopher Spinoza said, 'To be what we are, and to become what we are capable of becoming, is the only end of life.'

It is my hope that this book and the Wildmind website will be tools to help others find the purity in the depth of their own beings, and to live in full awareness of the loving and lucid warmth of their own Wildminds.

No easy path

If you want a quick and easy path to greater happiness, you've picked the wrong universe to live in. Since it may take some time to find a universe in which personal change is swift and straightforward, you may want to bite the bullet and experiment with letting go of any assumptions that you're going to be able to change without doing any work.

This isn't to say that there are not great joys to be found on the path. In fact, although changing has its challenges it also brings great joys – just as a hike in the countryside is both hard work and enjoyable. But the challenges are definitely there. Sometimes your patience is going to be tested. Sometimes you will despair at the rate at which you are changing. Sometimes you're going to be plain confused. Sometimes you're going to feel like giving up.

These obstacles are not really obstacles at all. They are not rocks blocking your way, but stepping-stones to change. They are opportunities to get to know yourself better, and to develop fortitude, courage, and patience.

Your difficulties are going to be your greatest teachers, for we often learn most about ourselves when we are stretched to our limits – or to what we think are our limits, since those limitations often turn out to be illusory. We are all capable of far more than we know. Having our patience challenged is an opportunity to expand our understanding of what we are capable of. It is a call to a greater depth of understanding and acceptance of ourselves and others, and a call to let go of resistance to change.

Despair at the rate of change we are experiencing is an opportunity to become more aware of our preconceptions about what we think should happen, and an opportunity to learn acceptance.

“If you want a quick and easy path to greater happiness, you've picked the wrong universe to live in.”

A true artist has to know his or her materials intimately, and understand how they will perform under various conditions. We have, as developing human beings, to learn the nature of the material with which we are working, and in meditation our material is our own mind. It would be wonderful if the nature of our minds was such that we could flick a switch and be happy, but that's not how things are. Despair arises when we have a false understanding of how quickly we can change or the conditions necessary for change. This is obviously one of the main areas in which we can learn through meditation.

Doubt and confusion can be looked at as a healthy part of change rather than experiences of failure. Confusion arises when we leave behind one set of preconceptions and suppositions without having yet found a way to make sense of what is going on. We've let go of a false certainty, and are on the way to finding a new and truer understanding. That is a sign of progress, not failure.

Ultimately, all suffering is a message that we have something to learn; that there is some skill we have not yet mastered, some idea we have that is false, or a pattern of behaviour that is not delivering the results that we expect.

In one psychological discipline, they say that in communication there is no failure, only feedback. I believe this is true in meditation. If what we experience in meditation is not to our liking, it is not a sign that we are not cut out to be meditators, or that we should give up or find a different meditation practice, but that we have something more to learn. Not only that; we are often being given an indication of what it is that we must learn.

This feedback can be very precise. Meditating can be a bit like scrutinizing our lives with a microscope. When we repeatedly experience tiredness in meditation, this can teach us about the need to look after ourselves and to guard our sources of nourishment. When our minds are making lists and anxiously planning, we can see that we need to become more organized in our daily lives. When we find that we are spending our meditation mulling things over, this can teach us about the need to set aside more time for reflection. Inner arguments show us that there are important conflicts that we have yet to resolve, whether by forgiving, and letting go of grievances, or by sorting things out with another person.

The concept of failure in meditation is profoundly disempowering. It leads to giving up. In meditation there is no failure, only feedback. Remember that your difficulties will turn out to be your teachers, your obstacles will turn out to be stepping-stones, and that the sometimes hard and rocky path of meditation will turn out to be the way to greater fulfilment and deeper contentment. Learning is not always easy, but it is always beneficial in the long term. Let go of the idea of failure, and embrace the notion that everything you experience in meditation is feedback, and the path will be immeasurably more enjoyable and enriching.

How to use this book

Feel free to use this book in any way you want. It is a playground for the mind and spirit. The following are only suggestions.

❖ This book is aimed primarily at complete beginners in meditation, but it can also act as a refresher for those who have been meditating for some time. All of us find our meditation becoming stale from time to time, and need fresh approaches to help us recapture the openness and wonder of the beginner.

❖ Meditation is a skill, and like all skills is learned only through practice. You will have to complete the exercises to gain the benefits. Even ten minutes of meditation a day can make a big difference to your life. So I would suggest that you do not read this book as if it were a novel. Make sure you take time to do the exercises.

❖ If a book is structured like a novel, most people will read it like a novel. Reading a book in that way isn't very helpful when it is teaching a skill, since you'll forget most of what you've read before you have a chance to practise it. The reason this book has been written in short sections is to encourage you to pause regularly, and reflect upon or practise the content. I suggest you read only as much as you need in order to do a few minutes of meditation. Then meditate. Take some time for yourself and actually do some meditation, following one of the exercises. The book will still be here when you come back.

❖ There is a companion website for this book: www.wildmind.org. Much of the material in this book can also be found on the website (and there is material on the site that is not in the book). The website also contains RealAudio files that will guide you, stage by stage, through the practices that we teach. You will also find Web addresses in some of the instructional sections of this book.

If you enter them in your browser, you will be taken straight to the guided meditations. You will need a program called RealPlayer to listen to these files, which you can download for free from the Wildmind website.

❖ Two of the meditation practices are in several stages. The Mindfulness of Breathing has four stages, and the Metta Bhavana has five. (The Walking Meditation has no formal stages.) I suggest learning these two practices one stage at a time. Each stage is a meditation in itself. If you are learning these practices for the first time, there is no advantage whatsoever in skipping ahead so that you learn all the stages at once. If you're an experienced meditator, however, it might be more appropriate to dip into the parts of the book that are most relevant to your needs.

Take your time learning the exercises, and frequently come back to the book to explore. You'll probably have some questions, and the book is organized to answer the most common ones. Some of the earlier material will make more sense once you've spent some time practising what's in the later sections, so it can be useful to go back and reread the earlier sections with the new perspectives you've gained through practical experience.

1

the examined life
an introduction to meditation

An informal description of meditation

Meditation is a natural method of working with your mind so that you can experience contentment and live a more fulfilling life in order to benefit yourself and others. It involves the cultivation of positive states of mind such as love, contentment, calmness, awareness, and patience. Through meditation we gradually change our habitual mental states so that they become increasingly characterized by these positive states of mind. As our mental states change, so does our view of the world. As our mind becomes calmer, for example, it becomes easier for us to see the connections between actions and consequences, for ourselves and for others. So meditation, as well as helping us to develop a calmer mind and a more loving heart, also helps us to develop wisdom – for what is wisdom but the ability to discriminate between actions that will lead to suffering and those that lead to greater fulfilment?

We all act out of negative states of mind at times – often to a greater extent than we realize. It often seems that negative emotions like anxiety 'just happen' to us, and frequently we aren't even aware that we have any choice as to how we respond emotionally. There may be circumstances in which you typically experience fear or anger; for example, when your boss summons you to talk about your performance, or when you are criticized. But this doesn't have to be the case. Even if you haven't yet realized it, you have the ability to choose your responses to the situations in which you find yourself. None of us has to be dominated by anxiety, or ill will, or self-doubt, or any of the other negative emotions that undermine us and interfere with our ability to be happy and fulfilled. Meditation helps us to develop greater awareness – or mindfulness – so that we realize we have these choices.

Mindfulness is a key term in Buddhist meditation. To exercise choice in the way we have been talking about, you have to develop a greater degree of purposeful awareness, or mindfulness. With mindfulness, you can become more aware of the way your habitual negative emotions are sparked off by external events. First of all you start to realize that much of the time 'you' are not in control at all. Instead, your actions are driven by habitual patterns of responses. This realization is sometimes rather painful. It can be hard to acknowledge the extent to which we are like string puppets controlled by an unseen puppet master. At this point people often turn away from meditation – the newly discovered awareness of our unawareness can be so painful that we'd rather not acknowledge it; we'd rather retreat into unawareness again. Of course, hiding from our problems doesn't help us to deal with them. In fact it just makes them worse. Meditation involves facing up to ourselves, even when it's uncomfortable. So meditation usually requires some degree of patience and courage.

"Meditation, as well as helping us to develop a calmer mind and a more loving heart, also helps us to develop wisdom."

So why choose to face these challenges? Why not just go about our lives in the way we always have done? Actually, we're perfectly free to do that. You should feel completely free to put this book down, walk away, and never think about meditation again, but you'd be missing out on some very great rewards.

When you choose a course of action, you also choose the consequences of that action. If you act out of selfishness, or ill will, or fear, you will experience the often unpleasant and limiting outcomes to which those emotions lead. But if you choose their opposites, a whole new world opens up. If you choose to take the challenge of becoming more aware of yourself, you will find that you begin to develop a whole new outlook on life. You'll find that your life becomes more fulfilling and rich. Your life will become a sort of artistic creation.

Possibly one of the first things you will notice when you start to experience the benefits of meditation is an increased sense of freedom. You will learn that there is a gap between stimulus (your boss saying he'd like to have a word about your performance) and response (your anxiety), and that you have the freedom to choose your responses – for example patience rather than anger, or calmness rather than fear.

This doesn't necessarily happen all at once. Sometimes we only become aware in retrospect that we have acted out a habit – we realize that we've just lost our temper, or that we've said 'yes' when we meant 'no', or that we've raided the fridge yet again, despite the diet we swore we'd stick to. In fact, it's often the case that we don't recognize our habits until after the fact. Practising mindfulness helps us first of all to become more aware after the fact, then to extend that awareness into the habitual action itself, and then to become aware of the potential action even before it takes place. As we develop our awareness in this way we start to have more and more choice and freedom.

"You'll find that your life becomes more fulfilling and rich. Your life will become a sort of artistic creation."

Over time, you will begin to shape your personality so that negative emotions become less and less part of the way you are, and positive emotions such as calm, contentment, joy, and love, become a natural part of the way you feel and act. You'll learn to be more patient, kind, and confident.

You'll also find that the world responds to you in a different way as you begin to change the way you act. Our ill will, for example, sets up patterns of reaction in other people – leading us into a series of conflicts. Usually we don't consciously set out to be aggressive – our habits simply take over. We create these conflicts, and because we're not aware of our part in them we tend to blame the conflict on other people ('she made me angry'). But as we begin to become aware of our unhelpful emotional patterns and create the freedom to choose more creative states of mind, we find that much of the conflict around us just disappears.

I had one meditation student called Bill who worked in a supermarket in Missoula, Montana. He told me he used to have two or three angry customers approach him every day. Perhaps they were in a rush and couldn't find what they wanted. Not long after Bill started to meditate, he noticed that these customers would quickly calm down after they'd approached him. He'd discovered that it was possible for him to choose to respond to them in a friendly and compassionate manner, and the lack of aggression and the positively friendly qualities in Bill's responses had a calming effect, reminding his customers that they too had choices. Bill wasn't aware that he'd ever been unfriendly to customers, but something had shifted in his behaviour that his customers could respond to.

That's a powerful enough indication of how meditation can change your relationship with the world, but Bill went on to tell me that after a while he stopped having any angry customers at all! I suppose it's possible that they just went to other staff members, but my feeling is that the angry customers somehow calmed down even before reaching him.

Another friend of mine, Pat, who runs a health club, became interested in meditation after seeing the changes that had taken place in one of his employees. This woman had a reputation for being difficult to work with. She was very prickly and defensive. But over a period of a few weeks she seemed to mellow; she smiled more, and became easy to get on with. Pat asked whether this employee was on some kind of medication – it was the only way that he could imagine her changing so fast. It turned out that it was not medication but meditation that had caused such a profound change in her personality.

Many people have noticed similar changes taking place in the world as they themselves change. Not only do their relationships with strangers change, but their closest relationships become deeper and more satisfying. People start to like them more. Doors begin to open, and the world may start to seem full of opportunities instead of frustrations and barriers. Many people begin to discern underlying patterns that shape many of the choices they made in their lives. Once they have brought these patterns into consciousness, they can start to see more clearly in what direction their lives are moving, and begin to take advantage of opportunities in order to pursue their dreams more directly. For some people it's like wandering in the wilderness, not knowing whether the path they are following is taking them home, and then discovering to their surprise that they have been carrying a map and compass all the time! Meditation can help us to develop the clarity to know ourselves more deeply – including knowing not only who we are, but also who we are destined to become.

These changes may take time. When the spring comes, the various seeds that have overwintered in the shelter of the soil germinate at different times, and the plants they form grow at different rates. Meditation is not a quick fix. Some people will notice changes almost immediately, while others may experience change happening more slowly. Sometimes other people will notice changes in us before we do, while at other times we'll notice internal changes that others cannot yet discern. Sometimes we'll feel confused and unsure about what we're doing and whether anything is happening at all. I believe that this is all part of the process of learning.

> "Meditation can help us to develop the clarity to know ourselves more deeply – including knowing not only who we are, but also who we are destined to become."

The most exciting and far-reaching consequence of meditation does not rely on any kind of external validation – such as having people like and respect you, or discovering that people will go out of their way to help you. As the Irish playwright Oliver Goldsmith said, 'He who seeks only for applause from without, has all his happiness in another's keeping.'[4] It's dangerous to place our well-being in the hands of another, and a sign of spiritual maturity to take our happiness into our own hands. Ultimately, every individual must validate his or her own life. Meditation can bring more of a sense of meaning and purpose into life than anything else I know. The most satisfying thing I know of is not the benefit that comes from personal development, but the path of development itself. It's the journeying that brings the deepest satisfaction, not the individual sights you encounter along the way.

John Butler Yeats said, 'And happiness … what is it? I say it is neither virtue nor pleasure nor this thing or that, but simply *growth*. We are happy when we are growing. It is this primal law of all nature and the universe.'[5] Your life itself can have a far greater sense of meaning and purpose if you embark on this course of personal development, and if there are activities that already bring meaning and purpose into your life, then meditation can help to deepen the impact of those activities. Many musicians, dancers, writers, and sportspeople have discovered deeper levels of richness in their chosen field as a result of meditation.

Development is natural to us. We were born to grow and mature, but although it is our nature to grow, this does not always happen of its own accord. We have to learn to take responsibility for our lives, we have continually to remind ourselves of where we want to go, and ask ourselves if what we are doing right now is taking us there. So often in our day-to-day lives we get caught up in relatively unimportant busyness and forget this. Meditation is a means to personal growth and also provides the awareness through which we can make every activity in our lives an opportunity for development.

It may sound as though meditation is rather magical. I'm tempted to say that meditation is not magical – that in fact it's rather an ordinary activity – but it would be more useful to say that what meditation does is simply help us to be aware of the miracle of everyday life, of the magic of existence; for there is nothing more miraculous than the fact that we exist, that we are aware, and that we can use that awareness to benefit ourselves and others. I urge you to make the most of your existence. A tremendous opportunity is available to you right here and now – it's up to you whether you want to make full use of that opportunity.

The raisin experiment

So far, we've been in danger of taking too intellectual an approach.
You might have noticed that there has been nothing practical to do
for the last few pages and you might have slipped into the habitual
patterns that emerge when you read a novel: taking in a lot of
information, and being carried along by the narrative, without pausing
for reflection. (Of course that's not necessarily the best way to read
a novel but it's how we often do it.) So here's a simple, practical
exercise in awareness.

For this experiment, you'll need one raisin. If a raisin is not
available (or you're allergic to them) then a similar small dried fruit
will do, though it's best if it's something ordinary, not exciting. Go
and get one now, or if you don't have one put this book down and let
what you've read so far percolate into your mind and heart.

Now you have your raisin. Sitting comfortably, begin to explore
your raisin with your senses. You can look at the raisin, perhaps
holding it up to the light. You can smell it. You can touch it. You can
listen to it. Give the raisin your full attention.

Once you have spent a minute or two exploring your raisin, you
can put it into your mouth and continue to use your sense of touch to
explore its texture – your tongue is a very sensitive tool with which
to touch something.

Once you bite on the raisin, really pay attention to the taste,
and continue to notice the changing texture of the raisin as it bursts.
If your mind wanders, let go of the thoughts in which it's become
entangled and bring your attention gently back to your experience of
the raisin.

When you feel you've thoroughly explored your raisin, you can
swallow it, but continue to notice the lingering flavour in your mouth.

Make notes about what you have experienced. In particular, think
about how other experiences you've had of eating raisins have differed
from this one, and think about the implications of this experience for
other aspects of your life.

Raisin experiment results

Describe the experience of eating the raisin.

What (if anything) did you learn about raisins from this experiment?

How do other experiences that you've had of eating raisins differ from this one?

What implications does this experiment have for other aspects of your life?

What we can learn from the raisin experiment

'I liked taking the time with my raisin. It made me appreciate all the raisins I have gobbled in my lifetime. How quickly I gobble without smelling – then the line between taste and smell blurs and I don't know if I smell or if I just taste (even though it's both). Yesterday morning I walked to work and I thought of my raisin and took long breaths and long easy strides. The sun was out and the buildings and the people and the sounds seemed distant but at the same time more fully realized than they had been before. Everything was magnified and it made me smile.'

The words above were written by Wilma, an actress and student of mine from New York. They beautifully illustrate how we can learn and change and have our experience enriched by something as simple as eating a raisin with awareness, for this experiment is an exercise in mindfulness. It's a sort of meditation practice in its own right, in which we pay attention to something that normally we would hardly notice. It's significant that we chose a raisin, since we tend not to regard these as particularly glamorous, and eat them in a pretty utilitarian way. We could do this experiment with a delicious treat – like a Belgian chocolate truffle – but that would reinforce unhelpful attitudes, such as the assumption that to have a special experience you have to do something special.

This exercise can show us that the quality of attention that we bring to an experience has at least as much effect on the quality of the experience as does the object of our attention. Most people find the raisin much more interesting than they had expected. We tend to assume that raisins are pretty dull and we take them for granted, so it can be a real surprise to find that there's a lot of flavour in a raisin, and that a raisin's flavour is rather delightful.

One of the ways in which the quality of experience was different was that we slowed down and paid attention. Typically, we might eat raisins without much awareness – perhaps while doing something else such as reading or watching television. But we generally find that when we give something our full attention the experience is richer, more enjoyable, and more fulfilling. And this applies even when the object we are experiencing is not something we would normally think of as interesting.

“ This experiment is an exercise in mindfulness. ”

Following this experiment, people often realize that they normally don't really experience raisins very fully. Many people eat raisins by the handful rather than individually and don't chew them very thoroughly. Handful follows handful, and the raisins are swallowed so quickly that the flavour hardly has time to register on the tongue. If we slow down and pay attention, we realize there is a wealth of sensation to be gained. One of my students said, 'One raisin can have as much impact as many.' I would go further, and say that a single raisin eaten mindfully has more flavour than a hundred eaten inattentively. This contrasts markedly with our normal attitude that the more we cram into life, the richer our experience will be. This simple exercise of eating a raisin mindfully has important implications and lessons for the way that we live our entire lives!

Sometimes people notice that their thoughts wander during the practice. Eating the raisin reminds you of something, and one thought leads to another until you entirely forget what you were intending to do. This is normal. Wandering is what minds do. If noticing this disappointed you, then you have a valuable opportunity to learn how your expectations can create suffering for you, and how liberating it can be to let go of them. A lot of what we do in meditation involves bringing our awareness back to the breath after noticing that it has wandered.

The very fact of having the purpose of eating a raisin as a point of reference for our experience helps us to become more aware of what's going on in our thoughts and emotions. This is all part of the practice. Having a reference point like this helps us to slow down and become more aware of ourselves, and that awareness is the starting point for every journey of exploration and growth.

We will take this attitude of slowing down and paying attention into the Mindfulness of Breathing meditation, which we'll be learning shortly. We are paying attention principally to our breath, but inevitably we start noticing other aspects of ourselves – for example, we might notice how a 'perfectionist streak' can actually interfere with our effectiveness, or notice how saying the word 'patience' to ourselves can have an effect upon us. (Normally, words are like raisins – we use so many of them that we don't realize that just one can have a significant effect.)

So in slowing down and noticing the breath, we start to notice the whole dynamic of our being. We start to realize how we construct our experience through our habitual actions and expectations, and how we can reconstruct our experience so that we live a life more like the life we want to live.

In Buddhist practice we're aiming to treat every experience in life like we treated the raisin – as being potentially full of riches and opportunities for learning. As you begin to meditate and pay more attention to your experience, you will begin to develop important insights about your life.

A more formal definition of meditation

Meditation is an activity involving the cultivation of mindfulness and the application of methods to change ourselves in order that we become more fulfilled and better able to see Reality.

We'll break down this definition and look at what each part implies.

Meditation is an activity ...

Meditation is something active. It's a skill that has to be learned, much like walking, skiing, playing a musical instrument, or participating in a sport. Students often think they will be handed a technique that will somehow change them without their having to do any work. Change may be inevitable; but growth is intentional. This book will require you to work, and some of you might find it rather challenging at times, but you've learned other skills and you can learn this one too.

Another common misconception is that meditation is simply relaxation. This is partly true, in that meditation promotes relaxation, and indeed requires us to relax in order to do it well. But relaxation is simply an absence of unhelpful activity, while meditation requires both the absence of unhelpful activity and the active cultivation of beneficial activity. (These activities are mainly internal, mental activities, of course.)

... involving the cultivation of mindfulness ...

This is the first internal, beneficial activity that we undertake when we meditate.

Mindfulness, or the act of purposefully paying attention, plays a key role in meditation. In the raisin experiment you can develop a feel for how a more conscious awareness of your experience can lead to greater fulfilment. In the first meditation we will be learning – the Mindfulness of Breathing – we'll be cultivating the faculty of awareness through paying attention to the physical sensations of the breath.

Awareness is fundamental to meditation, and to all other Buddhist practices. Without awareness there is no possibility of practice in Buddhism. Principally, awareness brings choice. A very basic example of this is when you are physically tense. If your shoulders are tense, the only way you can relax them is to become aware of that fact. Without awareness, there is no choice; with awareness, there is choice. With choice comes the consciously directed change that is personal growth.

... and the application of methodologies to change ourselves ...

Once we have developed awareness, we have more choices available to us. But what choices do we make? In Buddhist meditation we choose to cultivate skilful states of mind, and to eradicate unskilful states of mind; this is another level of the practice of internal, beneficial activities. Skilful states of mind include those based on love, contentment, patience, kindness, and awareness. Unskilful states of mind include those based on craving, ill will, and unawareness. These words 'skilful' and 'unskilful' are technical terms that you will encounter if you read about Buddhist practice (particularly ethical practice).

Everything we do has one aim: that of finding greater fulfilment or happiness. The problem is, of course, that we're often deluded. We might think, for example, that being aggressive is going to make us happier, but the conflicts to which such behaviour gives rise are more likely to lead to unhappiness. So the basic message here is that we want to be happy, but we're not very good at it. This is why Buddhism talks about mental states as 'skilful' or 'unskilful'. When we have skill in a particular field, we have the ability to create what we want to create – a skilled potter can envisage a particular vase and then create it. In our lives we want to create happiness but we frequently fail – so you could say that we lack skill in creating happiness. So Buddhism talks about mental states as being skilful or unskilful rather than good or bad. In fact the Buddha went as far as to say that if mental states like hatred and selfishness did lead to happiness, he wouldn't have advised us to abandon them.

This book will introduce you to a wide range of methods you can use to develop skilful states of mind – those that lead to greater fulfilment – and to eradicate unskilful states of mind.

... in order that we become more fulfilled ...

The Buddha said that he taught only one thing: unsatisfactoriness and the way to end unsatisfactoriness. The underlying purpose of Buddhist meditation, as with all Buddhist practice, is to help us experience less unsatisfactoriness (what in Pali, which is the language of the earliest Buddhist scriptures, Buddhism calls *dukkha*) and more happiness.

In the Buddhist understanding of psychology, all dukkha is caused ultimately by our unskilful mental states. By eradicating unskilful mental states – greed, hatred, and delusion – we lessen and eventually eradicate *dukkha*. Furthermore, skilful mental states are seen as inherently more satisfactory than their unskilful counterparts. The raisin experiment again illustrates this. Normally when we eat raisins we are strongly influenced by the negative mental states of unawareness and craving.

The raisin experiment might seem rather trivial, and not relevant to life's major issues. But Buddhist practice deals with the seemingly trivial issues of eating, moving, talking, and so on, since these are the activities that make up the bulk of our lives. Every great journey is composed of innumerable small steps, and so it is with our lives. As Vincent van Gogh said, 'Great things are not done just by impulse, but are a series of small things put together.'[6] It is precisely by bringing awareness into ordinary activities that we become happier and more fulfilled – and perhaps even make of our lives a 'great thing'.

... and better able to see Reality

There are two types of meditation: *samatha* (calming) meditation, which has the purpose of developing awareness and creating a calm, clear mind; and *vipassana* (insight) meditation, which applies our calm, clear mind to examining the nature of Reality. According to Buddhism, in order fully to escape from dukkha we need to learn to 'see things as they really are'. In this course, we'll be learning how we live within interpretations of reality that we ourselves create. We'll be learning how we can change our experience by changing the way we see the world, and that we can change the way we see the world by changing our experience.

66 Great things are not done just by impulse, but are a series of small things put together. 99

The value of mindfulness

The techniques you will learn here are straightforward – even simple. You can learn the basics in a few minutes. Although your mind is unbelievably complicated, the principles underlying those complicated workings are very simple to understand.

But although they are simple to understand, we can spend our whole lives learning to practise them on ever-deeper levels. The principles I am about to outline can be understood by a child, but the implications of them are so far-reaching that that child, as she or he grows up, will in all likelihood never entirely plumb their depths.

Those principles are:

1 There's a gap between stimulus and response

Between someone speaking harshly to us (the stimulus), and our getting angry (the response), there is a gap. Between any perception and any reaction, there is a momentary pause.

2 There is choice in the gap

We can choose how to respond. For example, we can choose to allow our anger to develop, or to exercise patience. In every moment these kinds of choice exist. We don't in any given moment have an unlimited menu of responses from which to choose, but there are always choices, and as we continue to practise meditation we become more creative and our menu of choices expands.

3 The choices we make matter

Some of our emotional states cause us (and others) grief. Getting angry when it's not justified, hatred, escapism, putting ourselves down, worrying, denial – all these attitudes impair our happiness by causing conflict in our own hearts and disharmony in our relations with others.

Other emotional states, like kindness, love, empathy, patience, and respect for ourselves and others, tend to enrich our lives –

bringing greater fulfilment and happiness. We can choose to cultivate these qualities.

4 We can only choose if we have awareness

Awareness, or mindfulness, is necessary. We have to be 'awake' to spot unhelpful emotional patterns emerging, and to exercise choice.

As I've already said, these principles are very easy to understand. You can learn them in two minutes – but you can spend the rest of your life putting them into practice. You'll never run out of situations in which to apply mindful awareness, and you'll never find an end to the satisfaction that this 'simple' practice brings into your life.

This book introduces a few simple meditation practices:

❖ Posture guidelines that will help you to sit in meditation. You need to be able to sit comfortably and use your body effectively in order to meditate. I recommend starting with the posture workshop before learning either of the two seated practices.

❖ The Mindfulness of Breathing, which will help you to develop the awareness to 'choose in the gap'.

❖ Walking Meditation, which will help you to take that awareness into your everyday activities more effectively.

❖ The Metta Bhavana (development of loving-kindness), which will help you to appreciate yourself and other people.

A planned second Wildmind book will show you how to work more effectively in meditation by working with distracted states of mind (known as the hindrances) and help you to develop positive states of mind. That book will also cover insight meditation, bringing a more existential slant to the Mindfulness of Breathing and Metta Bhavana, and introduces the Six Element Practice – a meditation that helps us to appreciate the ever-changing and interconnected nature of our existence.

Common problems for new meditators

Everyone's experience is different, but there are some problems that many people face when they are learning meditation. Telling you about them probably won't prevent them, but perhaps you'll recognize them more quickly if you know about them in advance. You might also be spared the agony of thinking you are the only person to have experienced these particular outcomes. Some of the most common are:

Feeling that you have to do it perfectly

You sit down to meditate, and it's supposed to be blissful, instantly – right? But instead, your mind is all over the place, your left knee aches, and there's an unbearable itch in your right ear. Obviously, you think, you're not cut out for this meditation lark, and you'd do as well to give up. Feeling that we have to do it perfectly turns into the realization that we can't do it perfectly, which leads to our beating ourselves up and quitting.

But as G.K. Chesterton wrote, 'If a thing is worth doing, it is worth doing badly.'[7] That is not a typographical error, and I believe there is great wisdom in this saying. If a thing is worth doing, it's worth doing badly. Anything that is very rewarding, from parenting, to painting, to meditation, is likely to be very complex. There is by definition always a lot to go wrong, so you'll make a lot of mistakes. It's natural and inherent in meditation that you will experience, for example, a lot of distraction and sometimes realize that you haven't a clue what you're doing. And that's all right. If you keep doing it, you will learn; you'll learn from your mistakes and learn to get results that you want rather than results you don't want.

The fact that you experience distractions in meditation is not a sign that things are going wrong. Here's a typical comment from one of my students, a management consultant. 'I certainly found my attention wandering – sometimes it focused on past events from today, at other times I was anticipating what would come next, at other times I was impatiently waiting for the meditation to end. But overall it was good; I certainly felt more calm and relaxed and centred when it was over.' Do you see how it's possible both to experience distractions and to experience beneficial effects from meditation? The more you can accept that distractions are inevitable, the more likely it is that you will appreciate those benefits.

We may feel that we have limitations that affect our ability to meditate, but so what? Who doesn't have limitations that affect their ability to meditate? What we have to do is simply keep on working within our limitations until we find we've transcended them.

I sometimes call Buddhist practice 'the fine art of making mistakes', since the point of practice is to pay attention to what you do, to learn from it, and to keep doing it differently until the results you get are more to your liking.

We need to learn to forgive ourselves if we are going to meditate, and if we commit ourselves to meditation we have a strong incentive to forgive ourselves in order to make life more enjoyable and less frustrating. Making mistakes is inevitable – so inevitable, in fact, that it seems ludicrous to me to think in terms of mistakes. When we walk we are always catching ourselves as we fall. That is how we move from one place to another. To single out the part of our meditation where we get distracted or frustrated, and to label it 'failure', seems to me about as helpful as to single out the part of our walking where we fall forwards and to describe it as a 'mistake'.

The poet David Whyte points out that 'to find the real path we have to go *off* the path we are on now, even for an instant, and earn the privilege of losing our way. As the path fades, we are forced to take a good look at the life in which we actually find ourselves.'[8] I believe this is absolutely true. The path we are following in meditation is not like one that is clearly laid out in front of us. The journey we are taking is an internal one, and although others have followed similar paths during their own spiritual journey they cannot leave trails where we need to go. We can only have a sense that we are following that invisible trackless track within by straying to its very edges and beyond – by losing our sense of balance and by stumbling on the rough ground of our own ego. As we begin to tread this inner path we cannot know where its edges lie without blundering into them. In fact, this inner path is not so much found as created.

Trying to make your mind go blank or chase thoughts (or noises) away

This doesn't work, and it isn't what meditation is about. In meditation, your mind will often become calmer and quieter. Sometimes you might even stop thinking in words. But your mind never goes blank (unless you are deeply unconscious); if it did, you wouldn't know you'd succeeded, would you?

When it comes to outside noises, there is no point in trying to push them away. If you push them, you are holding on to them. The harder you push, the more deeply entangled you'll get. Instead of trying to push noises away, just let them be. Allow them to pass through you unhindered. If you keep doing the practice, one day you'll realize that you just hadn't noticed them.

"This inner path is not so much found as created.**"**

The situation with thoughts is somewhat similar, except that we have more choice over whether a thought continues or not. In becoming more aware of our propensity to generate thoughts, we can learn to let go of those thoughts when that seems to be appropriate. Thoughts can be let go of, but they cannot be chased away for more than a few seconds. We cannot successfully chase thoughts away any more than we can chase clouds out of the sky because we prefer the sunshine. Instead we need to learn patiently to let go and accept that a busy mind is what we are working with.

Trying to make something happen

We may have expectations about what meditation is going to be like, and even try to make our expectations happen. We may strive, for example, to experience bliss because we think that meditation is supposed to be blissful. Or when we do begin to experience some rapture arising, in the form of energy or pleasure, we may try to grasp and hold on to it, convinced that this is the beginning of some deeply spiritual experience. But what happens is that we kill the developing positive quality as surely as if we'd crushed a small bird in the palm of our hand.

Sit loose to your experience. You'll have ups and downs, and your meditation will vary considerably. Observe these changes without attaching too much significance to either the ups or the downs. We often respond to these changes as if they were permanent – so we get elated when something pleasant happens and we become despondent when things don't go the way we'd hoped. In meditation, elation and despondency are unbalanced and unhelpful. Rather than become elated or despondent, maintain as much equanimity as you can, realizing that the changes you are experiencing are just part of the ever-changing flux of your life.

Confusing being aware of something with thinking about it

'Being aware of' is not the same as 'thinking about'. We can be aware, for example, of how our body is, without keeping up a running commentary. Being aware of your breathing (something we'll be doing a lot) is not the same as describing your breathing. Try simply to experience. If thoughts arise, don't push them away but also don't indulge them. Instead, just let go of them and let them evaporate. At first you might have to do this over and over again, but eventually the number of thoughts bubbling up will decrease, and your mind will become calmer.

Helpful habits in meditating

Over the years I've noticed a few traits that crop up in people who are successful at establishing a regular and long-term meditation practice. All these traits can be cultivated, so that any of us can learn, over time, how to set up a successful meditation practice.

Noticing and appreciating small changes

Many people give up meditation because they want to see major changes in their lives, and they want to see them now. They don't realize that most major changes are composed of a great many small changes – just as a long hike is made of many small steps. Each step might not get you very far, but when you add them all up they take you a long way.

The most successful meditators do notice and appreciate these small changes. They see every small change as important in its own right and take delight in it. Those who don't do this are likely to give up, which is a bit like giving up on a hike after the first few steps because they don't seem to be taking you very far. They then often look for some other form of meditation (or other method of personal change) and give up on that too. They end up getting nowhere. Meanwhile the meditators who recognize and appreciate the small changes they are making are finding they've come a long way.

An aspect of this quality of noticing and appreciating small changes is to describe your practice in terms of degrees on a continuum rather than as choices between good and bad. If you tend to describe your experience in terms of good and bad, this tends to be demotivating. Basically, you're working with a very crude descriptive system that doesn't allow you to notice small changes, and therefore you'll tend to place yourself and your progress at the 'bad' end of the spectrum. If, however, you see things in terms of better or worse, rather than good or bad, you'll be able to make finer distinctions. Rather than saying your meditation was bad, you'll be able to say it was 'worse than yesterday, but better than last month', for example. In this way you're seeing your progress as part of a continuum of possible states of mind. You're also implicitly reminding yourself of the possibility of better meditations, since you're making comparisons with those times.

Reminding yourself of progress
If you don't sometimes step back from your practice and note what changes have taken place, you may end up assuming that no changes have taken place. It is very useful, especially in the early stages, to take note of what you've learned. If you keep a meditation journal you can use the end of each week to summarize what you've learned. This will help you to maintain your motivation and your confidence.

Seeing opportunities, not problems
Successful meditators see opportunities where others see problems. Seeing problems as opportunities is almost a cliché in the business world, but clichés generally become clichés because they happen to be true. Frustration leads to breakthroughs; confusion leads to insights. Instead of moaning about something that's not going as well as you think it should, instead of assuming that you must be a lousy meditator, give yourself the opportunity to learn from any frustrations that crop up.

We all have access to intuitive wisdom, if we are prepared to listen to ourselves. In the midst of the random noise of our distractions there is often a quiet voice pointing the way forwards. Listen and learn. You know more than you think you know.

Tenacity
When the going gets tough, the tough keep meditating. Meditating when you feel like it will only take you so far – and that's not very far at all. What's needed is an attitude that you will keep meditating come what may. Meditation needs to be as essential as brushing your teeth. Most adults (fortunately) don't just brush their teeth when they feel like it – they see it as a regular and necessary part of life. If we keep on meditating even when it gets boring, or when it's positively

frustrating, we'll be able to make breakthroughs – such as the intuitive problem solving that we just talked about.

Having clear goals

Something that supports the ability to notice progress, to solve problems intuitively, and to stick tenaciously to practice, is having a clear goal. You may realize that you need to develop more happiness and enjoyment in your meditation. You may notice that you tend to be harsh toward yourself and that you could do with developing more kindness. Or perhaps you need to work on strengthening your concentration. If you're clear about what you want to achieve in life, and in your meditation, you can tell whether you are making progress towards that goal.

When you encounter obstacles your subconscious mind will be able to generate new approaches if you have a clear sense of where you want to go. It's hard to find a way from point A to point B if you have no idea what point B actually is.

And if you have a clear sense of where you want to go in life – what kind of qualities you want to have, what kind of person you want to be, what kind of achievements you want to be remembered for – it's much easier to stick to the path that is going to take you towards those goals. If you have an unclear sense of where you want to go, it's going to be hard to maintain any sort of regular practice.

At the same time you'll distress yourself if you cling to the idea of attaining your goals quickly. When we do this we tend to become upset and frustrated, but we can bear a goal lightly in mind, so that we use it as a guide to orient ourselves and don't beat ourselves up for not having attained it yet.

❖ Noticing and appreciating small changes
❖ Reminding yourself of progress
❖ Seeing opportunities, not problems
❖ Tenacity
❖ Having clear goals

These are all traits we can cultivate, both inside and outside of meditation. I'd suggest that you get into the habit of practising these attitudes in your daily life, thereby generating some momentum that will help you to take these qualities into your meditation as well. Notice small changes around you – in the weather and in the natural world, in the way people dress, in their moods – and within you – the ever-changing pattern of your moods. Whenever possible, comment on positive changes that you notice. Remind yourself of progress in your relationships and in your work by taking a few minutes to review your day. When problems occur at work or at home, see what you can learn from those situations. Keep going, even when the going is tough, and develop and stay focused on clear goals that you set yourself in all areas of your life.

Can anyone learn to meditate?

Yes, just about anyone can learn to meditate. Sex, age, nationality, religion, previous experience are all unimportant. Forget any ideas that you have to be 'spiritual' (whatever that means) to meditate. You don't need any innate ability, any more than you need special powers to be able to learn to walk or ride a bike.

People with mental illness should be cautious about taking up meditation. Those who have experienced schizophrenia, serious depression, or bipolar disorder should consult their doctor before learning to meditate, and discuss their history with their potential meditation instructor.

This book is written by a Buddhist, but it's not a book about Buddhism. I just want to share with you something that I (and many other people through the centuries) have found useful. You certainly don't have to be a Buddhist to do any of the practices you'll find in this book. You can continue to practise the religion within which you were brought up and make use of what you find here. You don't have to find a guru or make any radical change in your lifestyle, like shaving your head. Lots of normal people meditate. You could walk past them on the street and never know.

There's nothing in this book that will seem particularly 'religious' (in fact, many people think the term 'religion' isn't a very accurate way of describing Buddhism itself). Meditation is just a way of getting to know yourself better, and learning to take responsibility for what you find, so that you can learn how to be a happier, more fulfilled person.

"Lots of normal people meditate."

We so often label ourselves in ways that limit us. We say, 'I'd like to meditate, but I'm just too distracted. I could never do it.' These labels may start off as simple descriptions, but they end up as prison cells. Our description of ourself confines us and prevents us even trying. The truth is that you can learn to meditate if you want to.

A Buddhist teacher once explained the Buddhist path to a class. One young man said, 'What you've said sounds great, but I don't think I could manage to do that. It sounds too hard for me.' The teacher replied, 'Really? What makes you think you're so special?' From a Buddhist perspective it's just as conceited to tell yourself that you are special due to some supposed lack of ability, as it is to believe you are naturally superior to others. This is a challenging perspective, but we cannot grow without challenges, and possibly the first challenge we have to face is to accept that our growth is our responsibility, and that we have what it takes – simply by being an aware human being.

The most important thing is persistence – keeping at it despite the natural ups and downs you'll experience. Sometimes it will be easy; sometimes it won't. Some discomfort is to be expected when we step outside the known and undertake a challenge, but unless we go beyond what we have already mastered, we will never grow.

2

sit like a mountain
a posture workshop

Principles of posture

We might think that meditation is something we do with our heads (or if we're really on the ball we might think it involves the heart as well). Actually, meditation involves your whole being: mind, heart, and body. In order to learn to meditate you have to learn to use your body well by developing a posture that supports, rather than hinders, your attempts to change. Your posture has a huge effect on your mental states in general and on the quality of your meditation in particular, because your mind, heart, and body do not exist in isolation from one another (however much we might try to effect such a separation at times).

What happens in your body has an effect on what goes on in your head and in your emotional life, and vice versa. If you've ever had a good massage, you'll no doubt have noticed that afterwards, with the tensions gone from your muscles, you feel emotionally and mentally refreshed and relaxed. The work that the masseur did on your muscles also had an effect on your heart and head. And of course those physical tensions didn't come from nowhere – much of our tension is directly caused by mental overload and emotional conflict. So the interconnection between our bodies, minds, and hearts is not something mystical – it's something we all experience. And we need to make use of that interconnectedness in our meditation.

You don't have to be able to sit in the lotus position, or even to sit on the floor, but there are some important principles that you have to learn in order to meditate effectively.

Two principles

There are two things that we need to learn to do in our meditation posture.

First, we need to develop as much comfort and relaxation as we can. The more we are relaxed, the less will aches and pains in our muscles and joints distract us. Also, as we become more comfortable and relaxed we can let go of the mental and emotional counterparts of our physical tensions. If, in our meditation posture, we can let go of physical tensions, it will have an effect on our minds as well.

Secondly, we have to find a posture that will allow us to maintain alertness and successfully cultivate awareness. The best posture to help us achieve this is a dignified and upright one; that's why we sit upright in meditation. If we simply wanted to relax, we could just lie flat on the floor. Lying down is a very relaxing posture, but it's not a good one for maintaining awareness. If we lie down we'll probably feel sleepy, and might even doze off, so we need to learn to sit comfortably upright so that we can relax.

That's what this posture workshop will help you to do. This book will show you how to sit cross-legged, or astride cushions, or on an ordinary dining chair or office chair. Bear in mind the need to find a position that is comfortable for you. There's no point in trying to sit cross-legged if you don't have the flexibility to do so.

Just because you want to sit in a particular posture doesn't mean it's right for you. You need to pay attention to the principles of comfort and relaxation, as well as openness and uprightness.

Sitting in a chair

One of the simplest postures is sitting on an ordinary dining or office chair. The only thing you need to do to modify the chair is to raise its back legs by 1 to 1¼ inches (2½ to 3½cm). Books or blocks of wood can be used to raise the back legs, or you can buy special foam wedges to place on the seat.

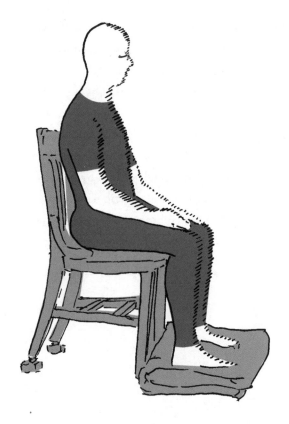

An unmodified chair has a flat seat, which causes your pelvis to tilt backwards, meaning that you have to lean against the back of the chair, or slump (and probably both). Having the seat sloping forwards allows your pelvis to sit in a position such that your back can rise straight up with little or no effort.

The tilt produced by raising the back legs of the chair or by sitting on a foam wedge allows you to sit upright without holding your back rigidly or leaning against the back of the chair. If you hold your back rigidly you'll become uncomfortable, and leaning against the back of the chair encourages a lazy attitude.

Your feet should ideally be flat on the floor. If your feet don't reach the floor, use a folded blanket (like Jeremy is using in the picture) or even a thick book to place your feet on. If your legs are longer than the length of the chair legs, raise your seated height by sitting on a cushion or something similar.

You can rest your hands on your thighs, palms down. Or you can have your hands resting in your lap, perhaps supported by a cushion, or even something as simple as a folded sweater.

Using an office chair

Some office chairs are perfect for meditating on.

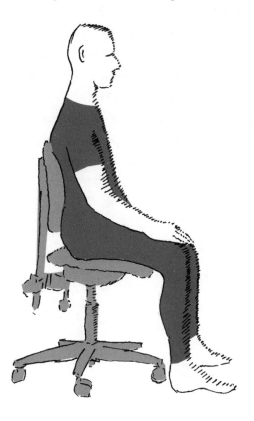

First of all, set the seat so that it is tilted slightly forward, and make
sure that the backrest is making only very slight contact with your
lower back. Make sure you are not leaning against the back of the
chair.

Then you can adjust the height of the chair so that your feet are
flat on the floor.

If you can't tilt the seat, it's probably not going to work well for
meditation, unless you're doing a very short sit of perhaps five to ten
minutes. With a flat seat it will be impossible to have a straight back
unless you hold yourself upright by sheer force – and that will lead to
painful tensions. Or you'll end up leaning back into the chair, which
will encourage a lack of effort.

Whatever kind of chair you use, I suggest the following exercise when you set up your posture. First, with a straight back, bend forward from the waist until your belly is close to your thighs. Then wiggle your bottom backwards as far as it will go. Then sit upright. What you should find is that you can now sit up with only the smallest amount of contact between the lumbar part of your back and the chair back. You'll probably notice a small amount of contact from the chair very low down in your lumbar spine without having any sense that you are leaning back or giving your weight to the chair.

If you search on the Web, you'll find other sorts of special meditation seats. (See pp. 80–1 for a list of websites.) Some allow you to meditate without sitting on the floor. Others offer back support to help you to sit on the floor more comfortably. Shrijñana is using such a seat here. Another popular type, called the Nada Chair, supports your lower back by using your knees as a brace. A lot of people prefer to find a way to sit on the floor since they feel rather ungrounded on a normal chair.

Using a stool

A meditation stool is an excellent way to sit comfortably on the floor if you're not flexible enough to sit with your legs crossed. You might be more comfortable with some padding on the floor to protect your knees, though this might not be necessary if your carpet is thick. Jeremy is using a special meditation mat called a zabuton, but a simple folded blanket will do. It's important to make sure that your hands are supported. You can rest them on a cushion, or you can have a blanket wrapped round your waist and make a sort of 'nest' for your hands out of the blanket.

You'll probably also need a small amount of padding under your bottom to stop the hardness of the wooden seat causing discomfort.

This is probably the easiest way to sit for people who are not very flexible. Most of your weight is on the stool, and the rest on your knees. If you want to move on from sitting in a chair, this is probably the place to start.

There is a list of suppliers of meditation stools at the end of this section, as well as a diagram of how to make a simple meditation stool. There are two basic styles: the one-legged stool, where your calves end up on either side of the leg of the stool, and the two-legged, where your calves lie between the legs of the stool. The two-legged variety tends to be more stable. Some stools have hinged legs to make transportation easier.

Sitting astride cushions

Another common form of this kneeling posture involves sitting astride cushions. Finding good cushions is important. They need to be really firm, and most pillows and household cushions compress too much and can't provide enough support. On the links page on the Wildmind website (www.wildmind.org/links.html) and later in this section we list several suppliers of meditation cushions.

Jeremy is using cushions (called zafus) that are specially designed for meditation. Most people who sit astride cushions need two (or three, depending on the height required and the type of cushion). You might also need another on which to rest your hands.

When you sit astride cushions, make sure your feet point straight backwards, and are not splayed out to the side. Having your feet splayed will twist your knees, and can cause cartilage damage in the long term.

When sitting astride cushions, you'll notice that you can make changes in your posture by varying the distance between your knees. This allows you to make subtle changes to the tilt of your pelvis – a topic we'll return to later.

Protecting your ankles

Sitting in a kneeling position (on either a stool or a cushion) may at first cause the front surface of your ankle to feel painfully stretched. This is simply the discomfort that comes from unaccustomed stretching, and shouldn't cause any physical harm. After a few sessions your ankles should stretch and adjust and you'll feel quite comfortable sitting like this.

If the pain does persist, place some padding between your ankle and the floor. You can use a rolled-up hand-towel. One friend of mine who had stiff ankles made some special pads by stuffing cotton into a pair of socks.

An alternative way to deal with this is to have your ankles hanging off the back of the zabuton or blanket that you're using to cushion the floor.

Problems with lower legs going to sleep

If you find that your lower legs go to sleep, this can be due to clothing being bunched up behind your knees. This puts pressure on your nerves and blood vessels. Jeans are especially bad for this, because denim is so thick, but if you happen to be wearing trousers made from thick fabric, you can lightly pull on the material above and below the knee in order to remove some of the folds.

It can also happen that your legs go to sleep just because you're not accustomed to sitting still. This should normally pass fairly quickly.

If your legs go to sleep while you're sitting on a wooden stool, make sure you have something soft between your bottom and the wood. The edge of the stool can put pressure on your nerves and blood vessels, cutting off your circulation.

This problem can also arise if you are sitting too low. The lower you sit, the more pressure your thighs put on your calf muscles. We'll look at how to choose the right height later in the posture workshop.

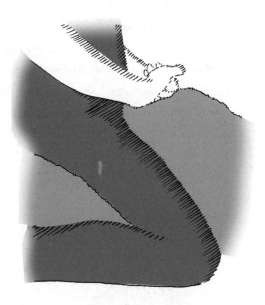

Sitting cross-legged

I'm not going to explain how to sit in traditional half lotus or full lotus position in this guide. If you have the flexibility to sit comfortably in those positions you can just go ahead and do that. And if you don't have the flexibility to get into those postures, a few illustrations and pages of text aren't going to help. So I'm just going to illustrate a basic cross-legged posture.

It should be clear by now that there's no need to sit cross-legged in order to meditate. In fact, if you force yourself into an uncomfortable cross-legged posture you may do long-term damage to your joints, and you certainly won't be comfortable enough to meditate effectively. However, if you have the flexibility then sitting cross-legged is a very stable and grounded posture.

It's very important for you to have both knees on the ground, to give you adequate support. Having three points of contact – your bottom, and both knees – gives you a lot of stability. Without three points of contact, there will be some tension in your posture because you'll have to hold yourself upright. This will lead to pain and discomfort, and will distract you from your meditation. So make sure that your knees are on the ground – or find another posture.

You can have your hands resting on your knees or in your lap so that the weight of your arms is supported. It's important that you don't have any tension in your shoulders due to their supporting the weight of your arms.

Padding under the knees

If you can't quite get both knees on the floor, you can use some padding (a thin cushion or folded scarf) under your knee to keep you stable.

If one, or both, of your knees is more than an inch (2½cm) off the ground, then it's probably better not to sit cross-legged. Try a more comfortable posture for now; you can always do some yoga or other forms of stretching, and come back to a cross-legged posture later on.

From time to time you might want to alternate which foot is in front. This is a good thing to do because any cross-legged posture is asymmetrical. If you sit with the same foot in front all the time, you'll always have the same subtle curvature to your spine, with the same tensions in the same places. Over time, you'll become habituated to these slight asymmetries, and think that you're sitting straight when you're not. If you alternate the position of your feet, however, you'll even out the imbalances and not 'build them in' to your posture.

Preventing sleepy feet

If you sit cross-legged, you may find that one of your feet has a
tendency to go to sleep. This is due to pressure being applied to the
nerves and blood vessels behind the knee. One way to help avoid this
is to make sure that you don't have any clothing bunched up behind
your knees. We dealt with this earlier, and I explained that you can
pull bundled-up clothing out from behind your knees. Better still, you
can wear soft clothing.

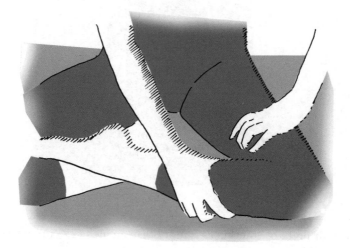

Another thing you can do is use your hands to create more space at
the back of the knee by rolling your calf muscle out and down, and
your thigh muscle out and up. When you release your hands, you'll
probably notice there's less pressure on the backs of your knees.

Elements of good posture

We've seen that there are several different ways to sit for meditation. I'm going to stress again that you need to find a position that is comfortable for you.

Listen to your body. Discomfort will distract you from your meditation and is also your body's way of telling you that something is wrong. Listen to your body, but don't indulge your body. We need to learn to distinguish – perhaps you can already – the discomfort of stretching from the discomfort of damaging pain. If you've ever done yoga you'll know that stretching resistant muscles can be painful – but it's a qualitatively different pain from the pain of damage. Being able to distinguish between 'good pain' and 'bad pain' is a useful skill.

Whatever posture you use:

1. Your spine should be upright, following its natural tendency to be slightly hollowed in the lumbar. You should neither be slumped nor have an exaggerated hollow in your lower spine.

2. Your spine should be relaxed enough for you to notice it moving slightly with your breathing.
3. Your hands should be supported, resting either on a cushion or in your lap, so that your arms are relaxed.
4. Your shoulders should be relaxed, and slightly rolled back and down, opening your chest.
5. Your head should be balanced evenly, with your chin slightly tucked in. The back of your neck should be relaxed, long, and open.
6. Your face should be relaxed, with your brow smooth, your eyes relaxed, your jaw relaxed, and your tongue relaxed and just touching the back of your teeth.

Common postural faults: slumping

In this picture, Leslie is sitting too low.

Sitting too low tilts the pelvis backwards, so the upper back has to slump forwards to stay in balance. This closes the chest and reduces the ability to breathe. If you sit in this posture you'll tend to feel rather dull and may even fall asleep.

This posture does not allow us to be alert and to remain aware while meditating. When you slump, you might experience tension in the neck and shoulders.

The solution is to adjust the height and angle of your seat – not to hold yourself upright by force of will. If you slump, and then force yourself to sit upright, your posture will look all right from the outside, but before long those clenched muscles will start to feel pretty painful from the inside.

Common postural faults: overarching

Here, Leslie is sitting too high (notice the exaggerated height of her cushions). What's happening is that the pelvis is being tilted forwards. In order to avoid falling on her face, Leslie has to lean back, causing an exaggerated hollowing of the back.

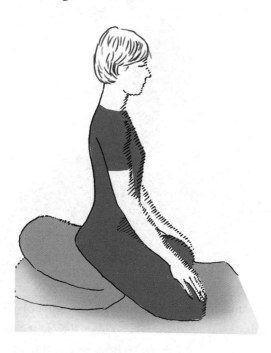

There should be a normal, gentle hollowing, called the lordotic curve, in the lumbar region, but exaggerating this curve causes painful 'pinching' in the lower back. This can also occur when the angle of the seat is too steep. (This also throws the weight forwards, so that the meditator has to lean back.)

The solution to overarching is usually to sit on something lower or to adjust the angle of the seat.

Avoiding slumping and overarching

To avoid either slumping or overarching you need to get the height of your stool or cushion just right. But how do you know? The best thing is to have someone with experience in adjusting meditation posture on hand to give you feedback. It's very hard to judge from the inside whether your posture needs to be changed, but here are some checks you can carry out yourself to see whether you are sitting too high or too low. First, set up your posture, and make sure you are comfortable and relaxed. Make sure you aren't holding yourself forcibly in what you think is a 'good' posture.

How does it feel? What shape does your back make? Feel your lower back with your hands to check. When you relax, do you find that you slump? If so, you need to be sitting higher, or to have more of an angle on your seat. If you're using a proper meditation cushion, you need to have your weight on the front of the cushion, not on the rear. If you're on a chair and find that you slump, you may need to raise the back legs of the chair a little more.

Slip your hands under your buttocks. You should be able to feel two little bones that protrude downwards through your buttocks. Meditation teachers have a technical term for them: we call them the 'sitting bones'. There's probably a more anatomically correct term, but we get by calling them sitting bones.

If the top of your pelvis tilts forwards, which causes your back to overarch, then the sitting bones will slide off the backs of your hands. If you tilt your pelvis backwards, causing the back to slump, the sitting bones slide off the fronts of your hands. When your pelvis is perfectly aligned, the sitting bones point straight down into your hands. And when you slide your hands out, the sitting bones are pointing straight down into the seat. So what you want is to have those sitting bones pointing straight down while your back is relaxed and at ease. This can be achieved when you have your seat at the right height, so play around with different cushions or whatever, and see when your back is relaxed and your sitting bones are pointing straight down.

Repeat the exercise of tilting your pelvis back and forth, but put your hands on the small of your back and notice how it slumps when you tilt your pelvis backwards, and overarches when you tilt your pelvis forward.

Shoulders

Make sure you're not holding any tension in your shoulders. Let them relax and roll back. Have your hands supported so that your shoulders can be free, allowing your chest to be open. That way you'll be able to breathe freely, and maintain awareness more easily.

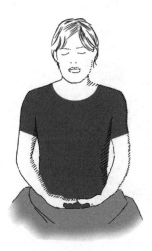
Tense shoulders

Relaxed shoulders

In order to create good conditions for being aware, you need to have an open chest, with a sense of spaciousness across the front of your chest between your shoulders. You can encourage this sense of spaciousness by taking a few deep breaths and filling your upper chest as you set up your meditation posture.

As you breathe in, the front of your body will rise. Feel the openness across the front of your upper chest, and at the same time relax your shoulders, letting them fall and roll back.

If you feel any stretching in the backs of your shoulder muscles, it probably means that you need to have your hands supported higher. Some people who are relatively stiff, or who have long backs, need to have their hands supported just above the level of the navel to avoid stretching their shoulders.

Supporting your hands

Your arms weigh a lot. If your hands are not supported, your shoulders have to carry all that weight. That means that either your shoulders will tense up to take the weight of your arms, or your shoulder muscles will be overstretched. Either way you're going to be uncomfortable.

Hands supported by a blanket

Hands supported on a cushion

So make sure your hands are supported. If you're in a low cross-legged position, you may be able to rest your hands comfortably in your lap. However, you may want to have your hands supported higher. This will allow your shoulders to roll back further and be more relaxed. If you're sitting in a chair, you can usually rest your hands on your thighs, but some people with long backs might need something to support their hands.

If you have stiff shoulders you might, as I mentioned earlier, have to have your hands supported quite high – perhaps even above your navel. A blanket wrapped around your legs, or a sweater or scarf tied round the waist, can be useful here. (A blanket can also be very useful in keeping your legs warm and comfortable.)

If you're kneeling, using cushions or a stool, you may need to have good support for your hands. In this case you can use another meditation cushion, or perhaps a sweater or blanket tied round the waist.

You may also want to try having your hands in the traditional meditation gesture – called the *dhyana mudra* (Sanskrit). This involves having the fingers of the right hand resting on the fingers of the left, with the tips of the thumbs lightly touching.

The dhyana mudra is a beautiful gesture to make and also has some practical uses. The contact between the thumbs, for example, can act as an 'effort meter'. If you are making too little effort in meditation then there will be a general, and very subtle, lack of muscle tone in your body, and the tips of the thumbs will tend to drift apart. When you are trying too hard there will be a corresponding increase in muscular tension and the thumbs will tend to press together.

The contact between your thumbs can also give rise to some very delicate and interesting sensations that can help you to appreciate the more subtle aspects of your experience.

Adjusting your head and neck

The position of your head is very important. Your head should be balanced, and should seem to float almost effortlessly on top of your spine. You can imagine the crown of your head being drawn upwards, as if it was attached to a helium balloon.

As you set up your posture, rock your head slightly back and forwards, noticing how the length and openness of the back of your neck change. Look for a point of balance where your head is supported almost effortlessly.

Your chin should be slightly tucked in, and the back of your neck long and relaxed. So as you tuck in your chin, feel the muscles on the back of your neck relaxing and lengthening.

The exact angle of your neck and chin when your head is perfectly balanced will vary from person to person. Some people's necks are habitually straighter or thrust further forwards than others. You'll have to play around and see what is right for you, although having an experienced outside observer check your posture can be invaluable.

If your chin is tucked in too far, so that your head hangs forward, you'll find either that you tend to feel dull and sleepy, or that you become caught up in a whirlpool of rather brooding emotions.

Chin too low

If your head is tilted too far back, so that your chin is in the air, you'll find that you tend to get very caught up in thinking and become rather speedy.

Chin too high

But when your chin is gently tucked in, you can be aware of both thoughts and emotions without getting lost in them. You'll also be more comfortable.

Chin just right

These effects are worth watching for in everyday life. You'll notice that when you feel depressed (caught up in loops of emotion) you hold your chin near your chest. And if you are walking along lost in excited thoughts, you tend to have your chin in the air – 'lost in the clouds'.

Posture checklist

In setting up your meditation posture, what you're really doing is using the mind–body relationship to help you develop a calmer, clearer, more focused mind. There is no escaping this relationship: if you want to change your mental states, you'll have to set up your posture in such a way that it supports rather than hinders your efforts.

Come back and revisit this posture workshop several times as you continue to practise. If you pay close attention to these guidelines and experiment with your posture, you'll be setting up ideal conditions for enjoyable and effective meditation.

1. Adjust your cushion height so that your back is relatively straight, and also relaxed.
2. Make sure your hands are supported, to let your shoulders be free.
3. Relax your shoulders, letting them roll back to open your chest.
4. Adjust the angle of your head, so that the back of your neck is relaxed, long and open, and your chin is slightly tucked in.
5. Begin taking your awareness into your body, relaxing every muscle.
6. Now you're ready to start meditating.

Body awareness and relaxation

Being aware of your body in meditation is vital. Setting up your posture is not something separate from the meditation, and is not an optional extra. It's an integral part of the process of meditating, and it's necessary to spend some time setting up your posture and taking your awareness through your body if you want to meditate well.

The more awareness you can take into your body as you begin your meditation, the better your meditation will go. It's like laying the foundation as the first stage of building the house.

Set up your posture

After you have set up your posture (see previous pages), take your awareness through your body.

Body awareness and relaxation

Start by becoming aware of your feet and your contact with the floor, really letting your awareness fill your feet. The more you become aware of your feet, the more you can allow them to relax. Let the muscles soften and lengthen as you become aware of them in a spirit of gentleness and curiosity.

Once you've done that for a few minutes, take your awareness from your feet up through the rest of your body, 'letting go' as you move through all the different muscles. Become aware of your legs, thighs, hips, back, shoulders, arms and hands, neck, head, and face. Each time you become aware of a particular part of your body, soften, relax, and let go.

Notice the subtle change in the quality of your experience as you first become aware, and then relax. Often you'll notice more energy, or tingling, or even feelings of pleasure, as your body relaxes. Notice those feelings and enjoy them in a relaxed way. Trying to hold on to those feelings will slow the process of relaxation, so try simply to notice and to let go.

You can listen to a RealAudio file that will guide you through the process of developing more awareness for your body, and of using that awareness to relax more deeply. You can connect to the RealAudio file by typing the following address into your browser: www.wildmind.org/realaudio/body.html

If you do not have the free RealOne player program that you need to listen to this file, you can download it from www.real.com.

Pay particular attention to the following parts of your body where commonly a lot of tension is stored:

❖ The back of your neck
❖ Your shoulders
❖ Your abdomen
❖ Your hips
❖ Your thighs and calves

You may find there are layers of tensions in those muscles, so you may have to repeatedly suggest that they relax. You may then find, to your surprise and delight, that a part of your body that you thought you had relaxed suddenly relaxes a little more.

Once you've been through your body, become aware of your body as a whole. Notice all of the sensations in your body. It's common to find that tensions have crept back into one area of your body while you've been focusing elsewhere, so continue to encourage your body to relax.

Then centre your awareness on your belly, sensing the calming, rhythmic motion of your belly as you breathe in and out. Follow your breathing flowing in and out, noticing how those rhythmic, soothing sensations have a calming effect on your mind and heart.

Relax. Soften. Let go. You've already begun meditating.

"It's necessary to spend some time setting up your posture and taking your awareness through your body if you want to meditate well.**"**

Dealing with discomfort

I almost hesitate to add this section in case I give the impression that meditation is always painful! Rest assured that it's not, but every meditator experiences some discomfort from time to time. It's good to be able to recognize how to deal with it.

I've already mentioned that there are two types of pain. There is 'good pain', which is the normal discomfort brought on by a challenge to our bodies – so if we are stretching there is likely to be some discomfort, and this is perfectly normal. If we sit with such pain, our muscles stretch and adjust, and the pain stops, so we've worked through the discomfort.

The 'bad' kind of pain occurs when something in our bodies is being damaged. It's very important to learn to recognize this kind of pain and deal with it appropriately, for example by stopping or modifying whatever it is that is causing the damage. You might feel this kind of pain (often a sharp pain) in your knees, for example.

It's possible for good pain to turn into bad pain if we don't deal with it correctly. A common source of discomfort, for example, is pain in the shoulders caused by not having your hands supported high enough. If your hands are too low, your shoulders have to bear the weight of your arms, and this causes stretching in your shoulder muscles (and perhaps also some pain in the neck). This isn't damaging in the short term, but in the long term it will lead to muscular and postural disorders. So don't put up with discomfort for so long that it gets really bad; experiment, or get some advice about how to change your posture.

The following may sound masochistic, but it's a good idea to take your awareness into areas of pain, rather than trying to shut out the discomfort. Often we have layers of discomfort. There may be a focus of pain, and then around that is an area of tension that is our response – our resistance to the pain. The initial cause of the pain might be some injury that you can't cure in the short term, or perhaps ever, but by becoming aware of the pain we are adding because of resistance and tension, we can learn to let go of that unnecessary, added pain.

Once we've done that, we may be able to deal more creatively with the original focus of pain. If you try to shut pain out of your mind, it will probably just build up outside of awareness until you can no longer ignore it, and by that time it's going to be very hard to deal with it.

One common way to deal with pain is to breathe into it. This can be part of the process of taking awareness into pain that I mentioned above. Imagine that your breath is flowing in and out of the area of discomfort. The awareness in itself can help you to let go of the tension around the focus of pain, but breathing into the pain also helps your body to move naturally, and the natural movement is almost like a massage, easing away your discomfort.

Remember that usually you can't let go of tension all at once. What happens is that you let go of it by degrees. The holding on is being done unconsciously, so it takes time to learn to consciously relax.

If you have the kind of focus of pain that I've been talking about, and you do try to be fully aware of that pain while letting go of any resistance to it, it can change its quality and cease to be pain at all, but simply energy.

Meditation equipment

The Buddha used to meditate sitting on a heap of grass under a tree. Those were the days! Of course he lived at a time and in a place where people usually sat cross-legged on the floor and he was very flexible as a result. Most of us Westerners need a bit more in the way of physical props when we meditate.

This picture shows some of the equipment you've seen being used by Jeremy and Leslie in the photographs.

The round cushion is called a zafu (that's a Japanese word and I suppose it means something like 'cushion'). Usually they are stuffed with firm cotton or kapok, which give much more support than the average household cushion, although zafus filled with buckwheat husks are also common. Cotton or kapok zafus give about 4 inches (10cm) of lift even when compressed. The buckwheat varieties give rather less lift and are more suited for those very flexible people who can get into half lotus or full lotus.

Most people who sit astride cushions need two cotton zafus. Sometimes a third is used to provide support for the hands. Zafus are not cheap, but they are a good investment.

The mat on which everything is sitting is called a 'zabuton' (Japanese for 'mat', at a guess). They're usually cotton-filled and protect the knees. A folded blanket does just as well.

The two stools illustrated represent the two most common designs: the one-legged and the two-legged. One-legged stools are marginally less stable and I find that my body is slightly less relaxed when I use one. The two-legged style provides more stability and is usually a little lighter — useful if you have to carry it around. In addition, the two-legged variety can also be found in a folding-leg variety, which makes it very portable indeed.

If the Japanese have a name for the small flat cushion at the front left, no one has told me what it is. It's placed on top of a stool to help prevent the buttocks from becoming sore and the legs from going to sleep and, as we've seen, it can also be used when sitting cross-legged to support a knee that doesn't quite touch the floor.

Sources of meditation equipment

Although meditation equipment is expensive, it is a very worthwhile investment. Zafus, zabutons, and most well-made stools will last pretty much a lifetime. I'd highly recommend that you treat yourself to some good quality equipment. You can purchase meditation stools and cushions by mail order or on the Web from a number of companies, including the following:

Garuda Trading (www.tibetanbuddhism.co.uk) supplies stools, mats, and cushions.

Meditation Designs (www.meditation-designs.co.uk) sells meditation cushions (zafus), mats (zabutons), stools, and small mats for supporting knees or ankles.

Putnam's (www.putnams.co.uk) sells a foam wedge that allows you to sit comfortably on an ordinary dining chair.

The above are UK based. The following companies distribute in the USA:

Carolina Morning Cushions (www.zafu.net) supplies zafus, zabutons, and stools – and even an inflatable zafu for travelling.

DharmaCrafts (www.dharmacrafts.com) supplies zafus, zabutons, stools, general meditation supplies, and also offers the 'backjack', which is the backrest in the picture on page 53.

The Nada Chair (www.nadachair.com) is a 'back-support system' rather than a chair. It has straps that run from a back-support pad to your knees, helping your body to support itself. A friend of mine highly recommends it.

Samadhi Cushions (www.samadhicushions.com) has an extensive selection of zafus, zabutons, stools, and other meditation supplies.

Making your own stool

Stools are expensive to buy, but cheap and easy to make. Here is a design for a very basic two-legged stool. Assemble it so that the seat slopes forward. The measurements are for someone about six feet tall (1.83m). You can make the legs shorter if the stool is too high. Someone who is five feet tall (1.52m) will probably want the legs about ¾in. (20mm) shorter. Put a cushion or padding on top if the stool is too low.

Materials: 3 pieces of 20mm (¾in.) pine board, four screws. The dimensions shown are in mm.

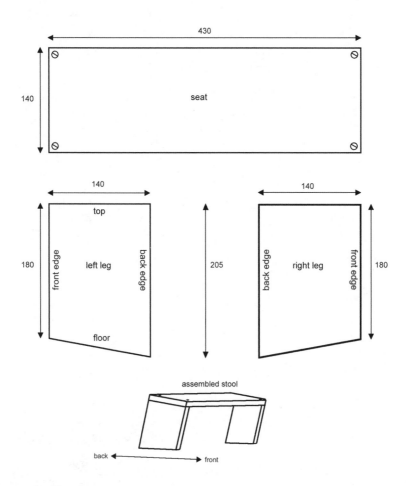

3

mind like the clear blue sky
breathing with awareness

Background

In the Mindfulness of Breathing practice we become aware of the physical sensations of our breathing as the air flows in and out of the body. We use the ever-changing sensation of the breath as an object of awareness, to which we return again and again. This isn't a breathing exercise. Unlike some yoga or T'ai Chi exercises, we don't try to control our breathing. We allow the breath to flow naturally, in a relaxed manner, and simply be aware of it.

One of the first things you learn when you do this meditation is how wild and distracted your mind is. All sorts of thoughts and feelings flow into your awareness, and then you find you've forgotten all about the breath. This is a good thing to learn; if you don't know you have this tendency you can't do anything about it. Most of what floods into our minds in this uncontrolled way is not very useful, and often it's actually bad for us. For example, we find ourselves worrying or getting angry, or putting ourselves down.

The simple principle behind this practice is that if we keep taking our awareness back to the breath – over and over again – our mind gradually becomes quieter and we experience more contentment. We'll gradually start to experience the calm, spacious, and pleasing depths of our minds – what I have called the Wildmind.

A common Zen saying is that we aim to have a mind 'like the clear blue sky'. It may seem at first that the mind is full of clouds, with no blue sky to be seen. There may even be a few storms present. What we have to learn to do is let go of the grey clouds, in fact to stop producing more clouds, and simply let them drift past, noticing the sky becoming clearer and more spacious. Eventually we will have a sense of the mind as being just as lucid, spacious, and beautiful as a blue sky on a summer's day.

This practice helps us not just to find a calmer and more fulfilling way of being, but helps us really to get to know ourselves. The Mindfulness of Breathing is the starting point of 'the examined life'.

The essence of the practice

The Mindfulness of Breathing is divided into four stages, which you'll learn one at a time. Before we get to those stages, we're going to do the meditation in its most basic form – a simple experience of our breathing. In order to do this, you'll need to know how to use your body effectively in meditation, so you'll also need to refer back to the posture workshop in Chapter 2.

Preliminary exercise

❖ Try setting up your meditation posture using the guidelines in the posture workshop.

❖ Close your eyes and become aware of the room around you, including any sounds. Just let these sounds exist, without pushing them away or latching on to them.

❖ Relax your body, taking a few deep breaths into your belly to help settle your mind. Then become aware of the physical sensations of the breath.

Hint: if you sense that you are low on energy and a little sluggish, pay particular attention to the sensations of the breath that you encounter in your head, throat, and upper chest – keep your awareness high in your body. If you feel you need to calm your mind because of a lot of racing thoughts, then pay more attention to the soothing, rhythmic sensations of the breath in your belly – keeping your awareness low in your body. If your energy feels balanced, just let your awareness settle on any part of the breath.

❖ Whenever you realize that your mind has wandered (which is quite normal and to be expected), bring it persistently, kindly, and gently back to your breathing.

You can listen to a RealAudio file that will guide you through a simple form of the Mindfulness of Breathing meditation. You can connect to the RealAudio file by typing the following address into your browser: www.wildmind.org/realaudio/mob_0.html

If you do not have the free RealOne player program that you need to listen to this file, you can download it from www.real.com.

❖ After a few minutes (it doesn't matter exactly how long you try this for), relax any effort you've been making and simply sit for a minute or two, noticing any changes that have taken place in your mind or emotions, before letting your awareness broaden out into the world around you. When you feel ready, you can begin to move your body and open your eyes.

I like to have students do this exercise just in order to appreciate how straightforward the essence of this practice is. All we do is pay attention to the breath, and keep bringing our awareness back to the breath when we realize it has wandered.

In effect, this meditation is simply another form of the raisin experiment, which I hope you've already tried. Here we use the sensation of our breathing as the object of awareness instead of a piece of dried fruit. Both these exercises have in common the fact that we are paying attention to something that we probably don't think of as glamorous or exciting. And just as the raisin, experienced with awareness, was full of surprising intensity, the experience of our breathing can be intense as well. This may not be so immediately apparent, however, when it comes to practising awareness of the breath. The sensations of our breathing are more refined and subtle than the intense dark sweetness of a raisin. It's easier for us to get distracted, and therefore it usually takes more persistent, patient effort in order to maintain our awareness of the breath.

"I want to stress once more that getting distracted is quite natural."

I want to stress once more that getting distracted is quite natural. It happens to everyone, and in fact it's part of the meditation practice. Just as alternating between being balanced and being unbalanced is an essential part of walking, so too is the alternation between distraction and concentration a vital part of meditating. We meditate by working with our distracted mind – by gently bringing it back, over and over again, to the breath. Meditation, as I've said, requires some effort – although that effort should be as light and as playful as possible.

Now we'll take an overview of the whole practice before we start refining it by introducing the four stages one by one.

Outline of the stages of the Mindfulness of Breathing

Here's a quick overview of the practice. After you've read this you can work your way through the meditation one stage at a time, reading the information on each section as you go, and listening to the guided meditations on RealAudio if you have the appropriate equipment. This is primarily intended as an overview of what you're going to be learning later in this section, so I don't recommend that you try the meditation by following only the instructions in the brief summary below.

The Mindfulness of Breathing has four stages. After setting up your posture you become aware of the physical sensations of your breath. Whenever your mind wanders, gently bring it back to the breath. Then:

1. Count after each out-breath. Start counting at one, placing a number after each exhalation. After you have counted ten breaths, start again at one. If you lose count, start again from one.

2. Do the same as in the first stage, but counting just before each in-breath.

3. Drop the counting, and just follow the breath as it flows in and out.

4. Narrow your focus until your attention is absorbed in the sensations of the breath flowing over the rims of your nostrils.

The first stage of the Mindfulness of Breathing

You may wish to review the posture workshop before starting this exercise.

Set up your posture, then take your awareness through your body, relaxing each muscle as you bring it into awareness.

Once you've taken your awareness through your whole body, begin to focus on the physical sensations of your breath. Let yourself become absorbed in the sensations of the breath flowing in and out of your body. Notice how the sensations are always changing. Then begin counting (to yourself) after every out-breath...

Breathe in ... breathe out ... 'one'

Breathe in ... breathe out ... 'two'

Breathe in ... breathe out ... 'three'

Breathe in ... breathe out ... 'four'

Breathe in ... breathe out ... 'five'

... and so on until you reach 'ten'.

If you make it to ten, start again at one. Keep following the breath, and counting, for ten minutes or so.

If your mind wanders, gently come back to experiencing the physical sensations of the breath, and begin counting again. Bring as much patience into the process as possible. Forgive yourself when your mind wanders.

Thoughts will arise from time to time. Just let go of them without adding to them.

At the end of the practice, spend a minute or so just sitting quietly, giving yourself time to appreciate any subtle changes in your mind or emotions.

You can listen to a RealAudio file that will guide you through the first stage of the Mindfulness of Breathing practice. You can connect to the RealAudio file by typing the following address into your browser: www.wildmind.org/realaudio/mob_1.html

If you do not have the free RealOne player program that you need to listen to this file, you can download it from www.real.com.

What's next?

Congratulations! You've just tried the first stage of the Mindfulness of Breathing. Perhaps, like many people, you're a little anxious about getting on to stage two?

Hold on a minute. Why not consolidate what you've already learned, rather than rushing to do the whole practice as quickly as possible? The chances are that you want to learn to meditate because life is so rushed and hectic, so why not start to relax? What's the rush?

Try doing the first stage of the practice over the next few days. Perhaps even try it more than once every day. Why not take a few minutes now to plan exactly when you're going to do it?

I suggest you do at least ten minutes in the morning, and perhaps the same in the evening, just before you go to bed. Or maybe a few minutes in your lunch break? There's no right or wrong time to meditate, so see what suits you.

Try that for perhaps three days, then come back and learn the second stage. Spend a few days doing both stages and then come back again. And so on.

While you're exploring stage one, you can read the following pages, which all deal with stage one or are likely to be relevant to you at this stage of learning. These pages will help you to deepen your understanding of this stage of the practice and help give you a solid foundation to build on.

Dealing with being distracted

Everyone gets distracted during meditation – even people who have been meditating for years. You're in good company.

The first stage in creating a beautiful garden is to realize how many weeds there are to be cleared up. If you feel a bit daunted by the sheer volume of trivia that your mind seems capable of creating, it's good to remember that you need to know it's there before you can do anything about it. Also bear in mind that dealing with it will bring you happiness.

It's as if you've just inherited a beautiful garden which is full of weeds. You can't just pretend the weeds aren't there – you have to do something about it. With a real garden you could always just get rid of it or hire someone to look after it. With your mind you don't have that luxury. Leave it alone and it will only get worse. The best thing to do is get started as soon as possible on clearing those mind weeds.

If you ever feel frustration with your distractions, remember that when you realize you've been distracted in meditation you have a choice – you can choose to exercise patience and gentleness with yourself. Getting mad or getting despondent will only make things worse.

When you do become frustrated or despondent because of the level of distraction you're experiencing, you'll find it useful to let go of the thoughts that arise from those emotional states. As thoughts such as, 'This is getting me nowhere' arise, let go of them and simply be aware of the underlying emotional state. Accept the presence of the frustration or despondence as best you can, and observe the emotion with as much kindness as you can find. This will help you to move beyond those emotions so that you can continue with the practice.

❝Everyone gets distracted during meditation – even people who have been meditating for years. You're in good company.**❞**

So relax, and patiently continue working at clearing the weeds from your wild mind so that you can reveal the splendours of your Wildmind.

Stage zero: the importance of preparation

Let's go back and look at what we did at the start of stage one. With any meditation practice, it's important to do a certain amount of preparation in order to help things go well. But all too often, this preparation is seen as an optional extra and is not done thoroughly, or at all. That's a bad idea.

Imagine you're baking a cake, and you want it fast. You want results. You want to get straight to the eating stage with as little time spent on fussing around with ingredients as possible. So you throw some flour and eggs and sugar into a cake tin (Who's got time for measuring?), give it a quick stir and slam it in the oven. Oh, the gas isn't lit? All right, let's just turn it up full now so that it cooks faster. Yum! Looking forward to your cake? I thought not.

If you want to get certain results (whether a delicious cake or a calmer, clearer mind) you need to set up the right conditions. This is an important Buddhist principle called 'conditionality': that if you want something, you have to provide the conditions that allow it to arise. There are no short cuts.

Preparation for meditation means setting up our posture, deepening our awareness of our body, and relaxing as deeply as we can. This is essential if we want to provide the conditions for the arising of a calmer, clearer, less stressed, more peaceful mind.

I call this 'stage zero' to emphasize that it's not an optional extra. Setting up the right conditions for your meditation is an essential and integral part of the meditation.

In a way it would be much better if we called stage zero 'stage one' instead. That way there would be less of a tendency to think you can drop the preparation and plunge straight into the practice. Unfortunately, that would be rather confusing, since the stage in which we count after the out-breath is universally known as stage one.

"Preparation for meditation means setting up our posture, deepening our awareness of our body, and relaxing as deeply as we can."

A sense of purpose in stage zero

One thing that you can add to your preparation for meditation in stage zero is the cultivation of a sense of purpose in meditation. As you go through your body, relaxing, and as you become aware of what you are taking into meditation, you may become aware that there are certain things that you particularly need to work on.

You may notice, for example, a lack of joy and inspiration in your experience. Perhaps you have a tendency to get annoyed right now, or perhaps it's just that your mind is a little restless and needs calming down. It's good to develop a clear idea of what you want to achieve in such circumstances. You can set yourself the goal of finding a way to enjoy your meditation more, or of calming your mind.

You can take this awareness of purpose into the other stages of your meditation, monitoring from time to time what progress you've made in moving towards your goals. Perhaps the first approach you take doesn't seem to be working, and you need to try another method. Or perhaps what you are doing works very well – perhaps even too well! You may try to calm your restless mind and be so successful that your mind becomes dull and sleepy. At that point you may wish to change your purpose for a more suitable one – in this case perhaps you could adopt the goal of balancing relaxation and energy.

Having goals like these can revolutionize your meditation practice. It's all too easy for our meditation to become stale and mechanical, as we unmindfully use some technique that was once appropriate but isn't now.

Having clear goals is another way of bringing more mindfulness into our practice. It helps us to become not only aware of what emotional, mental, and physical states are present in any given moment, but keeps us alive to where we are going and, very importantly, whether what we are doing is taking us to where we want to go.

The difference that makes the difference

In the short term, the Mindfulness of Breathing practice helps us to become calmer and (rather paradoxically) more energized and refreshed. In the long term, it helps us to develop more awareness so that we have more freedom to choose what our responses in any given situation are going to be. This means, for example, that we can find ourselves in a situation that would normally make us anxious, but we can choose instead to be patient and calm. Over time, we shape our habits instead of letting them shape us. Mindfulness allows us to take full responsibility for our lives, for our happiness.

Practising mindfulness is enormously enriching. Instead of being half-aware of what we're doing, we can fully and richly experience every moment of our lives. The mindfulness that we develop in this practice will help us to enjoy our food more, concentrate better at work, and be more present when we're talking to our friends. We can become more alive to the beauty inherent even in painful situations. And many people who practise this meditation last thing at night say it helps them to sleep and that their dreams are richer and more meaningful. Another paradox of mindfulness is that we become more fulfilled even while becoming more aware of unpleasant sensations or emotions. Instead of reacting to physical pain or to a disturbing emotion and thereby giving rise to more suffering for ourselves, we can simply observe these events with a friendly and curious attitude and accept their presence. The more we are able to do this, the more we can develop a sense of equanimity in the face of discomfort. Since this attitude of equanimity is healthier for us than denial or other forms of reactivity, we find we can experience discomfort and at the same time enjoy a form of contentment.

In time, mindfulness can help you to have a stronger sense of purpose in life as you begin to divine the direction in which your being is unfolding. The psychotherapist Viktor Frankl believed that man's deepest desire is to search for meaning and purpose, and that our purpose in life is detected rather than constructed. One of the most profound consequences of practising mindfulness – one that can take years to begin to take effect – is when we start to detect the gestalt – the underlying pattern – of our lives. At this point a deeper sense of authenticity can emerge.

We've come a long way from tasting that raisin! Mindfulness is a small difference that makes a difference – and the difference it makes can be truly life altering.

What's the counting for?

The counting has a number of really useful functions. (It's almost as useful as the breathing!)

It's very easy just to 'space out' instead of actually meditating. When we space out we get distracted without realizing it. We might start off following our breathing, but then a thought captures our attention and before we know it we're lost in thought. This happens to most of us rather a lot. The counting helps to give us a more objective sense of how much of the time we're distracted, and how much we're remaining aware.

Counting allows us to 'measure' how long we're maintaining our awareness. Sometimes it's hard to stay focused on the breath even for three breaths. At other times we can be aware for several cycles of ten breaths. So you can tell – by the counting – how long you're able to maintain your awareness.

Counting also gives us something to aim for. It's good to have goals. If you're getting distracted before reaching the tenth breath, you can try harder to reach it. If you make it that far, you can try to get to ten again. Without the counting it's harder to notice the effects of your efforts.

The numbers help us to see whether we're making progress. If you put the effort into your meditation, you'll see results. How could you see results if there was nothing by which to measure them?

"The counting helps to give us a more objective sense of how much of the time we're distracted, and how much we're remaining aware."

The numbers also subtly alter your perception of the breath. When you count after the out-breath, that's the part of the breathing process you're most aware of. So in the first stage of the practice you're more aware of breathing out. We'll talk more about this after you've done the second stage of the meditation.

Lastly, the numbers act as a kind of anchor. Just think for a minute: where in the cycle of your breathing would you think it most likely that you were going to get distracted? If you've considered this you will realize that there are two places in the cycle where there is very little happening, and therefore less sensation to occupy your mind. These places are, of course, the pause between the in-breath and the out-breath, when you have just inhaled and are about to exhale, and the pause between the out-breath and the in-breath, when you have just exhaled and are about to inhale again.

At these two points there is a slight pause when nothing much is happening. Because of the relative lack of stimulation at those times, your mind is more likely to wander. Actually, of the two pauses the pause between your exhalation and your inhalation is likely to be rather longer, and we place the number there because the longer pause means it's even more likely that our minds will get caught up in some stray thought. The number is a way of 'touching base' so that we can get through the pause between breaths without getting distracted. The number helps to anchor your mind so that it doesn't drift off into distraction.

Dealing with drifting numbers

Especially when they first try this practice, many people find that the number won't stay put. It merges with the out-breath so that you're sort of exhaling the numbers: oooooone, twooooo, threeeeee, and so on. This 'problem' is no big deal. The first stage is more connected with the out-breath, and the fact that the number has a way of integrating itself into the exhalation just reinforces that association. So if this is happening, then relax.

Having said that, it's good to work gently and patiently at getting the number to go where it's 'supposed' to go – in the space between the out-breath and the in-breath. There are good reasons for this. As I've already said, the number is placed at the point in the breath-cycle where there is least sensation and where you are most likely to become distracted, so placing the number there will help you to maintain your mindfulness.

Sometimes people see an internal picture of the number as they count it. If this happens to you spontaneously then that's fine. If you want to try this deliberately and find it helps you, that's fine too, although if it doesn't help then I suggest you don't spend too much time on it. If that kind of technique doesn't come naturally to you, it can cause more problems than it solves.

Sometimes I'm asked if you can replace the number with something else – like a colour. I'm not in favour of this. The numbers do have the quality of allowing you to be more objective about whether you're distracted or not. If you count up to thirteen, or don't get any further than five, then you know you've become distracted. But what does it tell you if you 'count' up to purple, or if you get lost at aquamarine? You've removed the numbers from the side of the ruler, making it ineffective at doing what it's meant to do.

The numbers have a variety of uses, and I think we need to learn to appreciate the discipline of the practice.

Facing the demons

Meditation can bring up fear – sometimes quite unexpectedly.
Annie, a student of mine from New York City, reported the following
fascinating experience:

'Today I went for a run, trying rather nonchalantly to meditate
with each step. I got an overwhelming feeling of energy – really good
energy. It was almost too much. I felt super-sensitive to every light,
smell, sensation, and so on. The best analogy I could come up with is
that it was like what you'd hope smoking pot would be, but far better.
Then when I sat down to meditate, it just intensified. It was almost
an out of body experience. I felt sort of disconnected from myself,
yet pretty centred. All this time, I was pretty frightened – there was
no shaking it off, and there was no denying that I was experiencing
something.'

New experiences can be frightening, as Annie's account shows.
When we have spent our whole lives believing that what we
consciously experience of ourselves is all there is to experience, it
can be very unsettling to realize there is more. It's like stepping into a
shallow children's pool and suddenly finding the water over our heads.
That kind of experience can promote fear – even panic.

At the meditation centre I first attended, there was a standing joke
among the teachers that if someone reported a particularly strong and
significant meditation experience one week, the chances were that
you'd never see them again. And as I hung around I began to realize
that this was not much of an exaggeration. It was as though people
became afraid to change, even though they could tell that the change
was beneficial to them.

It wasn't a surprise to me when Annie told me of a dream in
which she was having dinner with Hannibal Lecter from the film
The Silence of the Lambs. When Dr Lecter sent her out to buy a nice
bottle of Chianti, she took the opportunity to flee without finding
out what was on the menu! She was bemused at having the characters
of popular culture peopling her subconscious, but I suggested that
this dream pointed to the very striking truth that meditation involves

a degree of 'auto-cannibalism'. The energies that presently go into hatred, selfishness, and denial will eventually be 'digested' and reused as we go about the task of cultivating the positive.

"Many people find that they develop a subtle resistance to meditation, even though they know their meditation practice is generally enjoyable and that the days when they meditate go better than the days when they don't."

I have become convinced over the years that there are parts of us that are deeply resistant to change. 'We' – that is, the conscious part of ourselves that we identify with – might wish to change, but what about our more reactive habits? Our selfishness, for example? To those parts of ourselves, it must seem that meditation is something dangerous and threatening. Meditation is, in the long term, going to 'destroy' such parts of us. From the point of view of our more selfish aspects, it's no wonder that meditation is frightening – especially when it gives rise to particularly positive experiences, like Annie's.

You don't even have to have a powerfully positive experience in order to have a backlash of fear. Many people find that they develop a subtle resistance to meditation, even though they know their meditation practice is generally enjoyable and that the days when they meditate go better than the days when they don't. It's not that they've had some kind of powerful experience like Annie's. It's subtler than that.

In Buddhist iconography, most Buddhas can be seen in a peaceful form (beautiful, clad in silks, seated on a lotus, and quietly meditating) or in a wrathful form (with wildly distorted features, often clad in animal or human skins, and dancing wildly). The wrathful forms do not literally suggest that those who are enlightened experience rage – at that level of spiritual development such mental states are far behind. The two forms are the same qualities of wisdom and compassion seen from different viewpoints – that of the part of us that welcomes and embraces change, and that of the parts of us that resist and are afraid of change. Towards the selfish and reactive part of ourselves, wisdom and compassion threaten destruction and death, so the wrathful forms are actually the peaceful forms seen from another angle.

Perhaps we need to remember that destruction and creation are just different sides of the same process. If we fail to recognize this truth we will tend to lack an appropriate sense of compassion for those parts of ourselves that are resistant to change. We cannot grow without simultaneously dying. Meditation is a powerful process, and it's wise to remember that we might have to hold our own hand as we undertake the process of redirecting our energies in a more positive direction.

The meditation process

1 Following the breath

We start by following the breath. We've chosen, consciously, to perform this simple act: noticing the physical sensations of the breath. Perhaps there is a cool sensation where the breath flows into the nostrils, and a subtler sensation of warmth as the breath leaves. We can notice the movements in our ribcage and in our belly. We can notice whether our breath is quick or slow, shallow or deep, relaxed or laboured.

Following the breath seems a simple enough task, but after a while what tends to happen is that we forget all about the breath, and forget all about meditation, as we get distracted by some train of thought that is often nothing at all to do with meditation. We don't usually make a conscious decision to think about something outside the meditation practice, it just happens, as habitual patterns of emotion come into play, leading the mind into pathways of thought.

2 Becoming unaware

In fact, not only do we not choose to get distracted, when we get lost in thought we don't have much choice at all. Our habits are controlling us. It's more as though our thoughts are thinking us than we are thinking them. So one of the first things we learn in meditation is just how little control we do have – it's quite a disconcerting and perhaps even humiliating realization for many of us. However, the fact that we often aren't in control isn't cause for despondency – it's the same for most of us most of the time, it's just what we're going to have to work with, and we have to become aware how distracted we are before we can do anything about it.

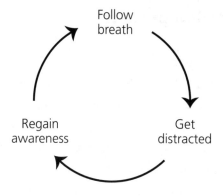

So what do we do when we're supposed to be meditating but we aren't? Often we're getting irritated, or fantasizing about things we'd rather be doing, or undermining ourselves, or dozing, or worrying. Most of these activities aren't very helpful or fulfilling. They're not things we've decided to do – they're simply the habitual things we do when we're unaware. This is what I call the 'wild mind' – the mind at its most disorganized, conflicted, unaware, limited, and chaotic. The mental states that characterize the wild mind are the opposites of meditative states of calmness, unified energy, purposeful awareness, and contentment, and it's often the chronic experience of such chaotic states that drives people to learn meditation in the first place.

The difference between being mindful and not being mindful is a big one, although we're often not very good at recognizing the difference between the two states. After all, we slip in and out of mindful awareness all day. But there really is a big difference between being mindful and not being mindful, as we'll learn to see.

3 Regaining awareness

So we get distracted, but at some point we become aware that we haven't been aware – that we've been distracted. In other words, we regain our awareness. This is a crucial point in the meditation process. Now we're aware again. Now we're no longer being driven by our habits. We have freedom again. We can decide that we don't want to re-enter the world of distractedness. We have choice. Rather than be

dominated by our habitual distracted states of mind we can choose
to exercise awareness. We have an opportunity to cultivate awareness
by maintaining our mindfulness of the breath. Once we realize we've
been distracted we can take our awareness back to the breath.

4 Making choices

But there's another important opportunity available to us the moment
we regain our awareness. We can choose not only what we do (taking
our awareness to the breath), but how we do it. There is often a
strong temptation to mentally beat ourselves up because we've been
distracted. Of course, if we do that we're going straight back into
an uncontrolled, unaware state of distractedness – we undermine
ourselves or get annoyed. A more creative response is to take our
awareness back to the breath with as much kindness, and patience,
and gentleness as we can. Instead of giving yourself a hard time
about having been distracted you can congratulate yourself on having
regained your awareness.

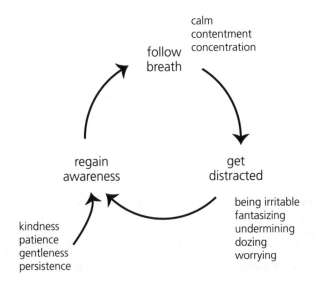

When you're taking your awareness back to the breath, bear in
mind that your mind is a miraculous and precious thing. Carry your
awareness back to the breath in the same way you would pick up a

young kitten in order to return it to its mother. Try to be that gentle and that kind. Your mind has a natural tendency to wander, just like a young, inquisitive animal, so there's no point in being harsh with yourself.

As well as gentleness, this is an opportunity to practise persistence, effort, and will. We need to learn to combine the persistence and the gentleness, so that we are taking responsibility and developing our will without becoming wilful. Wilfulness means exercising choice without sensitivity, and it usually ends up hurting someone. But once we learn to seamlessly blend kindness and effort we can make progress in developing our will and, at the same time, kindness.

Another meditation we'll learn later is the Metta Bhavana, or development of loving-kindness, which is all about bringing more of those qualities of kindness and appreciation into our lives. By repeatedly bringing our attention back to the breath, and by doing that with as much kindness as possible, we're learning to let go of unwholesome states of mind and develop a calmer and kinder awareness. This process of using our breath as an anchor for our awareness, combined with our ability to choose to act with more patience and kindness, are the two main ways in which we can lessen the influence of our wild mind and instead cultivate our Wildmind.

I've said that we're aware while we're following the breath, and that we're generally unaware when we become drawn into distracted states. This is true, but it's also a slight simplification. At times, you'll find that you are able to maintain a purposeful sense of awareness, and at the same time be aware of the presence of one of the hindrances, such as dullness, restlessness, doubt, craving, or ill will. You can sit there, with part of your mind steadily watching and observing, and perhaps even staying with the breath, but at the same time there are thoughts and emotions bubbling up incessantly. It is a definite sign of progress when this starts to happen. At this point your mind is both mindful and distracted, but your mindfulness has the upper hand. It may not seem like this – you might want all the distracted thinking to stop immediately – but if you keep up the effort to maintain your mindful awareness you'll inevitably discover that the hindrances do start to settle down. What you'll find, as this starts to happen, is that what's left isn't some blank, cold, clean awareness, but a delightfully warm, spacious, and joyful state of mind. It all takes time – but what better way to spend your time, since those positive states of mind increasingly begin to become a part of your normal way of being. You're starting to live in the Wildmind, and to embody its positive qualities.

The benefits of the practice

Developing awareness

The breath becomes a kind of anchor that helps us to stay in awareness, so we go back to the breath over and over again, and that has a number of important benefits. We're practising recognizing the difference between awareness and unawareness. We're also working on developing those qualities of patience, kindness, and gentleness that are so important when we realize when we've been unaware – when we've just come out of being distracted and regained our awareness. We're also training ourselves to stay out of the hindrances – to lessen the hold the wild mind has upon us.

Becoming distracted is a bit like falling over when you're a toddler. When we try to follow the breath it's as though we've decided to walk. But after a few steps we stumble and get distracted. We keep picking ourselves up by going back to the breath. The way children learn to walk is by taking a few steps, falling over, and picking themselves up, over and over again. The way we learn to be more aware is by following the breath, getting distracted, and then going back to the breath – over and over and over again.

In this natural way, through learning not to fall over into the emotional murk of the wild mind, we learn to live in a more balanced way. We learn to contact our Wildmind – the source of calmness, energy, contentment, and concentration.

Developing calmness

I've mentioned that the hindrances are not very satisfying states of mind. Being annoyed, or fantasizing, or undermining ourselves, all involve a lot of mental disharmony. They cause turbulence in our minds, so we find that we're not very calm. Learning to spend less time in the hindrances means that we develop a calmer mind. Note that this does not mean we are trying to make our minds go blank. This is a common misperception about meditation. It is probably not possible for our minds to become blank, but we do aim to make our minds quieter.

> **"**This does not mean we are trying to make our minds go blank. This is a common misperception about meditation.**"**

Developing energy

The hindrances are often states of conflict. We want something, but we don't have it. And we know it would be bad for us if we got it, but we can't help wanting it anyway. We have this person stuck in our heads and we keep thinking about things they've done that we don't like – and we wish they'd just go away. We know that what we said to our partner was harsh, but our pride won't allow us to apologize.

When two energies push in different directions in these ways, there is a tremendous loss of power. We experience a kind of inner friction whereby our energies are lost to us because they are tied up in internal struggles.

As we begin to let go of these emotional patterns, our energy becomes more available to us. Sometimes this energy is experienced physically: we feel currents of energy stirring, perhaps in our hands or in our spine. Sometimes we experience it mentally and emotionally – as inside and outside of our meditation we feel increasingly wholehearted, enthusiastic, and potent.

Becoming more content

Also, the hindrances are not states in which we're happy. If we're fantasizing, for example – either about things we'd rather be doing, or about things we're not happy about – there is emotional disharmony, because we're not happy about what we're doing. Spending less time in distracted states of mind means that we become more content.

Eventually we can be totally content just sitting being aware of our breathing, or anything else we happen to be doing.

Developing concentration

When we're distracted we lack concentration – our mind is flitting from one topic to another like a butterfly. This means we don't experience anything very deeply – like when we're having a conversation with someone but we're also preoccupied and then come to realize that the other person has been talking but we don't know what they've said. Or when we're eating handfuls of raisins but not really tasting them because we're reading and the radio is on. That kind of thing doesn't help us connect very deeply with our experience. And how can we reflect if we can't maintain a focused train of thought? And if we can't reflect then how do we learn? Practising mindfulness helps us to be more concentrated so that we can live more deeply, and appreciate life more fully.

The second stage of the Mindfulness of Breathing

Whenever I introduce a new stage to any of the practices, I'll briefly recap the previous stages. This will help to remind you to work systematically in meditation.

Stage zero

Set up your posture, as described in the posture checklist. Become aware of your body and relax as much as you can before taking your awareness into the physical sensations of your breathing.

Stage one

Spend a few minutes doing the first stage of the practice, counting after each out-breath in cycles of one to ten. When you feel you've begun to calm your mind down a little, move on to the second stage of the practice.

Stage two

In the second stage of the practice we continue to count in cycles of ten breaths, the difference being that this time we count just before each inhalation. Whenever you regain your awareness after being distracted, bring your mind gently back to the breath.

Ending

When you bring the second stage to a close, just let go of the counting and sit for a minute or two, noticing and appreciating the qualities of your experience. Allow yourself to be open to the fruits of the practice (which may not be obvious at first), and take your time coming out of the meditation.

When you feel ready, open your eyes and bring your awareness back to the outside world.

You can listen to a RealAudio file that will guide you through the first two stages of the Mindfulness of Breathing practice. You can connect to the RealAudio file by typing the following address into your browser: www.wildmind.org/realaudio/mob_2.html

If you do not have the free RealOne player program that you need to listen to this file, you can download it from www.real.com.

Varying the firmness of the numbers

You can use different amounts of effort while counting. It's good to play around with this – otherwise we can assume that the way we habitually count is the only way. You can place the numbers as delicately as an airborne feather settling in the palm of your hand, or you can place them as you would rubber-stamp an envelope. And of course there are infinite degrees of effort between these two extremes.

In general, I advise students to use as much effort as they need, but as little as they can get away with – in other words, to find a balance. If you place the number too lightly you'll probably find that your attention wanders. If you place the number too heavily, you'll probably lack sensitivity to the subtler nuances of what's going on in your meditation and either get bored or start to experience resistance to meditation.

At times your mind may be unruly and need a firm hand – with a firm number. At other times your awareness will be more subtle and you can use a lighter touch. What you need to do is learn to find an appropriate level of effort depending upon your state of mind.

Here's an experiment you can try:

Set up your posture, become aware of your body, and relax. Then let your awareness settle on your breathing and begin counting in the way you normally do.

Then gradually try making the numbers firmer, or louder and more definite, slowly increasing the amount of force. When you get to what feels like an uncomfortably loud and firm level of counting, begin to slacken off the counting until you return to the level of firmness with which you started. Notice the effects the various levels of firmness have on you.

Then start gradually to make the numbers lighter, slowly decreasing the level of force behind them. Keep on lightening the numbers until they are as quiet as you can make them. Again, notice the effects the various levels of firmness have on you.

You'll probably find, as most people do, that louder numbers really work at keeping your mind on track, but they also at some point start to seem intrusive and unpleasant. You'll probably also find that using very light numbers brings a more delicate and subtle feeling to your experience, but that your mind also has more of a tendency to wander (although if you didn't do this experiment for very long your mind might not have had much time to wander).

So what you want to do – to repeat the point I made above – is to use the least amount of effort you can get away with, keeping the numbers light and delicate. If your mind starts to wander you can start to increase the amount of effort in order to bring your mind under control. And you can keep making those adjustments as often as you need to.

In this way the effort that we put into the counting can become a very simple and effective way of altering our experience, bringing either more stability (through firmer counting) or more enjoyment and subtlety (through counting more lightly).

When the counting seems boring

Sometimes people find the counting boring, and want to drop it. There can be good reasons and bad reasons for wanting to drop the counting.

Sometimes we've really developed a strong current of stillness and it seems natural to drop the numbers. If so, just let go of the counting and enjoy that undistracted bliss. But often it's just a resistance to structure, or a desire to be passive, and we'd rather just daydream. Be honest about your motivation.

If the numbers seem mechanical, bear in mind that this is not inevitable – it's a product of the way your mind is working. The discomfort of finding the numbers mechanical is an opportunity to learn something about the way you operate. If you approach the numbers mechanically, they'll seem mechanical. On the other hand, if you approach the numbers gracefully and creatively, they'll seem natural and fluid.

One way to contact that natural fluidity is to place the number before or after the breath with as much care as you can. Imagine that you're kissing the cheek of a sleeping child. You want to make contact, but you don't want to cause any disturbance. Place the numbers tenderly, and with sensitivity. If you bring more care and attention into your practice, you won't experience boredom. A mind that is alive and curious finds things in which to be interested.

The differences between the first two stages

Most people find that the first two stages of the Mindfulness of Breathing feel very different from each other. You might have enjoyed one stage more than the other (though people differ on which is most enjoyable).

And if you enjoyed one stage more than the other, you might even have found there was one you really didn't like (more often the second stage, for reasons we'll come to).

People sometimes find that it's easier to remain absorbed in the breath in one stage or the other. Commonly, people will experience more mental chatter in the second stage, though sometimes the second stage will be more concentrated than the first.

The interesting thing is that both stages are structurally identical. How can that be, you might ask? In the first stage you count after the out-breath, while in the second stage you count before the in-breath; it's patently obvious they're different! Let me explain.

The structure of the first stage is:
in, out, 'one', in, out, 'two', in, out, 'three', in, out, 'four' ...

The structure of the second stage is:
'one', in, out, 'two', in, out, 'three', in, out, 'four', in, out ...

If you line both stages up, they look like:
in, out, 'one', in, out, 'two', in, out, 'three', in, out, 'four' ...
      'one', in, out, 'two', in, out, 'three', in, out, 'four' ...

Although you probably experienced the two stages as different in some way, you'll see that structurally they're exactly the same. So why do they feel different?

Why the first two stages feel different

The reason is that where you place the numbers (or more accurately, where you think you're placing the numbers) changes which part of the breath you're most aware of. In the first stage, because you're counting after the out-breath your mind links the counting with the out-breath.

Try taking a deep breath and letting it out. Go on, no one's watching. How does it feel? It feels like:

❖ Letting go
❖ Relaxing
❖ Moving downward
❖ Calming

Taking a deep out-breath (known to us professional breathers as sighing) is what we do when we let go of tension – you know, that moment you go 'phew' when you wake up and find you don't have to go back to school to take the exam you've just been dreaming about.

Now in the second stage you're counting before the in-breath, so your mind links the number more closely to the act of breathing in. So what does breathing in feel like? Try it. Do a big inhalation (remember to breathe out afterwards). It feels like:

❖ Expanding
❖ Opening up
❖ Rising
❖ Energizing

Relaxing before energizing

Breathing in deeply is what you naturally do when you wake up on the first day of vacation, step out on to the balcony of your luxury hotel overlooking the ocean, and notice how good it feels to be alive (as opposed to being in the office). It's also what you do when you look for your wallet and it's not there.

So while the first stage is a stage of letting go, the second stage is a stage of energizing. The first stage is the perfect thing to do when starting a meditation – we let go (hopefully) of all the tension in our bodies and (even more hopefully) all the thoughts flying around in our heads.

Once we've done that, the next stage (the second stage) is where you attempt to energize your relaxed mind and body. By encouraging your body to open up, and by feeling the energy that comes with the in-breath, you help set up the conditions for being aware. Maintaining your awareness requires an upright alert body, and an open chest (see Chapter 2 for more detail). That's exactly what happens in the second stage.

So there's a natural progression here – relaxing and then energizing – and it's important to get these stages in the right order. Of course, if you start meditation in a very tired and sluggish state, perhaps calming yourself is not the best thing to do – you might in that instance want to go straight into the second stage. And if in the second stage you were to realize that your mind was racing, you might want to revert to the first stage in order to slow it down.

In the first and second stages of the practice you have two tools – a brake and an accelerator if you will – which you need to learn to use appropriately.

When your breathing feels awkward

The first stage is meant to be more relaxing, while the second stage is more invigorating, and promotes awareness.

If you haven't managed to develop enough relaxation in stage one, the second stage can at first feel a little stiff and awkward. The problem is probably that you're exercising some kind of subtle control over your breath. Breathing is one of those things that are best done automatically.

In the first stage of the meditation we're just acknowledging the sensation, because we count after the out-breath. So there's less possibility of trying to control the breath – you can't control what's in the past. In the second stage there is a sense of anticipation – and it is possible to control what's about to happen. When your desire to control events meets a sense of anticipation, you find yourself taking charge of the breathing, rather than just watching it.

Since your unconscious is much better at regulating your breathing than your conscious mind, you find that your breathing is a bit stiff, and even uncomfortable. I remember one student saying it felt as though he was breathing backwards, and I know exactly what he meant. For him, it felt like writing with the wrong hand.

This problem will soon sort itself out. You'll find you relax into the second stage if you patiently keep working at it. At some point you'll become more concentrated and 'forget' to control your breath.

However, if you need to, you can always drop back into the first stage of the practice, and return to the second stage when you're more relaxed. Or you can consciously work in the second stage to develop more relaxation by really letting go on the out-breath.

"Breathing is one of those things that are best done automatically.**"**

Noticing after, noticing before

The differences between the first two stages arise from the fact that in the first stage we are acknowledging something that has just happened, whereas in the second stage we are anticipating something that is about to happen.

If you think about it, it's a much more difficult skill to be aware of something coming into being than it is to acknowledge that it has just happened. Think about something as simple as getting annoyed with another person. We all find that from time to time we get annoyed with others – sometimes with no justification at all. We may be acutely aware how unjust it is that we get annoyed, but it keeps happening anyway. It's easy enough to notice that the regrettable occurrence has just happened, but it's very hard indeed to notice the process beginning.

What we're doing in the second stage of the meditation is learning to notice our experience and anticipate the arising of some phenomenon that has not yet come into being. This is a skill that we can all usefully take out into our encounters with the world: learning gradually to notice the first stirrings of our emotional responses, and thereby beginning to have some freedom of choice so that we can decide whether or not it is appropriate to indulge in the response in question.

I've talked about there being a gap between stimulus and response, and that the principle of meditation is that we can learn to choose in that gap. The opportunity for intervention actually has a number of different aspects. Sometimes, as I have pointed out, we notice only in retrospect that we have acted and we have no real choice. At other times we can become aware how we are acting as it happens, and act to modify it. For example, we might realize we are starting to slip into an old habit of being over-critical and decide to drop the subject.

Sometimes we catch the emotion before we have acted on it, and decide not to do so. We find another gap between emotion and action and exert our will-power, our ability to choose, in order to desist from some course of action that our inner wisdom tells us would not be helpful. This is a real advance on blindly lashing out, but it can bring about painful tensions, caused by the fact that we are bottling up a habit.

Eventually, though, we can start to become aware of the way in which a particular stimulus gives rise to an emotional response before the emotional response even starts. We can have a sense of the energies beginning to manifest just below the threshold of consciousness, as a sailor might recognize by the patterns of waves that there is a dangerous reef just below the surface. A great advance indeed, for it means that we can take avoiding action before the emotion leads us into trouble.

"This is a skill that we can all usefully take out into our encounters with the world: learning gradually to notice the first stirrings of our emotional responses."

This is usually how our ethical practice grows out of our practice of mindfulness. We first start to regret actions after we have performed them, and then we start to modify the actions as they happen. Later on we can extend our mindfulness deeper into the flow of events from stimulus to response and choose not to act on an emotion that has arisen. Finally, we can begin to notice the incipient arising of emotions and choose instead another emotional response, for example, to exercise patience rather than anger. When we reach this stage there is no sense that we're bottling anything up, since we allow full expression of our emotional energies in a healthy and positive way.

Of course, there is a stage even beyond this. We are creatures of habit, but our habits cannot persist indefinitely once we decide not to feed them. Eventually, if we continue to practise mindfulness, our habits of selfishness and ill will cease to exist and our personalities become more open, patient, and kind. All this takes is the persistent cultivation of mindfulness.

Counting on your fingers

This suggestion is not based on an assumption that you don't know how to count up to ten unaided! This is a useful technique that I've used when my mind has been very distracted and I need a bit of a hand to get it under control.

What I do is very simple: in the first two stages I count on my fingers as my breath flows in and out. I don't move my fingers – simply take my awareness into each finger in turn, starting with the thumb of my right hand, working my way through each finger in turn, then continuing from the thumb to the pinkie on my left hand.

This really does help to keep your mind more firmly anchored than when you simply follow the breath alone. So why not use this all the time? You could, I suppose, but I find this technique mainly of use when I'm very distracted. Once I've managed to get my mind to settle down I let go of it. I do this because I find that counting on my fingers is effective but slightly crude as well. If you relied too much on this method it might prevent you developing more refinement and skill in your meditation. Perhaps it would be like never getting beyond using stabilizers when learning to ride a bicycle.

Although I said I don't move my fingers, I felt the need to do so when I first tried out this method. Unless I physically moved my fingers a tiny bit I found I had difficulty telling which finger was which (and that's despite spending years trying to learn to play the trumpet). Perhaps you won't have the same problem and can go straight on to counting your fingers without having to wiggle them. I stress that I don't do this all the time – only when my mind is particularly unruly and needs to be, well, taken in hand.

Stepping back from the process

At this point it might be a good idea to step back from learning meditation and reflect a little on how it's going. Learning meditation is not easy – in fact it's one of the more challenging and heroic things that a human being can choose to do with his or her life. Learning meditation involves learning to see ourselves – warts and all. It requires that we take responsibility for ourselves rather than using other people as scapegoats for our own failings (by saying, for example, 'you made me angry').

There are always ups and downs in learning any skill. Anyone who's learned something like skiing – or roller-blading, or ice-skating – as an adult will remember thinking, 'this is impossible', and regretting they ever started. It can also be like that with meditation, and I'd like to encourage you by reminding you that you are not alone and that you are going through a process that many other people have been through – and come out the other side.

One process that many people have been through is the discovery that meditation seems to give you problems you never thought you had. Before, you just had an irritating colleague. Now you realize that you are responsible for your own mental states and that your irritability is a construct of your own mind. It's not that meditation has created this problem, of course – it's just made you more aware of it. This can initially be a shock. At first it might seem that it would be more comfortable to retreat into unawareness – but that might not be an option. Once you've begun to realize that you are responsible for your life and emotions, it's hard to lose that perspective. You've looked behind the curtain and realized that the wizard is a little old man pulling strings, and can never again see him as the all-powerful Oz.

A related problem is that of getting more in touch with emotions that you hadn't previously fully acknowledged. Meditation can be a very accurate and unflattering mirror. Without meditation it can be very easy to delude ourselves into seeing ourselves as being purer, more patient, more socially competent, or kinder than we actually are. Meditation polishes the mirror, and this too can be a shock to the system. Cynthia, a child psychiatrist from New England, commented, 'I meditated today at the office and noticed that I can really slow down after meditating. I also noticed how irritable I was on arriving home when interacting with others. Ugh. I'm wishing I could be more mellow.' This is a common experience – slowing down enough to be able to see yourself in the mirror. Another student made the same connection: 'It may be just coincidental but I have felt quite emotional in a negative sort of way. I don't know if opening up in meditation has allowed an opportunity for my more repressed feelings to come to the surface (with some of the busyness out of the way).' This too is a phase that will pass. You'll still have a more accurate perception of yourself, but it will be tempered by a sense of the progress you're making. In a way, the mirror becomes four-dimensional so that you can see yourself not only as you are, but also as you were and as you will be. Seeing ourselves changing, and realizing what we can become, is the greatest antidote to self-doubt that I know of.

In the short term we need to have a sense of trust in the process. The path might at first seem hard and rocky, the way ahead almost impassable, but over time your stamina and resilience will improve, and so will your patience and forgiveness of yourself. The path has its own rewards.

Between the stages

Perhaps this is a good time to remind you of your body. I've emphasized that it's important to set up your posture at the start of a period of meditation. This provides you with better conditions. It's like making sure that your kindling is stacked properly and your matches are dry, so that you'll end up with a good blaze instead of a pile of smouldering wood and a bad temper.

When you take your attention away from your posture in order to be more aware of your breath, you'll often find that your posture starts to drift. You may find that some parts of your body start to sag, while others become tense, and these changes lead to mental and emotional changes. The tension in your shoulders may be related to some anger you've started to experience. The sagging in your spine may be related to a feeling of despair that's crept in. If you relax your shoulders, the anger will start to disappear; if you straighten your spine, you'll start to feel more confident.

As you become more proficient at meditation, you'll learn that you can periodically take your attention away from your breath for a few seconds in order to check your posture and make minor corrections. You'll get so good at this that you'll be able to effectively maintain a continuous awareness of your breath. Remember learning to drive? You probably found that at first you'd take your attention off the road to change gear and when you returned your attention to the road (several long seconds later) you'd find that you'd drifted to one side or that a red traffic light had appeared from nowhere. Later, you'll have found that you were able to shift gear without taking your awareness significantly from what was going on around you. The same thing happens in meditation – we learn to deal with the seeming complexity of managing our posture and what we're doing with the focus of our attention – elegantly, and even effortlessly.

A good way to start practising this skill of monitoring your posture without disrupting your meditation is to check and correct your posture between stages. You might want to do this every time you move from one stage to the next. Later, you'll find that you can integrate monitoring your posture into your practice in the way that I've described.

The third stage of the Mindfulness of Breathing

Stage zero
Set up your posture, as described in the posture checklist.

Stages one and two
Then spend a few minutes doing the first two stages of the practice. When you feel ready, move on to the third stage.

Stage three
In the third stage of the practice, drop the counting, and just follow the breath coming in and out. Do this for perhaps five minutes.

Ending the meditation
Let your awareness broaden from your breath into the rest of your body, and from there into your mind and emotions. Notice and appreciate any changes – subtle or obvious – in your mental or emotional states. Give yourself time to assimilate your experience.

Once you feel ready, open your eyes, and bring your awareness (your altered awareness) back into the world that surrounds you.

You can listen to a RealAudio file that will guide you through the first three stages of the Mindfulness of Breathing practice. You can connect to the RealAudio file by typing the following address into your browser: www.wildmind.org/realaudio/mob_3.html

If you do not have the free RealOne player program that you need to listen to this file, you can download it from www.real.com.

Balancing alertness and relaxation

While stage one helps us to develop more calm (by emphasizing the qualities of the out-breath), and stage two helps us to develop more energy and awareness (by emphasizing the qualities of the in-breath), the third stage emphasizes the in-breath and the out-breath equally. This helps us to blend the calm relaxation of the first stage with the energized awareness of the second.

Ideally, we are developing a sense of energetic calm awareness, or a calmly energized awareness.

In stage three you can be aware of the constant oscillation between the calming out-breath and the energizing in-breath, and allow the qualities of the out-breath and the in-breath to permeate each other.

Modifying an analogy the Buddha himself used, you can think about dough. When you're making dough, what you're doing is taking two contrasting substances – wet and dry – and combining them together in a perfectly balanced blend. If you add too much water, you'll have a sticky mess; if you add too much flour, you'll have a dry, cracked ball. Get the proportions just right and you'll have a dough that is pliable and workable. This stage of the Mindfulness of Breathing helps us to develop pliability of mind; to get our minds into a calm and energetic state in which we can work to develop a much greater degree of concentration and focus.

Thought trains

In the third stage, we've let go of the counting. The counting was a support to our mindfulness, a bit like the stabilizers from our bike. I remember being terrified when my dad told me it was time to take the stabilizing wheels off. Surely I would fall! And maybe I did. I can't remember. But if I did fall, it never did any lasting harm, I'm glad to say.

When we take away our stabilizers in the Mindfulness of Breathing, there's a greater likelihood that we will fall. Fortunately, we're not likely to hurt ourselves, since 'falling' in this case just means becoming distracted. Many people find they get more distracted when they start learning this third stage.

We talk about trains of thought. You can think of these as being like real locomotive trains that pull out of a busy station and go rattling off. Most of them don't go anywhere that we want to go. (Most of them are to do with worrying, getting angry, running ourselves down, and so on.) But our mind is like a restless and curious child who keeps going through the open doors into the carriages.

Before we know it we're miles away from where we wanted to be (often in dangerous territory), and it takes us for ever to get home.

You can teach yourself just to watch the trains pulling up and pulling away, being aware of them, and choosing not to board them.

Are there any trains we want to board? Yes. Some thoughts can be useful, if they are reflections on our meditation, for example. Such thoughts take us deeper into our meditation. One difference between these thought trains and those that take us into distractions is that when we're reflecting (as opposed to being distracted), we know what we're thinking and why, and what effect those thoughts are having. By contrast, distracted thoughts are like dreams – we don't know we're in them until we 'wake up'.

Using anchors

If the first two stages have gone really well, letting go of the numbers can allow us to develop a deeper and more balanced concentration. However, if we haven't managed to develop enough calmness in the first two stages, it's easy to get lost in the third stage.

This often happens because the counting has been acting as an anchor for our awareness: it prevents us drifting too far away from the breath. So if we let go of the counting we can often float off into distraction.

One way to retain an anchor while letting go of the numbers is to use a physical anchor. I sometimes use the physical sensations in my hands in the same way as I use the numbers. At the end of each out-breath and in-breath I take my awareness to my hands. This helps to keep me grounded. Basically this is similar to the technique of counting on the fingers that we looked at earlier, but this time we're not counting, so we don't need to be aware of each individual finger.

I maintain my awareness of my hands all the way through the cycle of the breath. When I do this I am still being aware of the breath, but I'm also keeping some of my awareness in my hands. This isn't as hard as it might sound. It's a bit like walking and chewing gum at the same time. How I experience this is that I feel my breath flowing towards my hands, and then flowing away from my hands, over and over again. This helps prevent me drifting away from the breath.

The physical anchor is a more refined anchor than the counting because it's non-verbal – it cuts down on the amount of thinking, so that your mind can develop a deeper level of stillness.

You can also vary which parts of the hands you are aware of. You can be aware of both hands in their entirety, or you can be aware of only the tips of your thumbs in contact with each other if you are using the dhyana mudra that we encountered in the posture workshop section. Being aware of only the thumb tips can bring a lovely sense of delicate energy into your awareness.

What's a good meditation?

If you've been doing the exercises regularly, you've been meditating for a few days now, and you will have seen some ups and downs in your practice. There are probably some meditations that you would describe as 'good' and some as 'bad'. But what does it really mean to have a 'good' meditation?

There are at least two answers to this question. Both answers given here are valid, but one is more useful than the other. The first answer would be that a good meditation is one in which you feel concentrated, where you're enjoying yourself, and where there aren't many distractions. There's an absence of frustration. This is the most common answer, and it's the less useful of the two.

The second answer is that a good meditation is one in which you have taken every opportunity to return your attention to the breath – no matter how distracted you have been. You might have become very distracted, but every time you realized this you took your awareness back to the breath. This is a much more useful way to assess a good meditation. Meditation is more of an activity than an experience. Meditation is the active cultivation of positive mental states. In meditation it's the effort you make towards change that is important. The results are important too, but to make them the priority is to put the cart before the horse.

Another reason that the second way of looking at this question is more useful is that 'good' meditations of the first type will come and go, whereas you can have 'good' meditations of the second type every time you sit on your cushion. Also, this is a more realistic way of looking at things. In meditation you're working to alter your mental and emotional habits. You're subtly changing your personality. In a 'good' meditation of the first type you might be having an easy time – your meditation is very enjoyable – but you might not be actively engaging with yourself, you might actually be rather passive. But a meditation in which you have really worked – even although you've experienced a lot of distractions and not had an easy time of it: that is a good meditation.

"In meditation it's the effort you make towards change that is important.**"**

Signs of progress

People who are new to meditation often need some reassurance that they're on the right path. It's often hard to tell whether you are making progress or not. I emphasized earlier that one of the things that will help you to stick with your meditation practice is the ability to notice and appreciate small changes. So here are some of the small changes that you might want to watch out for.

* **Other people noticing that you are changing.** Sometimes it's hard to have a sense of perspective on ourselves. We can easily concentrate on supposed failures to the extent that we completely miss positive changes. My meditation students often report that other people notice that they are changing: becoming more relaxed, less reactive, and more friendly.

* **Developing more concentration.** The counting can give you a sense of whether you are developing more concentration. Being able to count to ten even once can be a step forward. If you make it to there, you might want to aim to count to ten three times in a row. You might notice that you have the ability to count continuously and also have a lot of thoughts arising. That's great! Pay more attention to the fact that you have developed more continuity of awareness than you do to the fact that there are still lots of stray thoughts.

* **Having interesting experiences in meditation.** You may begin to notice unusual things – like a delightful sense of rhythm in your breathing, or the subtle way your body moves in response to your heartbeat. These are signs that you are developing more concentration and awareness in meditation, and you would be wise to pay attention to such experiences. Some of the things you experience might seem a little odd. Seeing patterns of moving lights is a common example. This is a good sign, in that you are moving into a deeper state of concentration, but it's best

not to pay much attention to those lights or they will become a distraction and slow your progress.

❖ **Spontaneous resolution of posture problems.** Sometimes you'll notice parts of your body relax spontaneously. Sometimes a problem with your posture might suddenly disappear.

❖ **Paying more attention to the outside world.** It's a very good sign when you start to slow down outside of meditation and notice the beauty in the world. After meditating, colours sometimes appear brighter and shapes seem more vivid.

❖ **Noticing your posture more.** You may become more aware of your body during the course of the day, and notice how awareness of your body grounds you. You may begin to understand better how your posture influences your emotions and mind.

❖ **Noticing you have choices.** You may start to notice the gap between stimulus and response, and realize that you have a choice about how to respond. You can choose not to respond habitually, and instead choose a more appropriate and creative response.

❖ **Becoming more aware of your actions.** Before we get to the stage of being aware of our actions *before* we perform them, we notice what we've done only *after* the event. It's tempting to feel frustration when you realize you've lost your temper once again, but it's a good sign that you're noticing it at all. With practice you'll be able to catch those responses earlier and earlier, until you're able to choose to respond more creatively.

❖ **Feelings of calmness.** You may have spells of greater than usual calmness in your meditation or afterwards. You may even experience some reluctance to end a period of meditation.

❖ **Interesting and vivid dreams.** When your meditation begins to 'bite', it often leads to more vivid and meaningful dreams. Pay attention to these and see what you can learn from them.

❖ **Time passing quickly.** When you're really enjoying something, time passes more quickly. It's common to notice that time passes faster in certain meditations.

Transcending time (just a little)

Meditation will take no time. In fact it will take less than no time. What I mean by this is that if you spend time meditating you'll actually have more time available than if you didn't. If our minds are clearer and more focused through meditation, we'll be more efficient and effective in what we do. If we are less flustered at work we'll have more harmonious relationships with our colleagues and spend less time in conflicts. If we are more mindful we are likely to notice when our attention is wandering. Perhaps we will notice when the quality of our work is beginning to slip and have a break. These things will more than repay the time we've invested in meditation.

While we're on the subject of time, I sometimes hear meditation students saying that they are 'having trouble finding the time to meditate'. This is an interesting metaphor, this idea of finding time. It suggests that time is something that we can find just lying around, unclaimed and unused. Perhaps sometimes it is – when we were children on vacation, for example. But this metaphor suggests to me some degree of passivity.

Students who do manage to establish a regular meditation practice (and therefore experience the benefits of meditation) tend to use the metaphors 'setting aside time' or 'creating time' to meditate. Of course you can't really create time, any more than you can create space or matter, but the attitude is that time is something you have to take charge of and make something of. You don't just wait for it to turn up, you reallocate tasks and schedule your priorities so that you can do what is important to you. And meditation is one of the most important things you can do with your time. We talk about time management, but there's really no such thing – what we manage is ourselves.

Parkinson's Law and meditation

Another thing I've noticed is that if you fit the important things in (things that make a real difference to our lives), you still somehow manage to get a lot done. This is the corollary of Parkinson's Law, which is that 'work expands to fit the time available.' If we try to fit our meditation around less important things, it won't work – the less important things will fill up the time because there is no end to the number of unimportant things to occupy our time.

Those things seem important while we're doing them, but that's because anxiety makes unimportant things seem crucial. If you meditate, you can develop a more realistic view of what is important and what is not. That's a powerful change to come from ten minutes a day.

In *The Seven Habits of Highly Effective People* Steven Covey tells a very illuminating parable concerning the difference between urgency and importance. He talks about coming across a man who is frantically sawing away at a pile of wood. He has a huge pile of wood to saw, so you can understand why he's going at it so hard and why the sweat is pouring off his brow. After a while, though, you realize the man isn't accomplishing very much. There's hardly any sawdust coming from the cut in the wood, and the small amount of sawdust appearing is just powder. You cough quietly to catch his attention and suggest to him that he'd get on a lot faster if he stopped and sharpened his saw. He doesn't even slow down from his fruitless sawing as he irritably tells you that he doesn't have time to stop and sharpen his saw: 'Can't you see how much work I have to do?'

We're very often just like that man. We're so caught up in 'urgency addiction' that we don't stop to see whether what we're doing is actually working or not. We concentrate on the urgent at the expense of the important. So what is important? What does it mean to 'sharpen the saw' of our lives? Many things are important but not urgent: improving our relationships with our friends and family, spending time listening to people, planning our time, reflecting on where we want to go in life, exercising, relaxing, renewing ourselves through creative pursuits – all these are important, but not urgent.

" Anxiety makes unimportant things seem crucial. "

Right at the top of the list of important (and non-urgent) activities, I would place meditation. I regularly tell myself that meditation is the most important thing I'm going to do all day. It's not urgent to meditate, but it sure is important.

Ultimately, you might find that meditation is not one more thing to fit into an already busy life, but a source of energy and guidance, helping every other aspect of your life to flow more smoothly.

Timing the stages

Beginners often assume that timing their meditation will be very distracting. They sometimes wonder if they should use an alarm clock, or some other mechanical method. Actually, an alarm clock or beeper can be jarring and unpleasant; most meditators just have a clock or watch in front of them. They'll open their eyes from time to time and see how long they've been sitting. It really isn't a great distraction. Just make sure to place your clock or watch where you can see it without having to move your head, or your eyes.

One problem with clocks is that we can end up 'clock watching'. Clock watching is a sign of restlessness or self-doubt, and both restlessness and doubt can be strengthened by frequently opening your eyes to look at the time. With doubt you reinforce the feeling that time is dragging faster than you can cope with it, and with restlessness you are physically restless in frequently opening your eyes.

When I feel like I want to look at the clock, I don't do it immediately. I breathe for another round of ten breaths or so, and only then do I check what the time is. This reinforces the fact that I am in control: I deliberately choose not to look at the clock. It reinforces a sense of potency. It also undercuts the physical restlessness by separating it in time from the desire to move.

If you want to avoid clocks altogether, and have a PDA that runs on the Palm Operating System, there's a handy meditation timer developed by Jan Exner. It's a free program, and you can download it from his site at www.jan-exner.de It's a nice little program that lets you just get on with the meditation without having to bother with a clock at all.

The fourth stage of the Mindfulness of Breathing

Stage zero
Prepare for the meditation by setting up your posture and relaxing.

Stages one to three
Do stages one, two, and three, first of all counting after the out-breath, then before the in-breath, and then letting go of the counting.

Stage four
In the fourth and final stage of this meditation, begin to narrow the focus of your awareness so that you're more and more aware of the sensation where the breath first passes over the rims of the nostrils or over the upper lip.

Ending the practice
Take your time, and enjoy coming out of the meditation. First of all, let your awareness expand from the tips of your nostrils into the whole of your breathing, then expand your awareness further into the whole of your body, continuing to encourage your posture to be upright, open, and relaxed. Then spend some time enjoying the fruits of the practice, noticing the subtle (or sometimes quite noticeable) changes that have taken place in your mind, body, and emotions.

Only after you have given yourself a minute of two to appreciate the changes that have taken place should you gradually start to broaden your awareness into the outside world. Notice the smells, the sounds, the touch of the air on your skin. Notice the sense of space around you. Then, when you feel ready, open your eyes and take your awareness fully into the outside world.

You can listen to a RealAudio file that will guide you through all four stages of the Mindfulness of Breathing practice. You can connect to the RealAudio file by typing the following address into your browser: www.wildmind.org/realaudio/mob_4.html

If you do not have the free RealOne player program that you need to listen to this file, you can download it from www.real.com.

A nasal experiment (best performed alone)

This might sound weird, but have you ever checked to see just how sensitive the rims of your nostrils are? Well, I didn't expect you were going to admit it.

Try touching the inner rims of your nostrils as gently as you can. Use the very tip of your finger, and try to find the lightest touch that you can still feel. You should find that you're able to feel your fingertip almost before it makes physical contact with your nostrils. You might even be able to feel the warmth of your fingertip from a short distance away.

The rims of your nostrils are covered with tiny hairs, a fraction of a millimetre long. Each hair has a very sensitive nerve at the root, and every time your breath passes through your nostrils, these nerves are triggered.

Of course we don't usually notice those sensations, but it's an excellent exercise to try to be aware of the breath passing over your nostrils. Having to pay attention to such a refined sensation encourages your mind to move on to a more subtle level of perception. And since it's not possible to remain aware of such a subtle sensation unless your mind is very still, the fourth stage encourages deeper levels of mental and emotional stillness.

Moving from stage three to stage four

In the third stage of the Mindfulness of Breathing, we're usually aware of quite a large area of the sensations associated with the breath. We might have been focusing primarily on the belly, or the chest, or the sensations in the head and throat. These involve large muscles like the diaphragm and collections of bones and muscles like the ribcage – fairly large anatomical structures.

In the fourth stage, however, we're focusing on a very small area of sensation: the rims of the nostrils.

I like to make a smooth transition from the third to the fourth stage in order to maintain a sense of continuity and to bring the quality of elegance into the practice. It's very easy just to suddenly (and inelegantly) 'drop' the strong sensations that you've been following in the third stage, and then have to scrabble around trying to find the much more subtle sensations on the nostrils associated with the fourth stage. This can be disruptive to your meditation, so it's better to try to make a smooth transition from one stage to the other.

I do this by narrowing my focus with every breath. Over a series of perhaps seven or eight breaths, I'll start to narrow down my focus, gradually 'homing in' on the sensations on the rims of the nostrils.

As I finish the third stage of the meditation, I might be focused on all the sensations of the breath, from the head right down to the belly. Then for a few breaths I might perhaps focus on the whole of the chest, throat, and head, leaving out the belly. Then just the upper chest, throat, and head. Then the throat and head. Then the head. Then just inside the nostrils, then the tips of the nostrils.

You might want to spend a few breaths on each stage of the homing-in process, though with time you'll find that you can accomplish a smooth transition more quickly.

Gradually homing-in in this way brings more elegance and smoothness into your mind and practice, and helps the stages flow together so that you can maintain continuity and deepen your concentration. Simply jumping from stage three to stage four is rather crude, and developing more of a sense of elegance can take your practice on to a new level of refinement.

Maintaining subtlety in the practice

Because the sensations at the nostrils are so subtle, there can be a tendency to breathe more forcibly in order to heighten the sensation. Try to resist this while allowing your breath to be light and delicate. Ideally you shouldn't be able to hear your breathing. (Sometimes you'll think you're hearing your breath, when it's actually a purely internal sound, that only exists in your head. This is fine, and you shouldn't try to get rid of that sound. Instead you should be aware of it as well as the physical sensations.) Instead of breathing more heavily, try to find the subtle sensations by allowing your mind itself to become more receptive – this is the purpose of this stage of the practice. Making your breath coarser by snorting (yes, it can get that bad!) can make it easier to feel the breath, but undermines the development of a more refined perception of it.

If you don't manage at first to find the sensations on the rims of the nostrils, you can be aware of the breath in your nostrils: cool on the in-breath and warm on the out-breath. Some people find it easier to detect the sensation on their upper lip, and that's all right as well. Over time, try to refine your awareness so that you become aware of the most delicate sensations possible – these are the true focus of this stage.

If you can detect the sensations of the air flowing over the rims of your nostrils, congratulations; now it's time for you to refine the meditation even more. For example, you can notice whether the sensations are more pronounced in the left or the right nostril, and you can try to take more awareness into any 'dead spots' where sensations are lacking. Or you can become more aware of the sensations just at the front of the rims of your nostrils, rather than all around – just to stretch your ability to detect very subtle sensations. There are always greater degrees of refinement to which we can take our concentration.

Occasionally, your mind will settle down and you'll notice some interesting and subtle sensations related to your breathing. For example, you might hear the soft internal sound I mentioned earlier

– a sound like the sound of your breathing but which isn't coming from any physical process. Or you might experience a sensation like silk associated with your breathing but not exactly a part of it. Or you might notice a delightful sense of 'flow' that accompanies the rhythm of your breathing. (These things can be hard to describe.) What seems to be happening is that your mind has moved to a more subtle level of perception, and found for itself objects of concentration that are correspondingly more delicate than the usual ones. Far from being a distraction, such sensations act as doorways into even deeper states of calmness and concentration. Cherish them when they arise, and let your awareness become absorbed in them.

Becoming a dragon

Your breathing is a gateway into your body — not so much in the obvious sense that the air you breathe starts on the outside before you breathe it in, but more in the sense that when you are being aware of your breathing you are being aware of your body. When you feel your breath entering and leaving your body, what you are experiencing is your body.

Most of us are not as aware as we could be of our bodies. We tend to spend a lot of time thinking, and not enough time exercising. And even when we are using our bodies, we might not really pay that much attention to them. I'm thinking of times when we're walking along the street, lost in thought — on autopilot. At those times we are barely aware of the world around us, never mind our physical experience. What we are experiencing is mostly our thoughts, and perhaps some emotion connected with those thoughts. In the Zen tradition they talk about 'dragon's head, snake's body' to describe this imbalance. It's as if we are these enormous heads floating along the street, trailing our feeble, atrophied bodies behind us.

So sitting down and becoming aware of our breathing is a way of getting back in touch with our physicality. As we become more aware of our bodies, we start to feel calmer. As our snake bodies begin to fill out and develop, and catch up with the development of our dragon heads, we start to ground ourselves. We begin to experience ourselves more fully, and this has a subtle but powerful calming effect. Slowly, gradually, our turbulent minds begin to settle down, and we begin to experience a joyful, lucid calmness. The snake body begins to fill out, to take on a more powerful aspect, until we're more truly balanced and complete.

66When you feel your breath entering and leaving your body, what you are experiencing is your body.99

Our breathing is also a gateway into our emotions. Our emotions and our breathing are intimately bound up with each other. When we are anxious, we tend to breathe rapidly; when we relax, our breathing slows and deepens. Becoming more aware of your breathing will help you become more aware of your emotions, and more able to influence your emotions. As you spend more time with your breath, you will learn that you can subtly, but powerfully, influence your emotions by changing the rate or depth of your breathing, or by using your imagination in combination with your breathing. Being more aware of your breathing gives you more choice: you'll be able to learn to tap into deep-rooted sources of energy by gently encouraging yourself to breathe in a different pattern.

Times to meditate

Although you can meditate any time, motivational psychologists have shown that if you want to establish a routine, the mornings are best. Many people find it useful to get up early and meditate before the pressures of the day begin to mount. They want to prepare for the day so that it goes well. Other people like to meditate before going to bed in order to 'unwind'. Both these approaches can work.

I'm far from being a 'morning person', but I do prefer to meditate early in the day. Perhaps it's not a good idea to limit ourselves with the labels 'morning person' and 'evening person'. Even those of us with an allergy to mornings can benefit from getting up a little earlier. The beneficial effects of twenty minutes' meditation before hitting the streets far outweighs the benefits of another few minutes in bed.

Among my students, those who meditate in the morning tend to get better results. This is because when you meditate at night you have to process all the day's events. Once you sit down there may well be a lot of restlessness as a result of all the stimulation you've received, whereas if you meditate in the morning you've just spent two hours or more processing the previous day's stimulation in your dreams. (You may sleep for seven or eight hours, but only about two and a half of those are actually spent dreaming.)

You might even want to experiment with meditating during the day. You could try closing the door, switching off the phone, and taking ten to fifteen minutes of relaxing and stimulating meditation.

And there's no reason why you can't meditate more than once a day.

Choosing a time

Probably the least effective thing you can do is tell yourself that you'll just fit your meditation in some time during the day. That time will probably never come, because you have implicitly made a statement that everything else in your life is more important than your meditation. In order to establish a regular practice you need to decide when you're going to meditate and stick to it. If you plan your week, then plan your meditation into your week to make sure it happens. When you are planning your time (and any time that you are considering skipping meditation), tell yourself, 'My meditation practice is the most important thing I'm going to do all day.' It's too important to leave to chance.

On a related note, many people (myself included) find it hard at times to schedule activities that we see as mainly benefiting ourselves. We may be infinitely flexible when it comes to accommodating the demands of work or family, but we find it hard to set aside time to go to the gym or to meditate. And that's despite knowing through experience how beneficial those activities are.

One thing you can do to help you commit to meditation, or other activities you see as being mainly for yourself, is remind yourself that doing those things actually benefits others too. If you're relaxed and easy to be around, that helps everyone you know.

But what I've found even more effective is the cultivation of a sense that it's good to spend time doing things that benefit mainly myself. As I go into meditation, I think to myself, 'Just for me!' in an inner tone of voice that conveys relish and warmth. When I do this my body relaxes and I experience a sense of delight and enjoyment. My meditation practice comes to feel as if it's a treat or reward, and I find that I'm now more comfortable spending time on myself.

Places to meditate

Although I've suggested you can meditate anywhere, like the office, it can be good to have a particular place to meditate regularly, and to make that place a little special, meaningful, and beautiful. You can do this by having pictures that remind you of why you want to meditate – whether religious imagery or natural imagery. You can have candles and incense. I find the ritual of 'lighting up' quite soothing and grounding, especially if I do it with mindfulness, and in a spirit of reverence. Sports psychologists have found that runners who see their running gear first thing in the morning are far more likely to run regularly than those who keep their gear out of sight. The same is likely to be true for meditators.

It will also help if you have your meditation equipment already set up so that you see it first thing in the morning. This will help cut through your early-morning torpor and remind you about your decision to meditate at the start of the day.

Should you listen to music while meditating?

The idea that you should listen to music while meditating is very common. It probably goes back to seeing meditation as little more than a means of relaxation. Of course, meditation does help you to relax, but it goes beyond that and helps us to be more alert and focused. Music is likely to get in the way of that. If you're trying to pay one-pointed attention to your breathing, you can't listen to music at the same time, and if you're trying to listen to music you can't fully concentrate on your breathing. I'm also wary that the enjoyment in our meditation practice may end up coming from the music we're listening to rather than from the inner sense of harmony we're bringing into being.

Focusing on music is fine, and I wholeheartedly suggest you try it; I also suggest you try doing it when you're not meditating. I'd go further and suggest that listening to music, if done properly, can be a meditation in itself, just as walking or washing the dishes can be. You can take many activities and make them richer and more satisfying by taking more awareness into them. Music is just one example. If you're going to listen to music as meditation, then try not to do anything else at the same time. Don't work, or read, or balance your accounts while you're listening. Just listen to the music. Sit or lie down comfortably, and just pay attention to the music. You'll probably find you enjoy it like never before.

Dealing with noise

Carol, one of my meditation students, lives in a very noisy apartment in New York. She says,

> 'The subway train is right across the street, the police/fire station is right around the corner, and to top it all there is a dance club on the bottom floor of my building! I've tried pretty much everything – earplugs, music, meditating at work instead of home. The only thing that really works is just to let it go and stop fighting it, but sometimes the noise will still yank me out of concentration.'

I replied as follows:

> 'I think I used to live in that apartment, except that it was in the city centre of Glasgow, Scotland. I think you're on the right track by stopping fighting the noise. Take that one step further and appreciate the noise – embrace it. As you prepare for meditation, really notice and appreciate all the noise around you. Call to mind the living, breathing, feeling human beings behind the noise and wish them well. Then accept that noise as part of your meditation practice. Stay loosely focused on your breathing, and let the noise be a sort of secondary focus – like the ring around the bull's-eye. If you stop seeing the noise as the enemy of the practice and instead see it as part of the practice, the conflict will vanish.'

Trying to fight the noise is unlikely to work. The noise is not going to go away because you don't like it. If you respond aggressively to it you're just getting yourself into a fight that you cannot win. In that apartment in Glasgow I had a dance club across the street, a taxi rank outside the window, and a washing machine just the other side of the wall from where I meditated. When the washing machine became noisy, what I would do was embrace the noise, just as I suggested to Carol.

"Trying to fight the noise is unlikely to work. The noise is not going to go away because you don't like it.**"**

I'd take this even further. What I'd do was reflect that the noise of the washing machine was a perception that existed in my consciousness. Since the noise of the washing machine was in my consciousness, and since my consciousness was meditating, I reasoned that the washing machine was also meditating. Realizing this made the washing machine noise just another part of my experience, like the sense of weight on my cushion, or my breath, or the emotions in my heart. It was no longer something separate from me that was interfering with my meditation, but was a part of my meditation. Doing this, such noises could cease to be a problem altogether, and actually seemed to enrich my experience of meditation.

Of course the logic in the above paragraph might not be entirely sound, but the important thing was that in creatively finding a way to stop seeing the noise as an enemy and start seeing it as just another part of my experience – and a possible aid to my meditation – it became an actual aid to my meditation.

Reviewing where we've been

In the first stage of the Mindfulness of Breathing, we worked on calming and relaxing the mind through focusing on the out-breath.

The second stage helps bring more energy and awareness into our relaxed and calmed mind, so that we are more alert (but in a relaxed way).

The third stage blends these two qualities or calm and alertness, to help us develop a calm, energetic awareness. When your mind is like this (you might not have got there yet but it will come with practice), it is very 'pliable', to use the traditional term. In other words, your mind has become a very powerful tool, capable of being applied to any object of concentration that you choose.

What we do with this tool in the fourth stage is develop one-pointed awareness. This isn't a forced concentration, but a natural absorption that is based on interest, even fascination.

Why is concentration so important? That's another story.

Why all the emphasis on concentration?

Concentration enriches life, while distraction dilutes life.

Have you ever had the experience of talking with a friend while you're distracted, and then realizing you haven't been listening because you've drifted off on some other train of thought? We all do this from time to time. How can we develop deep and meaningful relationships with others if we can't stay focused? How can we deepen our understanding of ourselves if we don't experience anything but our surface distractions?

Concentration allows us to go more deeply into our experiences. It allows us to experience more intensely, so that we can be more present with other people, and more present with ourselves.

Concentration allows us to really enjoy what we're doing, whether it's walking in the countryside, reading a book, writing, talking, or thinking.

Concentration allows us to think more clearly and deeply. When we can stay with a train of thought without wandering off, we can ask more penetrating questions of ourselves and, crucially, be able to hear the deep, considered, and wise answers that come from our depths. This power of reflective concentration becomes crucial when we move on to vipassana practices that require us to use thoughts or images as the objects of concentration.

Stage omega

We've talked about 'stage zero' as the important preliminary stage in which we set up good conditions for meditation by working with our posture and our inner attitudes. I've compared it to the stage of mixing the ingredients for a cake, as well as making sure that the oven is at the right temperature. In other words, we're making sure that the conditions are congruent with the outcome we want to achieve. But in baking a cake there are also some things you want to do at the end of the baking process to make sure the cake turns out right. You want to make sure, for example, that you have oven gloves on so that you don't burn your hands and drop the cake on the floor. You need to check that the cake is thoroughly cooked and doesn't need a few more minutes in the oven. You need to put the cake on a rack so that it doesn't go soggy.

Similar considerations apply in our meditation practice. It's possible to ruin a perfectly good meditation by hurrying out of the practice. So here are a few tips to help ensure that your meditation ends well. I call this process of ending the meditation 'stage omega', because it's the final stage of the meditation, although it isn't usually enumerated.

Give yourself time to absorb the effects of the meditation

If you don't pay attention to the effects the meditation has had on your mind and emotions, you might not realize that any changes have taken place. This can be rather dispiriting, to say the least. We often develop much more of a sense of calmness than we are consciously aware of, and if we don't give ourselves time to appreciate this we might immediately undo the positive states we've created by smothering it with despondent or frustrated thoughts and feelings.

Take your meditation into the world

In a way, stage omega is not really the end of your meditation. It's just a transition from meditating on a cushion with our eyes closed, to meditating with our eyes open in the midst of everyday activity.

Our meditation should have a beneficial effect on the way we live, and it's more likely to do that if we make the transition from sitting meditation to everyday activity as smooth and elegant as possible.

Under the heading 'Ending the practice' in the section that describes the fourth stage of the Mindfulness of Breathing (page 142), notice how I suggest that you gradually broaden your awareness. At the end of the fourth stage you're focusing on the subtle sensations at the rims of your nostrils. You can broaden your awareness from that narrow focus to become aware of the whole breathing process. Then you can become aware of the whole of your body, and then include other dimensions of awareness such as feeling, emotion, and your mind. Lastly, you can broaden your awareness right out into the world around you, becoming aware of your external sensations of space, sound, touch, and light.

> "It's possible to ruin a perfectly good meditation by hurrying out of the practice."

Actually, it's very beneficial to go further than that so that you try to maintain your mindfulness as you get off your cushion, bow to your shrine (if that's the sort of thing you do), extinguish the candles, tidy up your meditation equipment, and leave the room. Even then, you should try to maintain your awareness as you go on to the next activity.

When I'm leading group meditations, I can often tell how someone has been working in their meditation by the way they get up and move around. If they make a lot of noise and then drop their cushions with a loud 'whump' at the back of the room, it's a fair bet that either they haven't been making much effort or their effort has been rather crude. If their movements are elegant and they put their cushions down quietly and carefully, I have a good idea that they have been working internally with the same kind of grace, balance, and care.

Take your time moving on to the next activity

One very good reason for taking your time coming out of the meditation and moving on to your next activity is that it's possible to become emotionally jarred by rushing into the first item on your 'to do' list. As I mentioned above, it's often the case that you can develop more calmness than you at first realize. Another quality you can develop is a greater degree of emotional sensitivity, and if you do not respect this, the first encounter you have (which might be with someone who has not been meditating and is in a very different mental state from you) might be very unpleasant. Somehow this is less of a problem when you take a few minutes to allow the effects of the meditation to sink in. I don't know what happens in this process of assimilation, but I suspect that in some way your subconscious mind makes subtle internal adjustments that allow you to deal more effectively with these encounters.

If you do give yourself a few minutes to assimilate your experience, and take time to make a smooth and elegant transition from the cushion to the world, you will often have the experience of finding you can meet others, who may even be in a very antagonistic state of mind, and calmly absorb their emotions without even a ripple appearing on the surface of your mind. As the Buddha said, 'If your calmness is like a great lake, an elephant can jump in and the waters simply close over it. But if your calmness is like a small pool, when an elephant jumps in there will be such a splash that there will be no water left.'

A meditation toolkit

Here we're going to look at some of the ways we can use the breath to alter our mental and emotional states. Some, no doubt, you already know.

Remember that unlike physical tools – the kind that you use to fix your car or put up a shelf these meditation tools exist for you only if you remember them and use them. Of course, the best way to remember them is to use them.

Try setting aside a few sessions of meditation just to play around with some of these. It may take time to appreciate exactly what they do for you, but once you've begun to associate the cause with the effect, you can draw on these tools at any time – inside or outside meditation.

These tools work, so remember to use them appropriately. If you're anxious, for example, it would be a bad idea to do any exercises of the stimulating kind. And if you're feeling depressed or low, the calming exercises would not be a wise choice.

These exercises don't necessarily work immediately (though they often take effect very quickly), and you may have to give them time. Changing the method every couple of minutes will just lead to frustration and restlessness.

Using the breath to calm your mind	Using the breath to stimulate your mind
❖ Take a few deep breaths into your belly (this will help to centre you)	❖ Take a few deep breaths into your upper chest (feel the expansion)
❖ Take a few slow breaths before letting your breath return to normal	❖ Take a few quick, light breaths, then let your breath return to normal
❖ Keep your awareness low in your body, e.g., in your belly, for as long as you need to develop calmness	❖ Keep your awareness high in your body, e.g., in your upper chest, or even your head
❖ Pay attention to letting go on the out-breath	❖ Pay attention to the sense of your body expanding on the in-breath
Using the breath to promote pleasure	
… and calmness	**… and stimulation**
❖ On every exhalation, imagine a wave of relaxation flowing downwards into the earth, sweeping away your tensions and cares	❖ On every inhalation, imagine you are drawing energy upwards from the earth, filling every fibre of your being with awareness
❖ Imagine your whole body is floating on warm water. With every inhalation you rise, and with every exhalation, you fall	❖ Imagine you are inhaling light with every breath. On every exhalation you breathe out your distractions in the form of grey mist

Guiding, not controlling

The great hypnotherapist, Milton Erickson, told a story about how one day, when he was a boy, a riderless horse wandered into the farmyard outside his home. Milton had never seen this horse before, and had no idea where it lived, but very soon he had the horse back where it belonged. How did he do this?

Well, he sat on the horse's back, got it to start walking, then every time they came to a turn in the road, he paid attention to the almost imperceptible movements of the horse's body that told him where it wanted to go. Once young Milton had sensed in which direction the horse wanted to head, he encouraged it to do so. It turned out that the horse knew its own way home, and all Milton had to do was give it a little gentle guidance.

It's similar with our breathing. I've said that in the Mindfulness of Breathing meditation we're not controlling our breath. On the other hand I've also suggested that you can use deep breathing, or breathing into the belly, or breathing into the upper chest, as ways to alter your state of mind. This is not really as contradictory as it might sound.

When we change the pattern of our breathing, we don't have to exert any control. We can gently guide the breath without controlling it, as Milton did. Had Milton tried to tell the horse where to go, he'd never have got it home. Horses, after all, are trained to follow orders. Instead he used a more subtle technique of being aware where the horse wanted to go, then reinforced that desire with some gentle guidance. The horse soon got the idea.

We all are horse-riders, in a way. Our breathing is generally under the control of subconscious processes, and it has to be said that our subconscious, by and large, does a pretty good job of keeping our breathing going. The subconscious rarely fails to carry out its tasks, which is more than can be said for our conscious minds. (How often do we go upstairs to get something and then forget what it was we wanted?) So let your subconscious do what it's good at.

When you want to change your breathing, say by breathing into your belly more deeply, all you really have to do is take your awareness into your belly to give your subconscious a gentle hint, then let it do the work. In this way, we gently guide our breath rather than control it.

Four dimensions of mindfulness

In Buddhism there are several terms that are translated as 'mindfulness' or are closely related to the concept of mindfulness, and each of them has a different flavour. It's useful to get to know the different dimensions of mindfulness.

Sati

At its simplest, *sati* means 'recollection', both in the sense of memory and in the sense of 'having gathered together once more'. Sati is the aspect of mindfulness that knows what is going on at any particular time. For example, when we're aware of our posture, and that we're in a certain mood, and that our mind is alert or dull, this is sati. Sati is knowing what is going on, and we need to know this in order to be able to make any meaningful changes. If you don't know where you are, how can you get to where you want to go?

Sampajanna

Sampajanna is the aspect of mindfulness that extends over a period of time. It includes awareness of purpose (where we want to go), and awareness of where we've already been. In Buddhist texts, the terms sati and sampajanna are often joined into a compound term, sati-sampajanna, and it's this compound term that's often translated as 'mindfulness'. Sampajanna is necessary so that we can periodically compare where we are going with where we want to be. Sampajanna is like a compass which gives us our bearings.

Dhamma-vicaya

Dhamma-vicaya is the aspect of mindfulness that categorizes our experience in terms of some model or other. It is the act of comparing our inner experience to a mental map so that we can navigate more effectively towards our goal. The simplest kind of map you can have is something like a division of your emotional states into 'positive' (states that are constructive and helpful, like love, empathy, confidence) and 'negative' (those that tend to be destructive, like hatred, addictive craving, cynicism).

Appamada

Appamada is mindfulness in the sense of watchfulness or vigilance. It's mindfulness imbued with a sense of the importance of the task in hand. Some texts say that if you lose your mindfulness you should snatch it up again like a soldier who has dropped his sword in the heat of battle. Another interesting analogy is that we should act as swiftly as someone who has discovered their hat is on fire. Appamada is the dynamic aspect of mindfulness.

Standing back once more

Diane, one of my students, reported, 'This morning it was not as easy to concentrate; I had to make more of an effort to keep myself on track. I handled the situation quite easily, noticing that I was more distracted and being aware that it would take a bit more work today to keep myself out of distraction. I did not judge myself or get scared that my practice was falling apart, just acknowledged that it was not one of my better days and went on from there.'

Your meditation practice will always have its ups and downs. This is inevitable in developing any skill. You'll have good days and bad days, and at first both good and bad experiences may seem to arrive randomly, as gifts – welcome or unwelcome – of the gods. This can be dispiriting at first; you think you're doing so well, your meditation was so calm and enjoyable yesterday, yet here you are today struggling to count to three and feeling that it's all hopeless.

❝Meditation is, above all, the art of dealing with what is.❞

Diane's approach to her ups and downs is exemplary. Instead of getting lost in the distracted, reactive states of self-pity or fear, she simply observed what was happening and realized that the conditions in her mind, for whatever reason, had changed, and that the kind of effort she would have to make had also changed. Change is unavoidable, life gives us that challenge, and it isn't helpful to mourn the inevitable or to fight change. We have to learn to embrace change, accept it as part of our lives, and respond as creatively as we can – no condemnation, no self-recriminations, just a patient sense of working with whatever comes up.

As Diane went on to say, 'I guess I always get the good and the bad, and perhaps just have more awareness now of my state of mind, whatever it might be. I remind myself to be especially gentle with myself, that the "bad" is really no different from the "good", it just is.'

Meditation is, above all, the art of dealing with what is.

Where are you going?

I'd like you to set aside the next few minutes for an exercise. If you're tired or unable for whatever reason to give this exercise your full attention, I suggest you put this book down for now, or read a different chapter, so that you can come back and spend some quality time with yourself.

As you're reading this, noticing the sensations of your skin touching the paper, feeling the weight of your body being supported, and as you notice your breath flowing in and flowing out, feel your body begin to relax and notice your mind becoming calmer.

Imagine that it's now some years into the future: perhaps ten years, perhaps fifteen years – it doesn't really matter. You're walking up to the front door of your house, and as you open the door you notice that it's very still and quiet and dark inside. Then you hear some surreptitious sounds, and just when you're wondering if you should be worried, you realize to your surprise and delight that your house is full of people you know.

There are family members, some that you haven't seen for years. There are friends. There are colleagues. There are people from the spiritual community or community groups of which you are a member. And all these people are here to celebrate you and your life. One by one, they stand up and rejoice in your merits. They rejoice in your achievements, in your accomplishments, in the personal qualities you embody. They share the contributions you have made to their lives.

Now I'd like you to spend a few minutes listening to what these people say, and then write down some of the points that seem most significant to you.

If you've really done this exercise, then what you have just done is step beyond your normal sense of yourself to get in touch with your deeper values and beliefs. You've developed a clearer understanding of what is most valuable to you. You've become closer to the aspects of yourself that exist in potential in the depths of your being. You've developed a deeper understanding of who you are and who you are to become – or rather, of who you can become, since the unfolding of that potential will not take place spontaneously, but will be the result of your own conscious effort. You have given yourself the beginnings of a map to navigate by, perhaps for the rest of your life. You have developed a stronger sense of your ideals – not what you think you ought to be doing but a true sense of what your deepest values are, for those people who were extolling your virtues were, of course, not other people at all. The voices were the voices of your own depths – your own Wildmind.

❝Every decision we make in life … is an opportunity to make choices in the light of where we ultimately wish to be.❞

I've already talked about the aspect of mindfulness called sampajanna – our inner compass that tells us where we have been and where we are going. Now a compass is more useful when we have a map to help us navigate, so the reason we have just done this exercise is to help us have a deeper mindfulness of who we are and who we are becoming. We're providing a sense of direction so that we can use our sampajanna in order to navigate towards our ideals. Every decision we make in life – from how we are going to prioritize tasks at work to how we are going to deal with a difficult child – is an opportunity to make choices in the light of where we ultimately wish to be. We have an opportunity in every such decision to move towards or away from our ideals. The more we are in touch with those ideals, the wiser our decisions will be.

I suggest you write down those ideals in some form and put them somewhere you can easily and frequently review them. I have a copy of my own 'personal mission statement' (as I call my ideals) in my planner, and I consult it at least once a week. Other people put theirs on the bathroom mirror so that they can remind themselves of what is important even more frequently.

Frequently referring to your ideals is an excellent way of clarifying your goals, and an important step towards committing yourself to bringing those goals into the present. Over time you will learn to see yourself not just as what you currently are, but in terms of what you are becoming. This, I have found, is one of the most empowering experiences we can have. What we currently are may not amount to much, but what we are becoming can be truly wonderful and a source of constant inspiration.

Reflections in mindfulness

This section is not about reflections on mindfulness, but about the practice of reflecting while in a state of mindfulness. If you remember our definition of meditation, the whole point of the Mindfulness of Breathing is to help us to develop more concentration and calmness so that we can break through into a deeper understanding of the nature of reality. Having stilled our mind, so that it has become like a calm lake, we can begin to reflect. It's a happy coincidence (or is it a coincidence?) that, like a lake, our mind can only reflect when it is calm.

But what is reflection? We tend to assume that reflection is a constant flow of thoughts running through our minds, but this does not have to be the case – in fact it's best if it isn't. Imagine you are standing in front of a calm lake. It is still and tranquil, and you can see the reflections of the further shore. You take a small pebble and toss it into the midst of the reflections (toss it in with respect, as if it were an offering to the ancient gods that live in the depths of the waters). The stone plops into the water and disappears without trace, leaving behind waves of concentric ripples. Each ripple presents you with a slightly different perspective on the reflections of the other shore. You watch the ripples radiating from the place where the stone vanished, as they widen and fade and eventually disappear altogether. Once the surface is still once more, the reflections have returned to normal, and then you toss in another offering.

This is how we can best reflect in meditation: reverently dropping a thought into our hearts, then patiently watching the ripples of that thought until our mind has once more become still. The ripples that emanate from the thought pebble are not necessarily thoughts – they're more of an indescribable feeling of subtly shifting perspectives (like the distorted images at the edge of each ripple). You drop in the pebble of thought, and your emotions and your subconscious understandings respond with a subtle shiver.

"We all have a long way to go in cultivating that sense of awe and mystery that turns not-knowing into the most profound source of wisdom."

What kinds of pebbles can we drop into the waters of our hearts and minds? We can drop in the thought that each breath is precious – that it only lasts for a moment, never to return. This challenges our assumptions that we do the same thing over and over. We never do the same thing over and over. Every experience is unique, and it is deeply fulfilling to experience the uniqueness of each precious moment.

We can reflect on the fact that our breath connects us with every human being, plant, and animal in the world. Our breath is the living symbol of our interconnectedness with others. Your body, and the breath that sustains it, is made of forests, and fields, and birds, and animals, and oceans, and mountains. It is made of the air above, and the earth below. It is made from the remains of a long-dead star. We are vaster and richer than we think.

We can reflect on the impermanent and insubstantial nature of every experience. Thoughts come and go like rainbow apparitions, emotions coalesce like clouds and then dissipate. Feelings loom like shadows and then are gone. Where did they come from? Where did they go?

We drop such a thought into our hearts like a pebble into water, observe the ripples that radiate through our beings until the waters grow calm once more, and then we sit with the stillness until we feel ready to drop in another pebble.

The contemplation of such reflections can lead at times to a certain unease, although that unease should be seen as a creative force – a questioning of assumptions that are so close to us that we rarely, if ever, see them. But they can also lead to a sense of fulfilment, and a sense of awe and wonder at the majesty and mystery of life.

As a great Indian teacher said, 'Let these three expressions: I do not have, I do not understand, I do not know, be repeated over and over again. That is the heart of my advice.'[9] This might seem strange advice at first, but that only means that the path of reflection is deep and subtle, and that we all have a long way to go in cultivating that sense of awe and mystery that turns not-knowing into the most profound source of wisdom.

Keeping a meditation journal

Mindfulness is about knowing where we are (being in the moment) and also about maintaining an awareness of where we have been (reflection) and where we are going (having goals). A meditation journal can help us with all these areas of awareness, so helping us to have a more unified awareness of ourselves.

We might make efforts to be in the moment while we're meditating – to be aware of our experience as it unfolds in the eternal moment and allowing our own inner beauty to manifest. Or perhaps we become habitually vague in our practice, and spend a lot of our time drifting in thought, making insufficient effort to bring ourselves back to our current experience. Keeping a meditation journal helps give us a more definite sense of what is actually going on. When we sit down after meditation and take a few minutes to write down what we've been experiencing, it becomes more obvious how effective we've really been. If we examine our experience, honestly and with a desire to learn, we become much more aware of what our meditation practice actually is. We can become more aware of our weaknesses and our strengths, and have a much more penetrating understanding of what we need to be working on.

A journal also allows us to look back at our experience as it has changed over a period of time. We can review several days, weeks, or months of our practice and learn about the patterns that our consciousness follows. Perhaps we'll discover that we are lazier than we thought, or that we try too hard, or even that we fluctuate in our efforts. We might discover there are particular distractions that are much more common than we had recalled. We commonly also discover – especially when we're feeling a little down – that our meditation practice has been more effective and enjoyable than we had remembered.

And our daily writings can help us to set goals. It's not that we try to pin down our experience before it happens – that's rarely, if ever, going to work and is more likely to result in frustration than in any progress in our meditation. Instead, what we're trying to do in setting goals is to develop a stronger sense of where we want to go in our meditation. Through looking back at our past experience we can see what it is we need to work on. Perhaps it's forgiveness or patience that we need to develop. Perhaps it's more persistence or more calmness. Whatever changes we want to make, having clear goals will help us to attain them. Our goals become the magnetic north pole that allows us to navigate through our experience in order to get where we want to go.

Some people use checklist-style journals, with lists of distractions and positive factors that can be checked off. The advantage is that you can do your writing very quickly, and there are ready-made categories to help you analyse your experience. But I'm not fond of this; it can pigeonhole our experience and lead to a superficial understanding of what's going on in our practice.

"If we examine our experience, honestly and with a desire to learn, we become much more aware of what our meditation practice actually is."

I prefer a more unstructured form of journal in which you can write freely about your experience. For this style of journal a simple notebook will do. There are a few brief formalities that precede any entry: the date, the name of the meditation practice, and how long you meditated for. Then you can write more generally about how it went – what distractions you had, what you did about them, which positive factors (like calmness, patience, concentration, and so on) were present and what you did to strengthen them. You can write about factors in your life that had an effect on your practice, like lack of sleep, or a particularly busy day, or that you felt refreshed after a day's hiking with a friend.

All my students keep an online journal in which they write what's going on in their practice. I read their journal entries and can give them very specific feedback and encouragement. Most of them find this very useful, but unfortunately not everyone can get a teacher to read over their journals and make comments. You can gain some of the same benefits, however, just by rereading your own comments over a period of time and reflecting on them. It's an excellent practice to read your journal entries for each week and see what trends you notice. This helps you appreciate change and stand back from your day-to-day experience so that you can learn from having an overview.

A further refinement of this approach is 'double entry' journal-keeping. With this method you leave every second page blank – you only write on the right-hand page – then when you do your weekly review you can make notes on the left-hand page. Those notes might include further reflections on some aspect of your experience, or pick out particularly significant things you have learned. Or they might simply summarize what you've written on the opposite page so that you can look back over an even longer period – perhaps three or six months – and quickly review the major trends and learning experiences over that time without having to read each journal entry in full. Those notes also flag particularly significant experiences and observations so that you can easily find them later.

In short, keeping a journal helps us connect past, present, and future, so that our life seems more of an integrated whole rather than an assortment of disparate experiences. This helps us to develop more integration, or integrity – a sense of continuity of experience over time.

Being in the moment

I've mentioned that mindfulness can be seen as the practice of being in the moment – but what does this actually mean? Does it mean that if we're mindful we should never think about the past and present, never try to reflect on our past experience or anticipate the future?

Being in the moment means being truly aware of what is going on right here and now. Much of the time our experience does not have this quality of awareness or mindfulness. A lot of the time we are like robots, automatically living out habitual patterns of self-pity, anger, wish fulfilment, fear, and so on. These habitual tendencies take us over and run our lives for us – without our being able to stand back and decide whether this is what we actually want to be doing. It can be a real shock when you start to realize just how habitual and automatic your life is.

When we're in this robotic state, we're not aware of what's going on. We're angry without being aware that we are angry or that we have the option not to be angry. We fantasize without any discernment of whether what we're thinking about is making us happy or unhappy. In fact, a lot of the time when we are letting our habits dominate us we are not making ourselves or others happy; it's often quite the opposite.

Being in the moment is another way of saying we are aware of what is going on in our experience, that we are not just being angry (or whatever) but aware that we are angry and are aware that we can choose to be otherwise. Of course, a lot of the time when we are not being in the moment, we are thinking about the past or future. We might be dwelling on the past – brooding about some past hurt. Or we might be fantasizing about a future in which we have won the lottery and are living out our lives in some imagined paradise. As with all unmindful activity, we have no awareness that this fantasizing is pointless. All it does is reinforce unhelpful emotional tendencies that can never truly enrich our lives.

There are, of course, ways of thinking about the past or future mindfully. Being in the moment does not mean we are stuck in the moment; we can mindfully and creatively call to mind past events, or imagine what might happen in the future. We can think about the past and think about how we might have acted differently, or wonder why something happened in the way it did. We can think about possible futures, and how the actions that we perform now will make those futures more or less likely.

> "Being in the moment is another way of saying we are aware of what is going on in our experience, that we are not just being angry (or whatever)."

When we are thinking about the past or future while being in the moment, we are conscious that we are reflecting. We do not confuse fantasy with reality. We don't stray from thinking about the past in order to construct an imaginary past in which we said or did the right thing – or if we do so it's part of a conscious thought experiment to see what we might learn from the experience. We think about the future, but rather than idle daydreaming it's an attempt to find a creative goal towards which we can grow.

Sometimes daydreaming can be creative. It can be wonderful to relax the reins of consciousness and allow our creative unconscious the opportunity to express itself. But it's generally far more useful to have a part of our conscious mind standing by, observing, watching for any sign that the creative expression of the unconscious is turning grey – turning into the repetitive and reactive expression of old and unhelpful emotional patterns. The conscious mind can intervene at such moments with a light touch, a gentle redirection of our mental energies, so that we stay in the present, aware, mindful, and creative.

What's next, now that I've learned this practice?

It's an excellent idea to keep practising the Mindfulness of Breathing regularly. This is a meditation you could keep doing for the rest of your life and still keep finding benefits. You might also want to go on now and learn walking meditation, which will help you to take mindfulness into your daily life. Since you can do this practice any time you are walking, it means you can spend more time meditating. Or you can go on to learn the Metta Bhavana (the development of loving-kindness, page 218), which offers you a way of working with your emotions so that you can develop more patience, confidence, and love.

It's a good idea to alternate the Mindfulness of Breathing and Metta Bhavana practices, perhaps doing them on alternate days, or doing the Mindfulness of Breathing in the morning and the Metta Bhavana in the evening.

Meditating with others is an excellent way to support your practice. Most people find it's easier to meditate with others; they find their mind is calmer and they can sit comfortably for longer. When you meditate on your own, you can always give up when the going gets rough. You can always go and do something else instead, and who would know? When you meditate with others, that possibility is largely removed, since you can't get up without disturbing them, and if your meditation is more difficult than you expected, you're more likely to sit and work things out.

But more than this, we're social animals, and we're often more comfortable with shared activities. Take eating, for example: most of us feel happier eating with at least one other person than we do eating on our own, when we often feel the urge to read or to watch television to avoid feeling lonely. Meditating with others can bring about a sense of solidarity – a sense that you're engaged with others in a common endeavour. You're not going it alone, but sharing your aspirations and struggles with others, and that is comforting and supportive.

You might want to look for a local meditation group so that you can sit with them once a week, or you could start a group of your own. If you have friends who might be interested, you could invite them over to listen to a meditation CD or one of the RealAudio files on the Wildmind website (www.wildmind.org). Or you might want to lead the meditation yourself, or have the group members take turns. Teaching others to meditate is an excellent way of reminding yourself of important principles. When you teach others you also teach yourself.

We'll be adding material to the Wildmind website on a regular basis, and you can give us feedback or share your stories with us. We'd be delighted to hear from you! Tell us what you like about our site or this book, or suggest features you would like us to add, by emailing us at wildmind@wildmind.org.

"This is a meditation you could keep doing for the rest of your life and still keep finding benefits."

4

in beauty may I walk
walking meditation

What is walking meditation?

Walking meditation is a form of meditation in action. In walking meditation we use the experience of walking as our focus. We become mindful of our experience while walking, and keep our awareness involved with the experience as best we can. There are several different kinds of walking meditation. We'll just be looking at one of them in detail, although we'll touch on the others. Once you've mastered one form, you'll easily be able to pick up the others.

Obviously, there are differences between walking meditation and sitting meditation. For one thing we keep our eyes open! It would be rather unwise not to do so. That difference implies others. In walking meditation we are not withdrawing our attention from the outside world in the same way as we do when we are doing the Mindfulness of Breathing or Metta Bhavana. We have to be aware of things outside ourselves (objects we might trip over, other people we might walk into) and there are many other things outside ourselves that we will be more aware of than when we are doing sitting meditation – especially if we sit indoors – such as the wind, sun, and rain, and the sounds of nature and other people, and general human activity.

But one of the biggest differences is that it's easier for many people to be more intensely and more easily aware of their bodies during walking meditation, as compared to sitting meditation (especially when it's a led walking meditation). It is generally easier to be aware of your body when it is in motion than when you are sitting still. This can make walking meditation an intense experience of mindfulness. You can experience your body very intensely, and also find intense enjoyment in this practice.

The form of walking meditation we'll be introducing here is best done outdoors. For your first attempt, you might want to find a park or open space where you will be able to walk for twenty minutes without encountering traffic.

A guided walking meditation, led by Bodhipaksa, is available on CD. This can be ordered at www.windhorsepublications.com (UK) or www.wildmind.org (rest of world). For more information see page 340.

How to do the practice

I believe the best way to learn this practice is to be led through it. On the CD, I talk you through a twenty-minute session of walking meditation. This way of learning helps you to develop good habits that you can then practise on your own. To give you an idea what this involves, you might want to read this transcript, which represents the kind of thing I generally say when leading walking meditation.

Walking meditation transcript

To begin this period of walking meditation, first of all, let's simply stand. Just stand on the spot, being aware of your weight being transferred through the soles of your feet into the earth; being aware of all the subtle movements that go on in order to keep you balanced and upright. We very often take this for granted, our ability to be able to stand upright. But actually it took us a couple of years to learn how to do this. So just be aware of the constant, complex adjustments that you're making in order to maintain your balance.

And then you can begin to walk at a fairly slow but normal walking pace, and in a normal manner. You're not going to be changing the way that you walk; you're simply going to be aware of what happens when you walk.

So first of all, keeping your attention in the soles of your feet ... being aware of the alternating patterns of contact and release ... being aware of your foot as the heel first makes contact, as the foot rolls forward on to the ball, and then lifts and travels through the air.

Be aware of all the different sensations in your feet, not just the contact on the soles of your feet but also the contact between the toes, the feeling of the inside of your shoes, the fabric of your socks; and let your feet be as relaxed as possible.

Becoming aware of your ankles ... noticing the qualities of the sensations in those joints – as your foot is on the ground, as your foot travels through the air, and letting your ankle joints be relaxed. Letting go, making sure you're not holding on in any way.

You can become aware of your lower legs – your shins, your calves. Noticing the contact with your clothing … being aware of the temperature on your skin. You can be aware of the muscles … and noticing what the calf muscles are doing as you're walking. You might even want to exaggerate for a few steps what the calf muscles are doing, just so that you can connect with that. And then let your walking go back to a normal relaxed rhythm … encouraging your calf muscles to relax … and then becoming aware of your knees – noticing the qualities of the sensations in your knee joints.

Then expanding your awareness into your thighs … being aware of the skin – again the contact with your clothing – the temperature… being aware of the muscles … and noticing what the muscles on the fronts of the thighs, and the muscles on the backs of the thighs, are doing. And once more you might want for a few paces just to exaggerate what those muscles are doing – exaggerate the action of those muscles … and then letting your walk go back to a normal rhythm.

Become aware of your hips – the muscles around your hip joints – and relaxing those muscles. Really relaxing. Even when you think you've relaxed – relaxing them some more… And just noticing how that changes your walk. Notice how the rhythm and the gait of your walk change as your hips relax.

You can be aware of the whole of your pelvis – and notice all of the movements that are going on in your pelvis. One hip moves forward and then the other; one hip lifting, the other sinking. And you can be aware of the complex three-dimensional shape that your pelvis is carving out through space as you walk forwards.

The lowest part of your spine – your sacrum – is embedded in the pelvis. So as you feel your spine extending upwards – the lumbar spine, the thoracic spine – you can notice how it moves along with the pelvis. Your spine is in constant motion. It's swaying from side to side. There is a twisting motion around the central axis. Your spine is in constant, sinuous, sensuous motion.

Noticing your belly – you may feel your clothing in contact with your belly – and noticing how your belly is the centre of your body. Very often it feels like it's 'down there' because we are so much in our heads. So see to what extent you can feel your belly is the centre of your body, in the centre of your being.

Noticing your chest, just let your breathing happen naturally. Noticing the contact your chest makes with your clothing... Noticing your shoulders. Notice how they are moving with the rhythm of your walking. Notice how your belly, chest, and shoulders move with your breathing. Often our breathing naturally falls into a rhythm that matches our walking. You probably find that you take a certain number of paces per breath. There is no right or wrong number of paces per breath, so just notice what your particular pattern is.

Letting your shoulders be relaxed ... and letting your shoulders passively transmit the rhythm of your walk down into your arms, having your arms simply hanging by your sides and swinging naturally. There are all the motions in your arms – your upper arms, your elbows, your forearms, your wrists, your hands... And feeling the air coursing over the skin on your hands and fingers as your arms swing through the air.

Becoming aware of your neck – and the muscles supporting your skull... Noticing the angle of your head, and notice that as you relax the muscles on the back of your neck, your chin slightly tucks in and your skull comes to a point of balance. And you might want to play around with the angle of your head and see how that changes your experience. You may notice that when you tuck your chin close in to your chest, your experience becomes darker and more emotional – very inward turned, sombre. And if you lift your chin and hold it in the air you may notice that your experience becomes much lighter – that you become much more aware of the outside world and perhaps caught up in the outside world, or much more aware of your thoughts and caught up in your thoughts... And then bringing your head back to a point of balance, your chin slightly tucked in.

Relaxing your jaw, relaxing your eyes … and just letting your eyes be softly focused, gently resting, looking ahead, not staring at anything, not allowing yourself to be caught up in anything that's going past you. Letting the world drift by your eyes.

You can be aware of the feelings that you're having; not in terms of actual emotions, but just the feeling tone. Are there things that feel pleasant? Are there things that feel unpleasant – either in your body, or outside of you? And as you notice things in your body that are pleasant or unpleasant, just notice them. Don't either cling on to them or push them away, but just notice them. If you notice things in the outside world that are either pleasant or unpleasant, just allow them to drift by – just noticing them and letting them drift by without following them with your eyes or averting your gaze from them.

> **❝**I often find that if I can be aware of both the inner world and the outer world in equal balance, my mind settles at a point of stillness, and calmness, and clarity.**❞**

You can notice your emotional states. Are you bored? Are you content? Are you irritated? Are you feeling very happy to be doing what you're doing? Again just noticing whatever emotions happen to be present, not getting caught up in them but letting them pass through your mind like clouds through a clear blue sky. And noticing your mind as well. Is your mind clear, or dull? Is your mind busy, or is it calm? Are you thinking about things unconnected with this practice – or do whatever thoughts you have centre on what you're doing just now? Just notice these things with no particular judgement – just noticing, and letting go of your thoughts as they arise.

And you can notice the balance between your experience of the inner and the outer worlds. I often find that if I can be aware of both the inner world and the outer world in equal balance, my mind settles at a point of stillness, and calmness, and clarity. So see if you can find that point of balance, where you're equally aware of the inner and the outer, and your mind is calm, content, and quiet.

You can keep walking for a while, and when you're doing that you may want to keep your awareness centred in some part of your body. There's a point just two inches below your navel that's perfect for this. That spot is called the *hara* in Japanese, and it's regarded as being the physical and spiritual centre of the body. So you might want to keep your awareness there and to experience everything else – the rest of your body, your thoughts, feelings, and emotions, and your experience of the world – in relation to the hara. This will help you to stay grounded and focused while doing the practice.

So in a few seconds I'm going to ask you to stop. And I'd like you to come to a natural halt, so you're not freezing on the spot, you're just allowing yourself to come to a natural, comfortable, balanced stop. So do that now: come to a stop. And just experience yourself standing. Just notice what it's like to no longer be in motion. Notice once more the complex balancing act that's going on to keep you upright, feeling once again the weight travelling down through the soles of your feet into the earth, simply standing, and experiencing yourself, and finally bringing this meditation session to a close.

Why walking meditation?

Some students have a sneaking suspicion that walking meditation is not really meditation at all, or that it's perhaps a sort of watered-down meditation. These suspicions are completely unfounded, and are probably based on the misconception that in order to meditate you have to be sitting still. This is probably a very similar misconception to the idea that you can only really meditate properly in the full lotus posture. Both misconceptions are trying to define meditation in terms of what is happening outwardly, rather than in terms of what you are doing internally. Remember that meditation is a process of developing greater awareness so that we can make changes to our consciousness, become more deeply fulfilled, and have a greater understanding of life. Meditation is an internal process, and it's perfectly possible to meditate while engaged in activities such as walking. (There is, however, a need to keep up regular sitting meditation. It's possible in sitting meditation to cultivate states of concentration and bliss that are simply not available while you are engaged in external activities.)

Walking meditation is meditation in action. During walking meditation we are using the physical, mental, and emotional experiences of walking as the basis for developing greater awareness.

Walking meditation is an excellent way to develop our ability to take awareness into our ordinary lives. Any able-bodied person under normal circumstances does at least some walking every day, even if it's just walking from the house to the car, and the car to the office. Walking meditation is an excellent way to squeeze more meditation into the day – you can do it any time you're walking. Once we have learned how to do walking meditation, each spell of walking – however short – can be used as a meditation practice.

The great thing about walking meditation is that you can do it any time – even in a big city. In fact it's especially good (even necessary) to do it in a big city, with all the distractions of people and noise, and shop windows trying to catch your attention. When I used to walk through the city centre in Glasgow, I often used to practise this meditation. At first it would be very difficult to keep my awareness involved with my walking. Shop window displays and advertisements would beckon me, and my eyes would involuntarily flick to the side as if afraid of missing something. Attractive people would walk by, dressed in their most eye-catching clothes, and my neck would yearn to turn to squeeze every last moment of enjoyment out of the experience of seeing them. But I soon began to feel increasingly comfortable with my eyes directed forward, and I realized there was a kind of battle going on. Advertisers and shop window designers were trying to capture some of my awareness, and I was trying to hold on to it. When I began to realize that I was winning the battle, I would feel a surge of joy and confidence.

I then began to realize that the normal state of distractedness in which I would walk down a busy street was deeply unsatisfactory. When your attention is constantly seeking satisfaction outside of yourself – through glancing at consumer goods or attractive passers-by – your internal experience becomes fragmented, as if you're leaving parts of yourself strewn along the city streets. In this state of fragmentation, it is even harder to find sources of fulfilment within. This leads to a vicious cycle in which we feel increasingly hollow and fragmented as we seek fulfilment outside ourselves. In the consumerist mentality there is an implicit understanding that the only place we are able to find satisfaction is outside of ourselves, whereas from the Buddhist point of view satisfaction comes primarily from within.

“When your attention is constantly seeking satisfaction outside of yourself – through glancing at consumer goods or attractive passers-by – your internal experience becomes fragmented, as if you're leaving parts of yourself strewn along the city streets.”

Practising walking meditation is a way of defragmenting our minds. One of the literal meanings of the word sati (usually translated 'mindfulness') is 'recollection'. In practising mindfulness we are 're-collecting' the fragmented parts of our psyches and re-integrating them into a whole. As we become more whole, we become more contented and more fulfilled. This is one of the main aims and benefits of the practice of mindfulness.

You can also set aside special periods for walking meditation. At first, you might want to use the CD to help you get a better feel for what you're doing, but after a while it's good to leave the recording behind and develop your own individual method. Making the practice your own in this way allows you more flexibility. You can then do walking meditation for two minutes while walking from one room to another, or you can practise walking meditation for several hours during a hike.

You can even adapt the principles of walking meditation so that you practise mindful running. Some of my students have found that being in the moment helps them let go of unhelpful emotional states while running. One student recounted the following:

'Mindfulness helps me deal with fatigue. By noticing and relaxing my arms and shoulders and observing my breath, I can conserve energy and run more smoothly. I find my mind is on the running rather than negative self-talk: a constant enemy of marathon runners and similar maniacs.'

It's also possible to do a cycling meditation. Although the defensive attitude required in traffic can make it hard to be relaxed as well as alert, you can still practise being in the moment and let go of any irritation towards other road users. Swimming can also be an excellent meditation practice, especially early in the morning. A friend of mine who is paraplegic does a 'walking meditation' in his wheelchair. Once you make the meditation your own, it becomes a very flexible and useful tool.

Four areas for mindfulness

Unlike the other practices described in this book, walking meditation has no defined stages, but there is a logical sequence to the practice as I teach it here, and this sequence is rooted in a traditional formulation called the four foundations of mindfulness.

These are four areas of experience in which we can anchor our minds to prevent them from being fragmented and strewn around like leaves torn from a tree in an autumn gale. The four areas are our bodies, our feelings, our emotional and mental states, and objects of consciousness.

Mindfulness of the body

We begin by becoming aware of our bodies – the first foundation of mindfulness. It's useful to begin any meditation session (whether seated or walking) by paying attention to your body – in particular to those parts that are in contact with the ground. This helps to stabilize and ground the mind, making it calmer and less likely to wander. It's like lowering an anchor to prevent a ship drifting on the tide.

So in this meditation I usually start by becoming aware of my feet – first standing, then walking. Then I lead my awareness systematically through my body, relaxing each part of my body as I bring it to the centre of my focus.

Mindfulness of feelings

The word 'feeling' has a special meaning in Buddhist meditation. In everyday speech, we use the word to refer to a number of different levels of experience. We might say, for example, that we feel cold. Here we are referring to a physical sensation. We might also say we feel angry – here referring to an emotion. We sometimes even refer to thoughts as feelings, for example, if we say 'I feel he's up to no good.' In the specific Buddhist sense we mean none of these things.

The word 'feeling' (*vedana* in Pali) refers to a basic sense of comfort/discomfort, or pleasure/displeasure. (If you're not sure whether you like or dislike the object that they are associated with, feelings can also be neutral.) Feelings are gut-level responses that are less developed than emotions like anger, or love, or joy, or despondency. Can you see the difference?

Feelings are passive, while emotions are active. Feelings like pleasure or pain are closely tied to sensations, and arise automatically. In any given moment, you either find a particular sensation pleasurable or you don't. Emotions are active responses to feelings and perceptions. We may think our emotions arise automatically, but that, according to Buddhism, is a delusion. We may sometimes emote habitually and with unawareness, but the emotions we produce are our active response to situations in which we find ourselves.

Feelings stand between sensations and emotions. For example, you turn up in the office one day and find that a co-worker is using a particularly pungent perfume that you don't like. There is the sensation – the smell – of the perfume itself. Then there is a gut-level response that you don't like this particular smell (that's the feeling), and then there is a variety of emotions you might experience in response to that feeling, such as anger, compassion, or perhaps smugness (knowing that you would never be so tasteless). And of course our actions arise on the basis of emotions. We express our emotions in actions or words.

Sensations	→	Feelings	→	Emotions	→	Actions
colours, images, sounds, etc. (internal or external)		pleasant/ unpleasant, comfort/ discomfort, etc.		Love, hatred, joy, despair, compassion, patience, irritability, etc.		(Based on our emotions)

We probably experience feelings in relation to every sensation we perceive, whether visual, auditory, tactile, or whatever. Colours each have their own particular feeling tone. There are sounds we enjoy hearing (our favourite music) and some that we dislike (often someone else's favourite music). There are also odours and tastes that we involuntarily like or dislike. And physical contact can be pleasant or unpleasant too, of course. The same sensation can produce different feelings depending on the context. Our spirits might soar at the sight of fresh snow on our day off, but feel miserable about it if we have to drive to work.

When we are doing walking meditation, there will be feelings associated with our bodies, from a niggling pain to a pleasant feeling of relaxation. There will also be feelings associated with things that we see, and hear, and with all the other sensory modalities we experience – including imagined scenes and sensations that arise in our thoughts.

In paying attention to feelings, the important thing is simply to notice them without either clinging to them or pushing them away. When we are unaware, it is very common for our minds to start grasping after experiences associated with pleasant feelings. Take our example of walking past shop window displays. The shopkeeper has arranged goods and advertisements in the window in the hope that they will give rise to pleasant feelings. This isn't simply in order to make your life more pleasant, but in the hope that the emotion of desire will cause you to stop and look, and even to enter the shop and make a purchase.

Not all experiences are pleasant, of course. It is also common for our minds to reject experiences associated with unpleasant feelings.

So you might, as in another example above, feel anger or irritation when you encounter feelings of dislike that arise on the basis of certain sensations (perhaps on hearing some music that you dislike).

> "The feeling of living in the gap is a feeling of freedom – not the exultation that comes from being set free ... but a quieter, surer sense of being able to watch – confidently and without being judgemental – our being unfold."

In practising mindfulness, we're trying to be more aware of how our experience moves from sensation, to feeling, to emotion, so that we have more choice over what emotions we experience. Of course, the aim is to cultivate positive emotions and to eradicate negative emotions. The gap that I have talked about – in which we have choice about our response – actually lies between feelings and emotions, which is why I have been emphasizing the importance of being aware of feelings and how they give rise to emotions.

This gap between feeling and emotional response is actually more complex than a simple pause. By the time we have started to have a feeling based on one set of perceptions, we have already begun to have new perceptions that lead to yet more feelings. So we actually have a near constant torrent of feelings, one following hard on the heels of another; and at the same time, those feelings are flowing into emotional responses. If we are practising mindfulness, we notice not simply a gap between feeling and emotion, but an endless stream of gaps following on from an equally endless torrent of feelings. As soon as we step into mindfulness, we step into that stream of gaps and experience the wealth of choice that the gap brings.

Sometimes, of course, the torrent of feelings is too strong and our legs are swept from beneath us, leading back to that common state of unawareness in which our habitual emotional states play themselves out without the moderating effect of our inner wisdom, our conscience, and our sense of where we want to go in life. So initially, for most of us most of the time, our experience of living in the gap is sporadic – we're not able to sustain our mindfulness against the fast-flowing stream of feelings as they rush into emotional responses and then, further downstream, into actions. But with practice our mindfulness develops more strength. By repeatedly re-entering the stream, we learn to keep our footing, to live in the gap in a more sustained way. Choice becomes more constantly available and we are more easily able to live on the basis of wisdom and kindness.

The feeling of living in the gap is a feeling of freedom – not the exultation that comes from being set free (although that might initially be there) but a quieter, surer sense of being able to watch – confidently and without being judgemental – our being unfold. Living in the gap brings confidence, since we have an awareness of the power we have to shape our own destinies. We are actively engaging in shaping our personalities, but with such a gentle touch that it is more like play than work. We are able to withhold the stark judgements that we normally use to label our experiences. We are able to face what is less skilful, less desirable, in ourselves without feeling the need to recoil from it, or to try to conceal it, or to deny it by seeing it only in others. Similarly, we are able to recognize what is wholesome in ourselves without pride and without elation. We simply observe, and act with that light touch that redirects our energies in a more positive direction.

To sum up, in walking meditation we try simply to notice what feelings arise, without letting our consciousness stray unmindfully into habitual negative emotional patterns such as craving or ill will, or into excitement or despondency.

Mindfulness of emotional and mental states

The third foundation of mindfulness is awareness of our emotional and mental states. In Buddhism, the word *citta* (often translated 'mind') comprises both heart and mind. It refers both to mental processes and to emotional processes. So here we're becoming aware of our emotions, and of our state of mind. So as you're walking along, you can be aware of the emotions you're experiencing. These will almost certainly change throughout the course of a single period of walking meditation. A particular meditator might start off experiencing boredom, become slightly irritated as she wonders what this practice is about, start developing curiosity and interest as she begins to notice her body beginning to relax, and then start feeling intensely joyful as the practice becomes more and more fulfilling. Then the approach of a large dog might cause some anxiety, which might turn to relief as the dog passes. Then she might experience joy once more. Our emotional states often change very rapidly.

The quality of your mental states might also change. Your mind might be bright or dull. You might start off sluggish and then notice that your mind becomes more alert and interested. Or it might happen the other way round, with a burst of enthusiastic clarity as you start the practice, with your mind becoming duller as habitual responses come into play. Your mind might be focused or scattered. You might notice that you have a lot of thoughts at one time, and that your mind is very calm another time.

In our day-to-day lives it's very common for us to be quite unaware of our current experience. We are lost in thoughts about the past or the future. Being mindful helps us to be in the moment. In being aware of our emotional and mental states during walking meditation, we maintain this practice of being in the moment. By filling our mind with the richness of the experience of walking, we leave less room for daydreaming and fantasy. Instead, we are deeply aware of our present experience, which becomes far more fulfilling than any daydream.

Mindfulness of objects of consciousness

In dealing with the fourth foundation of mindfulness, we are aware not just of the general state of our emotions and our minds, but also of the specific contents of our emotions and thoughts. In being aware of this foundation of mindfulness, we categorize our emotions and thoughts in various ways. At the very least, we can be aware of whether our thoughts and emotions are those we want to encourage or those we want to discourage. A planned second Wildmind book will help you to categorize your emotions and thoughts in terms of the hindrances and the meditation factors, which are ways of classifying our negative and positive states of mind.

Why is this ability to categorize your emotional and mental states important? Well, the more skilfully you are able to do this, the more ability you will have to choose to alter your experience. An example might be useful: imagine someone comes up to you while you are working, and points out that your shoulders are tense. You realize they're right, and that you hadn't been aware that your shoulders were up round your ears. In fact, you now realize that your neck and other parts of your body are tense too – and that you're emotionally tense and thinking in an unhelpful way about your work. So you relax your shoulders and neck, and you feel more at ease, and you take a few minutes' break in order to unwind mentally and emotionally. You can now go back to your work without developing sore shoulders and a headache, at the same time maintaining a more balanced attitude.

In this example, it is being able to recognize physical and emotional tension, and knowing that tension is something you don't want, that allows you to make a change in how you are acting. Also implicit in this example is that you were able to recognize the absence of the positive state of relaxation, and knew what to do to bring it about (i.e., let go of the tension in your shoulders). So you had a model – a map of mental states – that allowed you to recognize that you weren't where you wanted to be.

"Being aware of objects of consciousness is rather like knowing which plants are weeds and which you want to cultivate."

Once you become more practised in meditation, and have read more of this book, you'll be able to recognize better which mental/emotional states are undesirable, and which states you want to experience more often. You'll also learn how to get rid of undesired mental/emotional states more effectively, and how to cultivate desired mental/emotional states more easily.

An analogy for this process of recognizing and choosing among mental and emotional states is weeding a garden. When you are gardening you need to make decisions about which plants you wish to encourage and which you want to eliminate. Being aware of objects of consciousness is rather like knowing which plants are weeds and which you want to cultivate. This kind of knowledge comes with study, reflection, and experience.

So in this walking meditation we start with the experience of our bodies, and then become aware of our feelings, and then our emotions, and then objects of consciousness. One thing I haven't mentioned in this sequence is our awareness of the outside world. Our awareness of the world is obviously dependent on our senses, which are part of our bodies. So you might think it would be best to focus on the outside world right at the beginning of the practice. However, I find it useful first of all to connect with my body, and only to focus on the outside world when I'm becoming aware of my feeling responses to what I perceive in my environment. Of course, I'm aware of the outside world for the whole of the period of the walking meditation (it would be dangerous not to be), but I only focus on the outside world once I have thoroughly grounded my awareness in my body, otherwise I'm likely to get distracted.

Balancing the inner and outer

Once I have been through the whole experience of my body, feelings, emotions, and objects of consciousness, I like to try to balance my awareness of the inner and the outer worlds. During walking meditation, there are some experiences that are purely internal (the sensations in your body, your emotions, and so on) and there are some that relate to the outside world (you are seeing trees, and grass, and rocks; you are hearing the wind, and birds, and vehicles).

❝I find that it is possible to have an awareness of both the inner and the outer worlds simultaneously, and that when I balance my awareness of inner and outer experiences my mind settles on a point of quiet, calm, lucid awareness.❞

It's possible to get lost in either internal experiences or external experiences: finding yourself caught up in the outside world and unaware of your inner world, or being lost in thought and scarcely responding to the outside world as you walk around on autopilot. However, I find that it is possible to have an awareness of both the inner and the outer worlds simultaneously, and that when I balance my awareness of inner and outer experiences my mind settles on a point of quiet, calm, lucid awareness.

One thing that will help you to establish a balanced awareness of the inner and outer is to pay very close attention to the angle of your head. When your chin is tucked too far towards your chest, you are likely to get caught up in your emotional states. It's as if you get sucked into a whirlpool of emotions, often of a rather dark and brooding nature. When your chin is too high, you are likely either to get caught up in a maelstrom of excited thoughts, or to get very caught up in the outside world. When you find a balance, so that your chin is very slightly tucked in, it's much easier to be aware of your body, your thoughts, and your emotions, and to be aware of the outside world, in quite a balanced way.

At this point of physical and perceptual balance, you'll notice that the muscles on the back of your neck are long and relaxed. Your skull is also balanced perfectly and effortlessly, with the crown of your head supporting the sky. The back of your neck feels open, and your chin is very slightly tucked in, with your head held level. Your gaze is directed slightly downwards, meeting the ground eight to twelve paces in front of you.

There can come a point where the very distinction between inner and outer ceases to have much meaning, and there is simply undifferentiated experience. When this kind of experience arises, it's very joyful. It feels almost like a huge burden has been laid down – the burden of self.

A little at a time

There's a lot you can be aware of while doing walking meditation. If you have the companion CD to this book, listen to it the first few times, then try the practice without the support of the guided meditation.

When you first start 'going solo' (doing walking meditation without an audio guide), or if you don't have the CD, you might want to keep the practice very simple – especially if you find you get distracted easily. You can start off just being aware of your body as you walk. You might spend most of your time being aware of just your feet. It's all right to do this, and to build up the practice slowly. Once you are better at keeping your awareness grounded in your body, you can start becoming aware of other elements of your experience, like feelings and emotions. When you can do that and remain mindful of the practice for most of the time, you can add the elements of mindfulness of objects of consciousness and balancing the awareness of inner and outer.

From time to time you might want to come back to the guided meditation in order to remind yourself of aspects of your experience you've forgotten to notice.

Making the practice your own

Some of my students find they want to do the walking meditation slightly differently from the way it's outlined on the CD. Some want to spend longer being aware of their emotions, while others want to pay more attention to the world around them, especially in the countryside. Some want to repeat a phrase of affirmation, or bear in mind a Buddhist teaching such as impermanence as they walk.

"There are no set stages in this practice. You can do it in your own way."

It's an excellent sign to want to adapt the practice in this way, and usually my advice is to make the practice your own. There are no set stages in this practice. You can do it in your own way. I would recommend always starting with awareness of your body, but you should make the practice yours and shape it to fit your needs.

Other students have adapted the walking meditation by applying it to running, cycling, skateboarding, playing rugby, and in-line skating. I'm always very pleased to hear how students have creatively applied the principles of meditation to other activities that are important to them.

Two really interesting examples have been to do with hiking and rugby. In both cases, the students concerned have been in very demanding physical situations, when ordinarily they might have found themselves getting into negative states of mind. Hiking can be tough going, especially when the weather deteriorates and you are exhausted. One of my students related how she just kept letting go of negative thoughts on a particularly long and challenging hike, and chose instead simply to be aware of her physical experience. Her usual tendency would have been to wallow in self-pity as she puffed her way up a steep hill, but through practising mindfulness she managed to stay in a balanced and positive frame of mind, even though her body was aching. Consequently, the hike actually became enjoyable.

My rugby-playing student talked about how by the last fifteen minutes of a match she would be physically exhausted and emotionally drained. Usually she'd think of nothing except how much she wanted the game to be over. But through practising being in the moment and simply being aware of her experience, she managed to enjoy finishing the matches – even when lying in the mud with someone standing on her head!

Walking meditation and the Metta Bhavana

At the time of the Buddha it was traditional for monks and nuns to practise the development of loving-kindness as they walked around. They would do this while begging for food. They'd radiate well-wishing in every direction as they walked through the streets and market places. They would also radiate loving-kindness towards wild animals as they walked through the forests. India at that time was heavily forested, and attacks by snakes and other wild animals were common. This practice was considered a good protection against snakebite.

Even if you're not at risk from cobras in your local park, you might still want to try practising radiating loving-kindness as you do walking meditation. It can be a lovely feeling to radiate love as you walk past people, and perhaps it has the same protective effect against large dogs as it has against tigers and snakes.

You can start doing walking meditation in the usual way, deepening your awareness of your body, feelings, emotions, and objects of consciousness. Then you can keep your focus on your emotions or on your heart centre, and wish everyone well. You can imagine you have a sun in your heart and you are radiating warmth and light in every direction as you walk. Or you can repeat the phrase, 'May all beings be well, may all beings be happy, may all beings be free from suffering.'

This might be an appropriate point to talk about what you do if you're practising walking meditation and you see someone you know. My suggestion is that you deal with the situation as you feel appropriate. If it's possible, and appropriate, for you just to say 'hello' and keep on going, then do that. If it seems appropriate to stop and talk to them, you can interrupt the meditation, but try to bring the qualities of awareness that you have developed into your conversation. You might want just to stop for a moment and say something like, 'Hello! I'd really like to stop and talk, but I'm practising my walking meditation just now. Can I call you later?'

On the one hand you have to watch out for rudeness through clinging to the idea that you are doing something so special that it can't be interrupted, that is to say, being precious about your meditation. On the other hand, we have to watch for using an encounter with another person to avoid the practice. Meditation challenges us in subtle ways, and sometimes part of your mind will look for a suitable distraction as an escape. ('Oh look, there's someone I vaguely know – let's stop and chat for half an hour about something completely trivial.') Sometimes also we act out of guilt: 'I *have* to stop and talk to this person because I feel guilty about spending time working on myself.' This is something we should work hard to overcome.

" It can be a lovely feeling to radiate love as you walk past people. "

If you do stop to talk to someone, and then resume your walking meditation, spend a few moments evaluating your motive for stopping. Perhaps there is something to learn.

Other forms of walking meditation

Thich Nhat Hanh style

The Vietnamese Buddhist teacher Thich Nhat Hanh recommends a similar walking meditation.[10] Become aware of your experience, and notice how the rhythms of your walking and your breathing synchronize. Then recite the following *gatha*, or verse, in time with the rhythm of your breathing.

In
Out

Deep
Slow

Calm
Ease

Smile
Release

Present moment
Wonderful moment

The first word of each pair occurs on the in-breath, and the second occurs on the out-breath. These simple yet evocative words can help to cultivate the actual qualities they refer to. In a further elaboration of the practice, you can imagine that each of your footsteps leaves the imprint of a lotus flower on the earth, and that as you walk on, a lotus flower grows from each footprint.

In Buddhism, the lotus is a symbol of unfolding compassion, and by imagining this exercise you will help to cultivate, within your own heart, the endlessly unfolding flower of compassionate love.

Indoors – group walking in a circle

This form of walking meditation also comes from the Zen tradition. I first learned to do walking meditation in a group, indoors, while on retreat. We'd start with a short period of sitting meditation. After perhaps five minutes, the meditation leader would ring a bell and we would silently stand. On the second stroke of the bell we'd put our meditation cushions mindfully into the centre of the room and stand in a circle, facing clockwise around the room. On the third ring of the bell we'd begin to walk slowly, following the pace of the leader.

This is the easiest way to teach walking meditation. Because everyone is in the same room, it's possible to give a few spoken instructions. At first the leader might guide people through the practice with a few words of explanation – drawing their attention to particular parts of their experience. Later, we walk in silence for thirty or forty minutes, then the leader rings a bell to bring us to a halt. In concluding the practice, we first of all just stand, experiencing what it is like to no longer be in motion. Then the leader rings the bell once more and we set up our meditation cushions and settle down for another five or ten minutes of sitting meditation – building on the mindfulness we've developed in the walking practice.

This kind of walking meditation is often done between two longer periods of sitting meditation – perhaps forty to fifty minutes before and after the walking meditation. The walking meditation therefore acts as a way of stretching your legs between meditations and also allows you to maintain your meditation for a long time; possibly up to three hours.

Slow walking to and fro

Another form of walking meditation, from the Theravadin tradition of South-east Asia, can be carried out either indoors or outdoors. This form of walking meditation is performed very slowly, as you walk between two fixed points. It might take thirty seconds or more to lift one foot from the ground and set it down again. In this form of the meditation you pay exquisitely detailed attention to your experience as you walk – noticing every detail as you observe your body, your feelings, your mental and emotional states, and objects of consciousness. All this is done, as in any form of walking meditation, whilst observing the breath.

In Theravadin monasteries there is often a walkway for this very purpose, and you can set aside space for this in your own back garden. When you reach one end of the designated route – which might be as little as fifteen feet (five metres), or as long as you want, depending on the size of your garden – you stop, slowly turn around, and then continue walking. It might take several minutes to walk from one end of the walkway to the other.

In some forms of this meditation, the walkway has symbols that evoke impermanence – I've heard of meditation walkways with a skeleton at one end, for example. You could adapt this principle and place any kind of meaningful symbol at either end of the walkway, for example, an image of a spiritual teacher, or simply a few flowers (a more attractive symbol of impermanence, as well as a symbol of the unfoldment of compassion).

A bridge into your daily life

Walking meditation can be a bridge helping you to take the mindfulness you are learning in your meditation into other activities in your daily life. As you learn to walk mindfully, you will see how you can apply the principles of the practice to everyday tasks like making and drinking a cup of tea.

You can pay attention to the details you so often overlook – like the beauty of the vapour rising from the cup, the sensations in your arm as you lift the cup, the heat of the china against your lip, and even the taste. (You might have realized through doing the raisin experiment that you often eat and drink without really tasting.)

"The practice of mindfulness immeasurably enriches our experience, helping us to be more present – more fully conscious."

It's particularly useful to become mindful of activities that most of us normally don't enjoy – like cleaning the kitchen or bathroom. When we have a clean-up period at the end of a retreat, I often volunteer to clean the bathrooms. It's an excellent opportunity to pay attention to the four foundations of mindfulness. I can notice the movements in my body as I wield the toilet brush and be aware of my senses – what I'm seeing and smelling. I can pay attention to the feeling tone of my experience, noticing the unpleasant feelings from getting up close to other people's mess. I can pay particular attention to my mental and emotional states, making sure that I let go of any emotional reactions that arise, learning to be comfortable with the discomfort of unpleasant feelings. Of course I can also enjoy the pleasant feelings – it's a pleasure to watch a stained and grimy lavatory begin to shine. I can notice what I'm thinking about as well, and maintain a sense of whether the specific thoughts I am having are helping me to become content. I might start to become distracted and remember some petty resentment from earlier in the retreat. I might start to think that I'm special because I chose to do the dirtiest job. I can notice these thoughts arising and let go of them if they are unhelpful.

You can be aware of the breadth of your experience in any activity – whether work or leisure. The practice of mindfulness immeasurably enriches our experience, helping us to be more present – more fully conscious – and helping us to direct the flow of our thoughts and emotions in a more positive and fulfilling direction.

In beauty may I walk

In beauty may I walk.
All day long may I walk.
Through the returning seasons may I walk.
. . .
Beautifully will I possess again.
. . .
Beautifully birds . . .
Beautifully joyful birds
On the trail marked with pollen may I walk.
With grasshoppers about my feet may I walk.
With dew about my feet may I walk.
With beauty may I walk.
With beauty before me, may I walk.
With beauty behind me, may I walk.
With beauty above me, may I walk.
With beauty below me, may I walk.
With beauty all around me, may I walk.
In old age wandering on a trail of beauty, lively, may I walk.
In old age wandering on a trail of beauty, living again, may
I walk.
It is finished in beauty.
It is finished in beauty.

A Navajo Prayer of the Second Day of the Night Chant[11]

5

heart like the sun
cultivating loving-kindness

The Metta Bhavana

Try this: Get a pen and paper, and then call to mind a friend – someone you like and feel warmth towards. Write down as many things as you can think of that you appreciate about your friend. You might appreciate their sense of humour, their kindness, their generosity, their ability to keep a sense of perspective, or many other things. Once you've included everything that springs to mind, underline the four or five things you most appreciate about them.

Then softly closing your eyes and beginning to relax, recall a specific memory of each of the things you most appreciate about them. If you really appreciate their courage in speaking their mind, for example, recall an occasion when you witnessed this. Recall the event as vividly as you can, and notice how your feelings change as you do this. You can also observe changes in your body. Perhaps you'll smile, or perhaps you'll experience pleasant sensations.

Once you've recalled all four or five events, sit with your experience for a minute or two, then gently open your eyes.

In the Mindfulness of Breathing we are learning to still the mind, to quieten the emotions, to develop a spacious and luminous sense of clear awareness. This next meditation goes a stage further, and helps us to develop a more loving heart. It's as if, in the depths of that clear blue sky, we have placed the sun, shining down on all beings without discrimination. The more we have cleared the sky of our mind from the clouds of selfishness, doubt, and anger, the more we can benefit others. Although the Mindfulness of Breathing meditation does benefit others, this new meditation has love at its heart.

"Empathy is the ability to share in another's emotions, thoughts, or feelings. When we empathize with another person we imaginatively step into their world to feel what it would be like to be them."

The first thing you might notice about the Metta Bhavana is that its name – unlike the Mindfulness of Breathing – is not translated into English. When you first read the words 'Mindfulness of Breathing' you'll have had some idea what it involved – perhaps a very clear idea. But 'Metta Bhavana' is often left untranslated, and there's a very good reason for this.

The meaning of *bhavana* is straightforward. *Bhavana* literally means 'to make to be', so it means cultivation or development. So this is the practice of the cultivation of *metta*. The word *metta* is harder to translate. There isn't a single English word that does justice to the original Pali. (Pali is an ancient Indian language that the Buddha may well have spoken. It's closely related to the classical Indian language, Sanskrit, in which language *metta* is *maitri*, so you might also sometimes hear this practice called the *maitri bhavana*).

Metta is an attitude of caring for the well-being of others. It's an attitude of empathic awareness of others in which their welfare is perceived as being as important as our own. Empathy is the ability to share in another's emotions, thoughts, or feelings. When we empathize with another person we imaginatively step into their world to feel what it would be like to be them. In doing this we of course realize that their concerns, fear, hopes, and passions are just as real as our own. Knowing this, our attitude to that person subtly changes.

All too often we know the mood of another person without empathizing with them; we might be all too aware that they are angry, for example. Without empathy we stand back from that person, seeing him or her as being absolutely separate from ourselves. Seeing them as separate we may act indifferently towards them and perhaps even be hostile, acting in such a way that it exacerbates their distress. But with an empathetic awareness of that other person we cannot help but care about how they feel, and are more inclined to take their emotional life seriously. In practising empathy (and empathy is a skill, to be practised like any other), we cease to see ourselves as absolutely separate from the other person.

Metta is unconditional love. We do not attach any conditions to metta. We do not withhold metta because we disapprove of someone. We do not withhold metta because we do not like someone's background, sex, race, or even because we dislike them. The most basic thing we have in common with another person is that they dislike the suffering that afflicts them, and they have a desire for happiness. All sentient beings share these fundamental drives of wishing to avoid suffering and to seek well-being. Metta is based on this awareness.

Metta is sometimes translated as 'friendliness'. This translation has some merit. 'Friendliness' has a nice, open ring to it. If we say that someone is a friendly person, we mean they are generally welcoming and considerate. They tend to treat whoever they meet in an empathetic and respectful manner. When they think of someone, they call them to mind in a way that is kindly. They take the other person's well-being into account, which is what metta does.

But the word 'friendliness' tends, in English-speaking cultures at least, to be rather too weak to convey the meaning of metta. Metta can be a very intense – even passionate – emotion, but can we really imagine someone being passionately friendly? In the way we usually understand the word friendliness, this would be a bit of a stretch.

The word 'love' is much better for conveying that sense of intensity of emotion. It's much easier to think of someone being intensely loving than it is to think of someone being intensely friendly. 'Love' can also have the same expansive, open quality as 'friendliness', but sometimes it doesn't, and that is one of the drawbacks of the word 'love'.

When we talk about love, we sometimes mean something very different from metta. Love can refer to a very exclusive type of relationship – a relationship built on sexual attracion, for example. Metta is based on an empathic awareness of another person in which we 'love' the other person in the sense of caring for them because they, like ourselves, want to feel happy and would prefer to be free from suffering. Metta is not based on physical attraction at all (although it's certainly possible – and even very desirable – to feel metta for someone towards whom we are sexually attracted). Usually we are 'in love' with only one person, but we can love many people.

Other forms of love can be very conditional as well. The love we feel for our children may well have a strong element of metta in it, but it may also have a lot of instinctive affection as well. To some extent we will always love our children because they are our children. (Again, it's quite possible to feel metta for our children, but not all of the love we feel for children is metta.)

Other forms of so-called love might have little or no resemblance to love at all. I had an unfortunate friend who got herself into a very confining relationship, in which her partner wanted to control everything she did: what she wore, to whom she spoke, what she did in her spare time, even what she did inside her own head (he disapproved of the fact that she meditated). He was convinced that he loved her (and she thought so for a while too), but in fact he wanted to control her – to have her as an extension of his ego. This kind of 'love' is simply a form of power, and a form of ego-reinforcement that is the opposite of metta. It can be rather confusing that we use the word love in ways that are diametrically opposed.

And yet, if we bear in mind these qualifications, 'love' is a good – possibly the best – translation for metta. If we bear in mind the senses of the word love that are closest to metta – the kind of love that is unconditional, and that seeks the welfare of others – we will have a good idea of what metta is. This is the kind of love that the New Testament encourages us to develop towards our neighbours. It's the kind of love that saints of all times and religions have sought to achieve and to teach.

The word 'loving-kindness' is often used as a translation for metta. I guess this term tries to include both love (the 'loving' part of 'loving-kindness') and friendliness (the 'kindness' part). To some people, this word has deep resonances, while to others it doesn't quite work. I personally find it less resonant than the word 'love'.

So this is why we tend to leave the word metta untranslated; it's easier simply to get a sense of what is meant by metta and to leave the word in the original Pali. This is why in this book I refer to the practice as the Metta Bhavana rather than the 'development of loving-kindness'.

Cultivating emotions

The Metta Bhavana helps us to bring more harmony into our relations with others, so that we experience fewer conflicts, resolve existing difficulties, and deepen our connections with people. This meditation helps us to empathize more, and to be more considerate, kind, patient, and forgiving. We can also learn to appreciate others more, concentrating more on their positive qualities and less on their faults. We can live more from our emotional depths than from the relatively shallow levels that breed irritability and lead to our taking people for granted.

Have you noticed how your emotional perspective can sometimes suddenly shift? I know a Buddhist who had a liver transplant operation. Having been so close to death radically altered his sense of what is important in life. When I met him just a few weeks after his operation he looked more relaxed than I'd ever seen him and commented that he was no longer worried about things like money. It just wasn't important any more.

You might not have had such a close brush with death, but you've probably had similar experiences. You might be caught up in petty concerns – the faults of others, the fact that things aren't going exactly the way you want – and then you discover that someone close to you has fallen ill or had an accident. Suddenly, all the things that were consuming you no longer seem important. You've realized what is truly important. That's what I mean by living from our depths. Such experiences allow us to drop the superficial concerns that we are often addicted to, so that we can live from a deeper level of our emotional life. The Metta Bhavana helps us to live from those deeper levels without the necessity of experiencing a trauma first.

The idea of cultivating emotions might strike some of us as being a bit odd: after all, don't emotions just happen? It often seems that they well up inside of ourselves unbidden, and come and go like the weather.

From a Buddhist point of view this is not the case. Emotions are habits, and are actively created. It seems as though they have a life of their own because we aren't conscious of exactly how we create them. If we can bring more awareness into our emotional life we can consciously cultivate the emotions we want to experience (those that make us and others happier), and discourage the arising of those we don't want (those that make us unhappy and generate conflict with others). This is what we aim to do in the Metta Bhavana – to cultivate the positive and discourage the negative.

Many people who have made meditation a part of their lives can give examples of how they have become more patient instead of acting from the basis of anger, or have become more confident in themselves rather than bogged down in doubt, or learned to let go of addictive behaviours that ruled their lives, becoming instead more content.

We cultivate emotions all the time

An example of how we unconsciously generate emotions is this: imagine you're with a group of people, and you get to talking about all the things that are wrong with the world: hatred, war, intolerance, terrorism, child abuse, pollution, and so on. As the conversation goes on, and we get more and more involved, what happens? The chances are that we get angry, or depressed, or feel self-righteous. By focusing on things that anger or depress you without creatively trying to see what you can actually do about these important issues, you actually cultivate these emotions.

"By calling a friend to mind, and recalling his or her kindnesses or other acts that you appreciate, you give rise to an emotional tone that is much more uplifting."

If you did the exercise at the start of this chapter, you have already had an experience of encouraging a sense of love and well-being. By calling a friend to mind, and recalling his or her kindnesses or other acts that you appreciate, you give rise to an emotional tone that is much more uplifting. You may have experienced a heightened sense of appreciation of your friend, with an increase of warmth and love. This is an excellent example of how we can positively affect our emotional states.

That's what the Metta Bhavana is about. In the Metta Bhavana, we consciously generate thoughts that are likely to give rise to positive emotions. Over time, and with practice, this has a nurturing effect on our faculty of love. We encourage the development of our patience, kindness, and understanding, and in this way we become more loving.

In this meditation we also cultivate metta towards ourselves, so that we experience less internal conflict and learn to appreciate ourselves more. This is very important, since in the West we are often afflicted with self-hatred. We also cultivate metta for those we are close to, towards people we don't know, and towards those with whom we are in conflict.

What metta is

Metta is an attitude of recognizing that all sentient beings (that is, all beings that are capable of feeling), can feel happiness or unhappiness, and that, given the choice, they will all choose the former over the latter.

Metta is a recognition of the most basic solidarity that we have with others; acknowledging that we all share a common aspiration to find fulfilment and happiness and to escape suffering.

Metta is empathy. It's the willingness to see the world from another's point of view; to walk a mile in another person's shoes.

Metta is the desire that all sentient beings be well, or at least the ones we're currently thinking about or in contact with. It's wishing others well.

Metta is friendliness, consideration, kindness, generosity, patience, understanding, considerateness, love, helpfulness. These qualities are only some of the facets that make up the jewel of metta.

Metta is the basis for compassion. When our metta meets another's suffering, our metta transforms into compassion.

Metta is the basis for shared joy. When our metta meets with another's happiness or good fortune, it transmutes into an empathic joyfulness.

Metta is potentially boundless. We can feel metta for any sentient being, regardless of gender, race, nationality, or even species.

Metta is the most fulfilling emotional state we can know. To wish another well is to wish that they themselves be in a state of metta. To wish others well is thus to wish that they wish others well.

Metta is the fulfilment of the emotional development of every human being. It's the potential emotional maturity inherent in each one of us.

Metta is more than just an emotion. It's an attitude of friendliness or love. We can act out of an attitude of metta even when we do not ourselves feel happy, or even when we don't subjectively feel loving. We can embody kindness so much that it becomes just the way we are – nothing special. In fact the more loving we become, the less outstanding love might be, on a subjective level, although we still benefit from the richness that comes from living on the basis of metta.

Metta is the answer to almost every problem the world faces today. Money won't do it. Technology won't do it. Where there is no good will, there is no way to make positive change. Metta can positively transform the world like no other quality.

What metta isn't

Metta isn't the same thing as feeling good, although when we feel metta we do feel more complete, and generally feel more joyful and happy. However, it's possible to feel good and for that not to be metta. We can feel good but also be rather selfish and inconsiderate, for example. Metta has a quality of actively caring about others.

Metta isn't self-sacrifice. Although putting others before ourselves is a good thing to do, a mettaful individual is not someone who *always* puts others before themselves. Metta has a quality of appreciation, and we need to learn to appreciate ourselves as well as others. With self-sacrifice, there seems to be an underlying view that if you keep denying yourself and keep giving to others for long enough, then your reward will come. But often it doesn't – the saviour never arrives. If we never give to ourselves, and keep denying that we have our own needs, other people will learn to relate to us as if we do indeed have no needs. In fact, part of developing metta for ourselves is the realization that we have, at times, to let others look after our needs. For many of us, this can be hard, especially if we live with the view that to admit to a need is to show weakness.

Metta isn't all or nothing. Sometimes people think they haven't experienced metta because they haven't ever experienced an all-consuming love for all sentient beings. Metta can indeed be an overwhelming and powerful emotion but, like all emotions, it can be experienced in subtle and delicate ways as well. Just as our anger can reveal itself in a multitude of intensities from mild irritation to incandescent fury, so too can our metta make itself known as anything from polite behaviour to a passionate love for all that lives.

"Metta isn't a denial of your experience. To practise metta doesn't mean 'being nice'."

Metta isn't something new or unknown to us. We all experience metta. Every time you feel pleasure in seeing someone do well, or are patient with someone who's a bit difficult, or are considerate and ask someone what they think, you're experiencing metta. In the Metta Bhavana, you are cultivating what is already there, you are learning to make your patience and kindness deeper and stronger – like a tree sending roots deep into the soil so that it is strong enough to withstand life's storms. You are learning to make kindness and patience manifest more often, and quite spontaneously, so that they are an enduring aspect of your personality.

Metta isn't a denial of your experience. To practise metta doesn't mean 'being nice' in a false way. It means that even if you don't like someone or disapprove of their actions, you can still have their welfare at heart. This, to me, is one of the greatest miracles in the world, since an awareness of this truth liberates us from the seemingly endless round of violence and revenge, whether on a global or on a purely personal level.

Emotion is a river

Rivers carve their own valleys. Water flowing over soil and rock cuts channels that grow deeper with every passing year. The contours of the channel then define the course of the river. The river creates the banks, and the banks create the river.

Our emotions also follow patterns. They give rise to thoughts, and our thoughts reinforce our emotions. For example, when we're in an irritable mood, our thoughts tend to find fault. We notice things that we don't like about ourselves, about others, and about the world in general. We overlook the good and the positive even when it is staring us in the face. This sense of being surrounded by faults reinforces our irritability, so our emotions shape our thoughts (the river bank), and our thoughts influence our emotions (the river). It's a disturbingly circular dynamic!

How do we ever escape from a mood once we get into it? Why don't we get into a particular mood and just stay there?

Thankfully, there are other influences on our feelings that can break in to the cyclical patterns that I've outlined above. There are five of these influences that we'll look at each in turn:

❖ Your environment
❖ Your body
❖ Your will
❖ Your thoughts
❖ Communication

Emotions and your environment

Our environment has an effect on how we feel. For example, an untidy room can make us feel bad about ourselves, and this can give rise to the attitude that tidying up is a waste of time anyway, because we're not that important. On the other hand, a well-organized and attractive space can help bring about a calm and pleasant mood.

If you want to change how you feel, you can alter your environment. If you're in an emotional rut you can do something as simple as take a new route to work. Or you can clear up. You can take a walk in the park, or in the woods, or take a hike in the hills. If you normally drive to work, park your car further away and make time for a walk. Eat your lunch somewhere new. Go and see a good movie. All these little things can help to shift a settled mood.

You can make your environment supportive of your efforts to develop metta by creating a beautiful space in which to meditate. You can make a shrine that expresses your ideals. Candles, incense, flowers, and images that are meaningful for you can all help to uplift your emotions. You don't have to use Buddhist images, of course. You can use images from nature, or pictures of people that inspire you. Keeping the space tidy will help you to have better mental states when you go into meditation as well as helping you to keep the positive mental states that you develop. What you see when you open your eyes after meditation can have a strong effect – and we are often more sensitive after meditation than we at first realize. So make sure you have a tidy and attractive environment to come back to.

Incense can be a simple but powerful way of evoking a sense of peace and spaciousness. Over time, the smell of particular kinds of incense can help you recall the peaceful states of mind you created in meditation. Chinese and Japanese incense are the most refined. Indian incense is often full of rather sickly-smelling chemicals, while Tibetan incense can be rather pungent (although it is also very natural).

Emotions and your body

How you hold your body has a big effect on how you feel. When
you're depressed, you collapse. Your chest caves in, your shoulders
slump forward, and you end up staring at the ground in front of you
because your chin is coming down to meet your chest. When you
hold your body like that it's almost impossible to feel anything but
depressed. Try it now and see what happens.

On the contrary, when you feel strong and positive and confident
your chest is open, your shoulders back, and you look the world right
in the eye. When you hold your body in this way it helps you develop
confidence and feel good about yourself. Your body has a memory that
you can tap into. If you recall what your body feels like when you are
at ease with yourself – relaxed, open, and alive – and then allow your
body to find those qualities, the emotional states associated with that
posture will take root. Again, try this now and see what changes it
brings about.

Smiling also has an effect on our mental states. It's said that
smiling changes the pattern of blood flow in the brain, promoting
the release of natural opiates called endorphins, and helping you to
feel more at ease and full of well-being. When you meditate it can be
useful to allow a gentle smile to settle on your face.

These are some of the reasons why posture is so important in
meditation. In setting up our postures it's not just a matter of being
comfortable – you're working on your emotions through your body.

It's important to be aware of your body outside meditation too,
and to make sure you're setting up physical conditions that will
support positive emotional states.

Emotions and your will

At every moment of your existence – any conscious moment, that is – you have some degree of choice about how you feel. Whether you realize it or not, you can let go of negative emotions and find more positive responses.

For example, if someone is rude or unpleasant, it may be that you feel crushed and hurt and withdraw in resentful silence. Or perhaps you lash out in self-defence. Neither of these responses is particularly useful, either for ourselves or for the other person. Retreating into resentment perpetuates the pain you initially experienced, and you may end up hurting yourself more than the other person did. Lashing out may lead to a seemingly endless round of tit-for-tat bickering. When you recognize the limiting nature of this kind of reactive response, you may feel inclined to let it go and find some softer, more appropriate, and more productive emotion – like patience, or forgiveness, or even the courage to challenge the other person while respecting their feelings and needs.

Another unhelpful emotional reaction is the burying of emotions. If you simply deny frustration, anger, inappropriate desires, and so on, this produces an unhealthy effect. Unexpressed emotion can damage us physically, leading to tension, ulcers, heart disease, and even cancer. In the long term, acknowledging your emotions is healthier than denying them.

There is a balance to be struck here: sometimes we see venting our emotions as the only alternative to bottling them up. But there is another option: that of fully experiencing your emotions and learning to work with them: transforming them through awareness or, when appropriate, learning to express them more skilfully.

The more mindfulness you have, the more you realize that you have these choices. What you are feeling at any given time is not what you have to be feeling. You have the choice of letting go of that emotion (to some extent at least) and finding other emotional responses. It's as if we all have an inner emotional menu from which we can make choices at will. When we lack awareness we're not able to sense the presence of our emotional menu, and it seems as though we're stuck with one particular response, but even a little mindfulness opens up the possibility of choices.

The choices we have are not unlimited. If you are feeling extremely anxious you can't usually just decide that you're going to be confident and then find that your emotions do what you want. But you can decide, following through this example, to let go of some of your fear and discover greater confidence. This will almost always create some change in your emotional state, and having made that initial change you can go on to make further changes. In this way, step by step, you can make substantial changes in your emotional states.

We can use this principle in the Metta Bhavana meditation at any time, but it's particularly useful to make these choices as we go into the practice. When we begin meditating we become aware what emotional states we bring into the meditation session. These emotions will sometimes be negative – sometimes strongly and sometimes subtly. It's useful to seek within ourselves and try to find elements of patience and kindness. In this way we create good conditions for cultivating metta.

Emotions and your thoughts

What you think about has an effect on your emotions, and fortunately we have some degree of choice over what we think about. This is largely the basis of the Metta Bhavana – we encourage the conscious development of thoughts that will give rise to positive emotions, rather than those that will reinforce negative emotions. The most widely used thought in the Metta Bhavana practice is, 'May I be well, may I be happy, may I be free from suffering.' This thought encapsulates the spirit of the meditation, and repeating it will encourage the development of positive emotion. There's no need to stick to this particular phrase – you can repeat phrases such as 'may I live in safety', 'may I live in peace', or 'may I grow and develop.' The possibilities are almost endless.

The thoughts that we'll use to cultivate metta aren't always verbal ones. We can also use visual imagery, such as a light radiating from your heart. Or of course we can use words and imagery together. Thoughts and feelings are deeply intertwined. I truly believe that everything we think has some effect on how we feel. Every image that passes through our minds, every half-formed sentence that trickles through our consciousness, has some small, unnoticed consequence for our emotional life. Our emotions will be affected even if we aren't aware of it – and usually we are not.

It's therefore essential that we learn to cultivate more mindfulness so that we can become more sensitive to the connections between our thoughts and our emotions, and also so that we can choose which thoughts to encourage and which to discourage.

Over time, these thousands of small changes create a huge change in our emotional life. Listen to the stories you tell yourself, and ask whether they are helpful. If they are not helpful, change them.

> "Listen to the stories you tell yourself, and ask whether they are helpful. If they are not helpful, change them."

Sometimes a shift in our understanding will transform our emotional state. Steven Covey relates how on one occasion, during a train journey, he and his fellow passengers were annoyed by a bunch of children. Their father seemed oblivious to the disturbance. Eventually Covey could contain his irritation no longer and pointed out to the father how disruptive the children were. Covey was stunned when the man apologized and explained that their mother had just died and none of them really knew how to handle what they were going through. Of course, when you stop simply apportioning blame and actually start to understand the stresses in people's lives, it changes how we feel about them. The more we understand others, the more we can forgive.

Most of the methods that we'll use in the Metta Bhavana involve cultivating thoughts that encourage the development of positive emotions.

Emotions and your communication

Our communication has a direct and powerful effect on our emotions. One way to change a mood is to talk to someone. Even if they don't respond, the feeling of being heard has a potent effect on us; it can help to put things in perspective and give us more of a sense that our emotions are manageable. When the emotions we express are positive, they can become much stronger through communication. Everyone has had the experience of thinking about saying something, then finding that when they try to say it, they have difficulty in getting the words out because of the power of the emotions welling up in their throat. It seems that through communication we often get more in touch with our emotions.

Communicating with ourselves has a lesser, but still useful, effect on our emotional states. Many people use a journal to help them manage their emotional states. Writing can help us untangle our experience so that we can begin to make more sense of what's going on in our emotional life.

Communication that alters our emotions need not be verbal. Non-verbal communication – a reassuring touch, a hug, holding hands – can have an enormous effect on how we feel.

In the Metta Bhavana we imagine we are communicating with others, and we actually communicate with ourselves. We call others to mind: those we like, those we have difficulties with, and those we are indifferent to, and we wish them well. We might find ourselves communicating to a friend exactly what it is that we appreciate about them. We might call to mind someone we're in conflict with and imagine apologizing to them. We might even imagine non-verbal communication as well.

This might seem very similar to the category of using thoughts to change our emotions, but communication is such an important part of being human that it's worth singling out. Thought is inherently an inner phenomenon, while communication goes beyond this. It can have an inner aspect that starts in thought, but by definition it involves reaching out to others and letting them into our hearts and minds as well.

Contacting your emotions

Introduction

It's best not to try to force emotions to happen – instead, patiently set up the conditions to enable them to arise and then see what happens. It's a bit like growing seeds. You can't make a seed grow; all you can do is provide warmth, water, and soil, and then be patient.

In cultivating loving-kindness we're wishing ourselves and others well. So how do we set up the conditions for doing this?

Emotional awareness exercise

The first thing is to become aware of how we are actually feeling just now. This is essential groundwork.

Try this exercise:

- ❖ Sit quietly and comfortably, and take your awareness into your body.
- ❖ Relax each muscle in your body as you become aware of it.
- ❖ Take your awareness to your heart area, and take time to notice what emotions are present.
- ❖ Smile, and notice what happens to your emotions and in your body.
- ❖ Remember: it's all right to be experiencing whatever emotions happen to be present, whether they're good, bad, or neutral. You can only start from where you are, so look for a sense of contentment with experiencing whatever is present. Where you are is the perfect place from which to start.
- ❖ Keep bringing your attention back to your emotions for at least five minutes.
- ❖ Notice any subtle changes that take place in your body, mind, or emotions.
- ❖ When you feel ready, bring yourself slowly and gently back to the outside world.

You can listen to a RealAudio file that will guide you through this emotional awareness exercise. You can connect to the RealAudio file by typing the following address into your browser: www. wildmind.org/realaudio/emotion.html

If you do not have the free RealOne player program that you need to listen to this file, you can download it from www.real.com.

When we do the first stage of the Metta Bhavana we'll begin with the above exercise, which is 'stage zero' for this practice. Having got more in touch with how we're feeling we can then begin to work with it. It may be that you aren't entirely sure what your emotional state is. Sometimes we feel rather neutral – perhaps because our emotions are rather weak at that particular time or because we haven't yet developed our ability to sense and identify our more subtle emotions. This is fine; as we do this meditation more often we will become more sensitive to our emotional states.

An outline of the Metta Bhavana meditation

In the Metta Bhavana meditation we cultivate love, friendliness, loving-kindness. Eventually we want to become like an emotional bonfire: a steady blaze of emotional warmth that will welcome any sentient being we become aware of. This is an attainable goal for every human being. All it takes is time and some persistent effort.

The practice is in five stages. We cultivate metta for:

❖ Ourselves

❖ A good friend

❖ A 'neutral' person – someone towards whom we don't have any strong feelings

❖ A 'difficult' person – someone with whom we have conflicts or towards whom we hold feelings of ill will

❖ All sentient beings

We'll learn these stages one at a time, but this outline of the practice will help you to know where we're heading. I suggest you practise each stage for a while before moving on to the next.

Nurturing seeds of emotion

We all experience metta – it's not some new emotion, but a new way of describing emotions that every healthy human being experiences. Every time you are patient with someone, every time you perform a small act of kindness, every time you are happy at someone else's good fortune – that is an experience of metta. We already have a propensity for metta. This practice takes our seeds of metta and nurtures them so that they grow and strengthen and send deep roots into the soil of our being. Eventually we produce a canopy of leaves and branches that provide shelter and nourishment for others, but for now we mostly need to protect and nourish those seeds.

For those seeds of metta to grow, we need soil and water. The soil is our awareness: we need to keep our emotions in our awareness in order to cultivate positive emotions. So while in the Mindfulness of Breathing meditation our focus is on the physical sensations of the breath, in the Metta Bhavana our focus is on our emotions.

But what is the rain? The rain represents the variety of methods we can use to encourage the development of the seeds of metta. There are four main methods that I've found useful: the use of words, memories, creative imagination, and body memory.

We'll look at each of these methods in turn. Some of them will work for you, and possibly others won't. It's best to try a few methods and see which suit your personality, but make sure you give any method you try sufficient time to work. Like seeds germinating in response to water, your emotions might take time to begin unfolding in response to the method you choose.

Using words to cultivate metta

Let's say we're cultivating metta towards ourselves. (This is the first stage of the practice.)

The use of phrases is the classic way of doing the Metta Bhavana meditation, and I use this method more often than any other. There is no limit to the words or phrases you can use, but the traditional phrase for the first stage is 'May I be well, may I be happy, may I be free from suffering.'

You need to say the phrase to yourself as though you mean it. You will also need to remember to keep your focus on your emotions: repeat the phrase, over and over, but observe its effect on how you are feeling. This is true for any word or phrase you use.

Leave time between each repetition of the phrase to absorb its effect. I often fit the phrase in with the rhythm of my breathing and say, 'May I be well', on an out-breath, and for the next in-breath, out-breath, and in-breath, I tune in to my heart and see what effect it has had. Then on the next out-breath I say, 'May I be happy.' Then two out-breaths later I say, 'May I be free from suffering.'

When you're thinking these words, you're being active. When you're listening for the effect they're having, you're being receptive. This practice needs you to be both active and receptive. You are actively working with your emotions, and receptively being aware of the effect of your actions. Both are equally important. Without active cultivation, your mind will tend to wander aimlessly and your emotions will follow old, habitual patterns. Without receptivity, you have no way of knowing whether the effort you're making is taking you in the direction you want to go.

Incidentally, you might want to try saying the phrase to yourself on an in-breath instead of an out-breath. This produces quite a different effect. Try both methods and see which works best for you.

This is a very good phrase to use as it so neatly encapsulates what the Metta Bhavana meditation is about, but if you prefer, you can just repeat a word like 'love' or 'kindness' or 'patience'. Or you can use a series of such words. I've recently developed a liking for the phrase,

'May I love and be loved', which seems to sum up the essence of this meditation.

Or you can come up with your own affirming phrase. I believe it is best to use affirmations that are true. If you say 'I am happy and content' when you obviously are not, it will be hard to do it wholeheartedly. On the other hand, if you use a phrase that expresses a wish, such as 'May I be happy and content', it is more likely to be effective in the long term.

Another thing you can do is remind yourself of your positive qualities, and rejoice in your own merits. You can recall appreciative things that friends have said about you, or recall acts of kindness you have performed.

Using memories

We're all familiar with the power of memory to evoke certain emotions. You remember something said by a child and feel a rush of warmth and love. You remember doing something foolish and blush with shame. These evocations take place all the time, as our minds meander through our memories, often prompted by free association with a word or image. The power of memory is such that our recollections often provoke a stronger response than the original incident.

We can consciously use the evocative power of memory to help us cultivate an attitude of metta. Let's say we're cultivating metta towards ourselves (i.e., we're doing the first stage of the meditation). You can recall a time when you felt appreciative of yourself. You might have been in a very good mood for no apparent reason, and found yourself at ease with yourself. You might have been in the countryside and felt a great sense of harmony and peace. Or you might have just made a significant achievement in your life.

Recall every detail about that time. Remember what you were wearing, what you saw, how you held your body, any scents you were aware of, what people were saying. Call to mind the details: the texture of your clothing, the brightness of colours, tones of voice. The more vividly you recollect the experience, the easier it will be to re-experience those emotions and be able to feel metta for yourself. The more senses you involve, the more vivid and evocative the memory will be, so remember to use sight, hearing, touch, and smell.

Sometimes you'll find it hard to remember a particular incident. At such times don't spend a lot of time trying to dig up some past experience; simply use one of the other methods discussed here.

Remember that the point of doing this is not just to feel good. What we're trying to do is wish ourselves well. Feeling good is very pleasant – you can do any number of things to make yourself feel better – but cultivating our ability to wish ourselves well is life-changing. So rather than having a hedonistic experience, what we're doing in the first stage of the Metta Bhavana is consciously connecting with our innate need for well-being, and finding ways to acknowledge that need. When we do this, we radically alter our relationship with ourselves. We may actually find that as a result of this kind of practice we indulge in less mindless hedonism because we're meeting our needs to value and appreciate ourselves in a more healthy way.

Using creative imagination

Again, let's say we're cultivating metta towards ourselves. One way to use your creative imagination in cultivating metta is to think of an experience that would make you feel well, happy, and free from suffering. Sometimes I imagine I'm snorkelling on the Australian Great Barrier Reef. I've never actually been snorkelling, but when I imagine the feeling of buoyancy, and the warm currents of water caressing my skin, the light rippling down from above on to the beautiful corals, and the shoals of vividly-coloured fish swimming past, I feel a sense of well-being. It's happening now, as I write, and it happens every time I tell people about it.

In the other stages of the meditation, you can invite others to join you. You're generously offering them the benefits of the environment you've created for them.

Again, the point is not simply to have a pleasant experience. Remember that metta is a desire for well-being and not just a pleasant feeling. It's possible to have pleasant feelings that have nothing to do with metta. (You can have pleasant feelings while being unkind to someone, for example.) What we are meant to be doing in the first stage of the Metta Bhavana is wishing ourselves well. In subsequent stages we go on to wish others well by imaginatively sharing our inner world with them.

By imagining that we are well, happy, and free from suffering, we are actually wishing these states upon ourselves. Through imagining a scenario in which we would be well, happy, and free from suffering, we are actually bringing about these states of being. Our subconscious minds are not particularly concerned with the difference between fantasy and reality, so our imaginations can actually bring about real changes in our state of mind. Indeed, we bring about changes in our emotions all the time – every time we daydream we're cultivating some emotion or other. Sometimes they are creative and helpful, sometimes they are destructive and undermining. If we're not conscious what we're doing, anything can happen. What we're doing in the Metta Bhavana is consciously and carefully bringing into being the particularly useful emotions of love, appreciation, patience, and so on.

During the meditation you can think of anything that brings you a true sense of joy and well-being. You could imagine flying over the Andes in a hot-air balloon, and feel the sense of spaciousness and perspective that comes with that experience, or you can imagine the awesome beauty and lightness of walking on the moon, or you can just imagine lying on a beach. As with the memory exercise, bring as many of your senses into play as possible, and make your sensory imagination as vivid as you can.

While we're using methods such as creative visualization and memory, we have to make sure we're still receptive to our emotional experience. Remember the lake: your focus should be mainly on the waters of your emotions, the memories or visualizations are like flowers dropped into it. If you ever sense you are in some way repressing a painful emotion or trying to stick another emotion over the top of it, then pull back from your effort for a while and just sit with your experience. Only once you're comfortable with your emotional experience should you try to use memories or imagination to work with it.

Using your body

We've already mentioned that the way you hold your body has a big effect on the way you experience emotion. You can use this principle in your Metta Bhavana; use your posture to help you cultivate metta by making sure that you avoid tension or slumping. It's almost as if our bodies have memories. As you sit in your meditation posture, recall what it is like to feel confident, happy, and full of energy. Let your body help you access these states by relaxing and maintaining an upright spine with an open chest. Imagine that your body is full of energy – when I start to access my body's memory of what it feels like to be full of well-being, I often start to feel potent energy in my arms and hands.

Allowing yourself to smile slightly will also make it easier to cultivate metta. If deliberately smiling feels false, however, then just allow your face to relax. As the practice of metta starts to result in perceptible and positive changes in your emotional states, you'll probably start to smile spontaneously.

Be flexible in your approach

I tend to use memory, creative imagination, or the body memory method to contact a sense of well-being, and then switch to repeating, 'May I be well, may I be happy, may I be free from suffering.' For a while I'll use two methods simultaneously. For example, I might use my imagination to experience myself by a still pool of water deep in a forest, and then imagine I am dropping flowers into the pool as I recite the traditional phrases. Later on, the visualization seems less important, so I let go of the imagery and simply let the phrases have their effect on my emotions.

This might just be a personal preference. Not all methods work for everyone. As I've suggested, try out several methods and see which work for you. Some people seem to respond more to words, while others find that adopting an open and expansive posture is more effective. An image that works for one person might leave another person cold.

While experimenting with a particular method, give it a good try. Beware of restlessly moving from one method to another without really giving any of them a chance to work. You need to balance the need to find an appropriate method with the need to allow each of them time to work.

Remember that your focus should be on your emotions. It's possible to become so absorbed in a visualization that you forget why you're doing it. In such cases guided visualization has slipped back into mere daydreaming. Your daydreaming may or may not help you to generate metta. If it does, you'll be able to slip back into the meditation practice without having lost any momentum. But if your daydreams drift away from the cultivation of metta into the cultivation of impatience, or guilt, or craving, then you'll have lost some ground. That's not the end of the world, of course; it's inevitable that you'll become distracted from time to time, and it's important to learn to be patient with ourselves when this happens. After all, becoming kinder and more patient is what the Metta Bhavana is about.

Metta Bhavana, stage one

This is the stage in which you cultivate metta for yourself.

Stage zero

In the first stage of the practice, set up your posture and deepen your awareness of your body.

Then become aware how you are feeling. What emotions are present? You don't necessarily have to label them, just be aware they are there. These emotions will be your focus during the practice. Keep your attention focused on your emotions throughout the practice. If you get distracted, come back to your body, and then to your emotions.

Stage one

To work with your emotions, use a word or phrase, or a memory, or your imagination. The simplest method is to repeat, 'May I be well, may I be happy, may I be free from suffering.' As you work with your particular method, be aware what effect it is having on your emotions, which are your focus.

You can do this meditation for as long as you wish, but ten minutes would be a reasonable length of time.

Stage omega

Once you have cultivated metta for yourself for ten minues or so, slowly begin to let your awareness broaden so that you become aware of your whole body, continuing to let your muscles relax.

Then slowly broaden your awareness so that you are more aware of the outside world, including the sounds and space and light around you. Then, when you feel ready, you can open your eyes and come fully back into the world.

You can listen to a RealAudio file that will guide you through the first stage of the Metta Bhavana. You can connect to the RealAudio file by typing the following address into your browser: www. wildmind.org/realaudio/mb_1.html

If you do not have the free RealOne player program that you need to listen to this file, you can download it from www.real.com.

More on the first stage

I suggest you learn this meditation one stage at a time, ensuring that you are comfortable with each stage before moving on to the next. After all, there's no hurry. This book is not going away, and if you spend more time on each stage the deeper understanding of the practice gained will help you to meditate more effectively.

So why not spend a few days just doing stage one for ten or fifteen minutes? You might even want to do it more than once a day – the more often you do it, the more effect it will have.

At the same time you can read the material on the following pages, which will give you valuable information about this stage of the practice.

What's supposed to happen?

Think of it like this. Every thought you have has an effect on your emotions. Those effects are often subtle, so one thought might have little perceptible effect. Most thoughts are like water drops falling on stone. Over time they carve channels. (Some thoughts, of course, can have a big effect – more like a dam bursting – but these kinds of changes are less common.) But the barely perceptible effects of all these thoughts are cumulative – over time our thoughts strongly affect the way our emotions arise.

Most of the time we're not even particularly conscious of what we're thinking, never mind what effect it has on our emotions and attitudes. That is why also doing the other main meditation in this book – the Mindfulness of Breathing – is so important. We need mindfulness in order to see how our minds work, and to notice how thoughts and emotions arise.

During the Metta Bhavana we're being more conscious of how our thoughts affect our emotions. And we're consciously encouraging words, phrase, images, and memories, which will re-inforce positive emotions and undermine negative emotions.

This has the short-term effect of altering your mood (you can lighten up for a while) and the long-term effect of altering your personality so that you become more emotionally positive – less prone to anger and despondency, and more inclined to love, empathy, confidence, and contentment.

This all takes time, of course. Those drips have to wear away at the stone of your established habits. But it works. That dripping water is inexorable. Water is, ultimately, stronger than stone, and all you have to do is keep the water dripping by practising regularly.

Dropping flowers into a still forest pool

Earlier, I touched on a particular image that I'd like to revisit. When you contact your emotions, think of them being like a still pool of water in a forest. Like a pool of water, your emotions are alive and vibrant, and ready to quiver at the slightest touch, although you might not always be consciously aware of that sensitivity.

Awareness of the vibrations in the pool of your emotions is receptivity. You're being receptive to whatever influences your emotions.

The thoughts you are consciously generating – the words, phrases, memories, and guided fantasies you are using in the Metta Bhavana – are your activity. You're using those methods in order to have an effect on your emotions.

Activity is like the hand that drops flowers, one by one, into the pool. Receptivity is like watching the ripples as they spread out across the water. Both activity and receptivity are necessary in meditation. You need to act, and you need to be aware of the effect your actions are having, so that you can, if necessary, modify what you are doing.

You can use this image in your meditation. It's an analogy that can help you to deepen your appreciation of what the practice is achieving.

When I use the phrases 'May I be well, may I be happy, may I be free from suffering', I like to drop each part in separately, like an individual flower. I drop in 'May I be well', then pause for a complete breath to watch for the ripples in my emotions. Then I say, 'May I be happy', and pause again to feel any effect from the phrase. Then I do the same with 'May I be free from suffering.'

❝Both activity and receptivity are necessary in meditation.❞

Be patient. It may take time to attune yourself to the effects of the meditation, but as you strengthen and deepen your awareness you'll be able to feel the effects on your emotions every time you repeat, 'May I be well.'

The other love that dare not speak its name

Loving oneself has a bad press in the West. Many of us have been encouraged to associate loving ourselves with self-centredness and lack of care for others. In fact, many people have a tendency to want to put themselves down to avoid being thought of as self-centred, in a sort of over-compensation.

But in the Buddhist tradition, which has produced countless outstandingly generous and selfless individuals, there is an emphasis on developing love for oneself as an indispensable prerequisite for loving others. In the Christian tradition we can also bear in mind that the injunction is to love others as yourself, implying not only that loving yourself is an OK thing to do, but that it is assumed you will naturally love yourself. Telling people to 'love others as yourself' would make no sense if it was assumed that the proper attitude to ourselves was to be unloving!

Self-hatred seems to be a peculiarly Western phenomenon. Apparently Tibetans simply can't grasp the concept of self-hatred. Buddhism teaches that if you don't love yourself, it is hard, if not impossible, for you to love other people. If you think about it you might already suspect that some of the most selfish people you know don't really like themselves deep down. Their selfishness is often a compensatory mechanism – they are trying to prove they are worth something by constantly rewarding themselves. On the other hand, many warm and generous and loving people are able to be at ease with themselves without being at all narcissistic or selfish – they are perhaps aware of their faults, but willing to be forgiving towards themselves.

If there are aspects of yourself you don't like, your tendency will be to dislike those same things in others. Psychologists talk about 'projection', meaning we dislike some part of our personality so much that we refuse to admit it exists and instead see it in other people. (If you think only other people do this, you're projecting right now.) We see in others the characteristic we refuse to see in ourselves, so we project our unacknowledged dark side on to them. So a lot of our ill will towards others is actually a dislike of ourselves. It stands to reason that if we want to improve our relationship with other people, we have also to improve our relationship with ourselves. You can't be harmonious and loving on the outside and full of conflict on the inside.

Of course, if our metta started and ended with ourselves it wouldn't really be metta – it would be selfishness. So although the first stage of the practice is concerned with ourselves, it moves on to others for the remaining four stages.

It's important to make sure you do the first stage. Don't skip it – if it's difficult that means you definitely need to do it. The cosmos will not award you extra brownie points for leaving yourself out. But make sure you do the other stages as well, once you've learned them.

"You can't be harmonious and loving on the outside and full of conflict on the inside."

The need for nourishment

Reflect on the way you live your life. Do you look after others, but let yourself get run down? Have you taken on views that lead you to sacrifice yourself? This is very common. Sometimes the view we hold runs along the lines of 'if we keep giving to others and ignore our own needs, then eventually those others will reciprocate and start looking after us.' Of course, what usually happens is that we successfully communicate to others the impression that we have no needs, and that we're happy to sacrifice ourselves in order to look after them, so the hoped-for saviour never comes.

“Balancing giving to others with giving to ourselves is one of the wisest things we can learn to do.”

Imagine a field of wheat. For a few years the field provides abundantly, but nothing is ever put back into the soil. Eventually the crop becomes more and more meagre, and if the field continues giving without receiving it will in due course become a dust bowl.

This is what some of us are like. We give (to our jobs, our families, and so on) but owing to insufficient self-metta we forget to give to ourselves. We don't give ourselves time to relax or to reflect. We don't spend time learning and growing. Many of us don't give our bodies the exercise they need in order to remain vital and energetic. And all too often we throw (appropriately named) junk food into ourselves because we are too busy doing things we think are more important. (More important than staying healthy?)

It's good to give. Giving creates connections of love and gratitude. And in order to give on a long-term basis you need nourishment yourself. Just as a field needs to be fertilized, so you need to be fed by sending yourself metta. If you keep fertilizing the field – perhaps occasionally letting it lie fallow – then in the long term it will be able to give far more than the field that is becoming a dust-bowl. Balancing giving to others with giving to ourselves is one of the wisest things we can learn to do.

Procrustes' bed

Procrustes was a character in Greek mythology who had a bed that he claimed would fit anyone – no matter how tall or short you were. If you were too long for the bed your feet would be chopped off, and if you were too short, you'd be stretched until you were the same length as the bed. This was the ancient Greek equivalent of 'one size fits all.'

The world around us can be like that bed. We can mould our environment to a particular shape that will accept us as long as we in turn continue to fit ourselves to the parameters our environment provides. We talk about this kind of thing when we say we are a square peg in a round hole. This can be very painful when it happens to us, especially when the corners of our personalities are brought into conflict with our environment.

The Procrustean bed (or the round hole) environment is partly composed of other people, who have developed expectations about how we will behave. They've usually based these expectations on how we've behaved in the past, so in a way we've created our own environment. Once we start to change, people will often happily accept those changes. If we've become a bit happier and friendlier, few people are likely to complain.

But there are times when changes that seem important to us will simply be met with indifference, though I suspect this is often disguised fear or hostility. So we cannot assume there will be help and reassurance from others, even from those who are most dear to us. As the poet David Whyte said, 'In my experience, the more true we are to our own creative gifts the less there is any outer reassurance or help at the beginning.'[12]

Then there are certain circumstances in which people might react with active suspicion and hostility to our changing – and this includes times when we are developing more of the assertiveness that comes with increased self-esteem. By assertiveness I don't mean aggressive behaviour; I mean standing up for ourselves in a mettaful way – a way that respects the needs and feelings of both ourselves and others. When other people have become habituated to our being compliant or passive, it threatens them when we change, and they may well act like Procrustes and try to cut us down to size.

Diane, one of my students from San Francisco, who is the very dynamic director of a research institute, had mentioned that self-metta had caused her problems in the past. I was curious and asked her to say more.

'You asked about how self-love hadn't worked for me. Obviously that is not actually the case, self-love can't actually cause harm, but it has always appeared to me that any time I ever tried to act on my own behalf, or feel some self-respect, or proud of myself, I have been smacked down or reminded in some way – either directly or indirectly – "who do you think you are?" Either verbally, or the situation I was in turned on me, or whatever.

'After years of reflecting on this, I have come to believe that this is an inside job. In other words, I think it's always been more about my attitude than about what others were actually doing to me. I think my self-regard was so low that (a) it probably ended up manifesting itself as arrogance, and (b) push-back from any quarter was enough to make me retreat back into self-loathing, with every situation re-proving to me that I (or whoever) was right, I was in fact worthless except as some kind of slave to work or other people or to my own dysfunction, and that I might as well not try. Thus another slide back into the swamp.'

❝In the end, you are confined not by others' – not by Procrustes' bed – but by your own fears and low expectations of life and what you are capable of.**❞**

Diane had inadvertently constructed a Procrustean bed for herself. When she tried to assert herself, she sometimes became aggressively arrogant rather than truly assertive, and that, not surprisingly, caused reactions in the people around her. If we've behaved passively in the past, it's almost inevitable that we'll exhibit some compensatory aggression on the way to becoming more assertive. But even when Diane was being more truly assertive, standing up for herself in a respectful way, others would respond aggressively to her in an attempt to limit the change that she was undergoing.

I think it's a very useful practice to notice how the changes you are going through have an effect on others. As I've said, those changes will often be welcomed with open arms. David Whyte qualifies his statement about the lack of outer reassurance that follows from our being true to ourselves by saying that this happens 'at the beginning'. Later on, as our confidence in ourselves becomes more outwardly visible, other people are more likely to help us than to oppose us.

But at first, our changes might meet resistance, and at those times I would counsel you to beware of the danger of retreating back into the limited form that people are trying to keep you in. It may well be that you need extra support at such times. You may need to talk to friends or a counsellor. You may feel an extra need for prayer or meditation. You may even want to think about changing your environment, which might mean changing jobs or ending a relationship. Sometimes our growth – even our very survival – can require such drastic steps and the extraordinary courage that these steps might require.

Ultimately, you are responsible for your own happiness. You have a choice about how you respond to others' reactions to you. As Diane wisely pointed out, she came to realize that her capitulation to others' hostility was an 'inside job'. In the end, you are confined not by others' – not by Procrustes' bed – but by your own fears and low expectations of life and what you are capable of. Only *you* have the power to create the conditions you need for happiness, and this means you should be prepared to respond as creatively as possible to others' objections to your changing.

What if I find it hard to like myself?

Many of us find the first stage of the Metta Bhavana the hardest, probably because some of our societal conditioning trains us to think that liking ourselves is bad.

Traditional Buddhism says it's very important to learn to like ourselves, otherwise we can never truly love others, nor are we likely ever to be happy, because we don't value happiness and well-being. So never skip the first stage of the Metta Bhavana. Always do it!

If you start the first stage and don't feel much, don't panic. Stay calm. It's perfectly normal not to feel much. When I was first learning meditation I sometimes spiralled down into a pit of despair because I didn't see any metta for myself being developed. The cultivation of metta can be a slow process. It works, but it's not a quick fix.

Think about things you do well. Think about your achievements. Think about what other people like in you. This will help you to realize your good qualities. Reflect: do you want to be happy and avoid suffering? Those desires are an expression of metta, or at least the basis for such expression. You probably don't appreciate your self-metta because it's too familiar and close to you. So you may well have plenty of self-metta but have not realized it. Sometimes we have a habit of overlooking the obvious.

Think about the qualities you would like to develop, the achievements you would like to make. What really matters to you? I'm willing to bet that you came up with some pretty high ideals for yourself. If you can have such worthy ideals then you must be, to some extent, a worthy individual. Respect that in yourself. If you do, it'll help you to develop those qualities and make those achievements.

Metta Bhavana, stage two

In this stage we cultivate metta towards a good friend.

Stage zero

Set up your posture, and deepen your awareness of your body.
Become aware of your emotions, accepting whatever you find there,
and not being in a hurry to label exactly what's there.

Stage one

Begin the first stage of the practice, wishing yourself well by using any
method that works for you. Once you have spent five to ten minutes
wishing yourself well, move on to stage two.

Stage two

In the second stage of the meditation, call to mind a good friend,
and wish them well. Decide in advance who you're going to choose,
otherwise you might waste time during the practice. You can use the
same phrase you used before, changing it a little so that you say, 'May
you be well, may you be happy, may you be free from suffering.'

You might visualize your friend, or you might just want to have a
feeling of your friend's presence. Imagine that your friend is well and
happy.

Stage omega

Once you've wished your friend well for ten minutes or so, let go of
the act of well-wishing, and relax back into an awareness of your body,
your mind, and your emotions. Spend a minute or two assimilating
the effects of the meditation before taking your awareness into the
outside world and opening your eyes.

You can listen to a RealAudio file that will guide you through the first two stages of the Metta Bhavana. You can connect to the RealAudio file by typing the following address into your browser: www.wildmind.org/realaudio/mb_2.html

If you do not have the free RealOne player program that you need to listen to this file, you can download it from www.real.com.

How to choose this friend

There are some traditional suggestions about who to choose and who not to choose for the second stage of the Metta Bhavana. You don't need to stick rigidly to these guidelines, but there are sound reasons behind them, and it's useful to follow them in the first few weeks or months of your experiments with this practice.

Choose someone who is roughly the same age as yourself

We want to make sure that it is metta we develop, rather than sentimentality (which can crop up if we choose a younger person in the second stage), or the desire to please an authority figure (which can occur if we choose an older person).

So choose someone who's within a few years of your age.

Choose someone you won't be sexually attracted to

The reason for this is that if you get lots of warm emotions flowing towards your rather attractive friend it might turn out to be sexual or romantic feelings that you're cultivating, rather than metta. It's not that there is anything wrong with those feelings, just that they're not the feelings we're trying to cultivate. Romantic or sexual attraction is very conditional (dependent on our finding the other person attractive) and can't be broadened out to all sentient beings in the way that metta can.

Choose someone who is alive

You might have had a friend who died, and whom you still have a lot of warm feelings towards, but there might also be lots of other emotions associated with that person – like regret, sadness, or guilt. These will complicate your meditation, and when we're first learning the Metta Bhavana it's best to keep things as straightforward as possible.

In the later stages of the meditation you can include all the people I've suggested you don't use in the second stage. Also, once you've been doing the practice for a while, and have a better sense of what metta feels like, you can use your own discretion a bit more. For now, let's make it easy on ourselves, and keep the practice simple by not introducing unnecessary complications.

Should you choose the same person every time?

You can vary the people you choose in this stage. You might want to choose the same person in the friend stage for a while, but it's good to work your way round all of your friends. Some students of mine have reported that they felt guilty the first few times they did this stage of the practice. They felt by paying special attention to one friend, they were ignoring others. It shows how insidious a lack of self-metta can be if we can experience guilt as a result of doing something as worthwhile as deepening our appreciation of a good friend. These responses are obviously a bit irrational, so bear in mind that in time you can include everyone with whom you have a special bond of friendship. You can simply think of this practice as a way to spend quality time with one friend, without having anything to distract you – including other friends.

When it comes to the other stages – for example when we're developing metta for someone we don't get on with – you may find that you have to stop putting a particular person in that stage because you no longer have any ill will towards them! The same can happen with the third stage – when we cultivate metta for a neutral person. Once we start having more of a real sense of that person and they are no longer neutral, we might want to start on another neutral person.

Watch out for restlessness – the desire to constantly change things to 'keep it interesting'. This can be a hindrance in itself, and it's fine to work on the same person for weeks or even months. If you do choose the same person for a while, you're also more likely to notice the changes in your attitudes towards them as your meditation begins to have its effects.

Levels of friendship

The question might arise: how much of a friend should a friend be in order for you include them in the second stage of the Metta Bhavana? Sometimes we call people friends when they're really just colleagues or acquaintances, rather than people we have a genuine concern for.

Aristotle outlined three levels of friendship: friendship based on utility, on pleasure, and on love of the good. Friendships based on utility would be like hanging out with your work colleagues – there may be genuine affection present but if the basis of the association is removed (for example, you change jobs) those friendships end.

Friendships based on pleasure would simply be two people hanging out because they enjoy some common pursuit, or perhaps they just like each other's company. If the common source of pleasure ceases – perhaps because the evening class you were both involved in stops over the holiday season – the friendship stops as well.

Friendship based on the pursuit of the good means that the people, although they like one another, really get a kick from seeing each other grow and mature – and like to help each other achieve that end. This kind of friendship is more enduring and more able to survive ups and downs.

Friendships of the third kind are, both for Aristotle and for the Buddha, the ideal. This is what we should be working towards, but we may not be there yet. We may be at the stage of maturity where most of our friendships are based on utility or pleasure. In that case, we just need to start from where we are and put those people in the second stage of the Metta Bhavana. It's possible – even likely – that as we cultivate metta towards those people our appreciation of them will deepen to the point where we develop a more substantial connection with them: a friendship based on a common pursuit of the good. For now, start where you are.

What's meant to happen in stage two?

In the second stage of the meditation we're strengthening the metta we already feel for our friend.

The word 'metta' comes from a classical Indian language called Pali, and in Pali the word metta is closely related to the word for friend: *mitta*. A mitta is someone for whom you feel metta, so a friend, by definition, is someone towards whom you feel metta. A friend is a friend because that person is important to you and because their welfare is a concern of yours. You want them to be happy rather than unhappy.

It's important to remember that metta is something you already experience. It's not some new emotion you've never felt before. What we're developing, or strengthening, is the metta we already experience towards our friends.

We experience this metta in ordinary life by such actions as being considerate to our friends, wanting them to be happy, putting ourselves out to meet their needs, expressing our affection for them, and being spontaneously generous towards them.

This stage of the meditation helps to deepen our friendships. Since our friendships with others are one of the factors that most contribute to our health and happiness, the second stage is a major step towards physical and emotional well-being.

What if you don't feel much?

When you call your friend to mind, be emotionally honest with yourself. If you don't feel much at that particular time, that's fine – it's just where you're starting from. It's quite normal to feel a bit neutral, and you may even (sometimes) feel some irritation towards your friend. These things happen. Your love (metta) for your friend is still there somewhere, and you can still strengthen that love, even if it isn't immediately apparent, simply by continuing the practice of wishing them well. In such cases the meditation helps put us in touch with our true feelings for our friends.

The worst thing is to try to force some kind of feeling to arise. That won't get you very far – it's better to look for a sense of patience. Remember that developing metta is like growing seeds. Forcing a feeling to happen is like trying to pull a seed apart to make it grow faster.

Be patient, be kind. Allow your emotions to develop at their own pace.

Metta and imagination

You'll have realized by now that the Metta Bhavana is very different from the Mindfulness of Breathing. There is a much wider variety of methods available, giving you a much broader scope for the use of your imagination. Allow yourself to be creative. For example, I was recently listening to someone leading the Metta Bhavana, and as we got to the second stage it occurred to me that wishing someone well was a bit like becoming their guardian angel. So I imagined myself invisibly following my friend around and seeing him with all his joys and sufferings, and wishing him well. This reminded me of the Wim Wenders film, *Wings of Desire* (later remade in Hollywood as *City of Angels*) in which two angels travel around a city helping to relieve people's suffering. I imagined myself like that: lifting the chin of someone who is depressed, giving someone a reassuring touch, listening to their thoughts and dropping in a more positive perspective.

Now you might find an approach like this to be interesting, and you might want to try it yourself. I found it a very beautiful imaginative practice. But you have the capacity for coming up with your own imagery and analogies. This is something that you can't force. You can't sit down and demand that you be creative. It'll happen if you just keep meditating, and especially when you start to feel a sense of creative discomfort – the sense that you could be getting more out of your meditation. It's also more likely to happen if you strive to explain the meditation to others. I've learned a lot through teaching, especially in response to questions and even objections. Having someone not understand you is a powerful spur to creative thinking.

A question might arise: when does the use of our imagination become distraction? Is there even a difference? There is. When we get distracted, we lose touch with what we're meant to be doing. We get lost in thought and stop meditating. When we're using our imagination in the way I've suggested, we're still aware of our emotional connection with whoever we're cultivating metta towards.

We're aware what effect our imaginative method is having on that emotional connection. We're mindful of our purpose in meditation. That's exactly what we lose when we become distracted.

Of course it's possible that an imaginative exercise that starts out helping us to deepen our meditation can turn into a distraction – we can get distracted any time – but in my experience we're no more likely to get distracted while involved in such an imaginative exercise than we are at any other time. In fact such exercises are so engaging that we're probably less likely to get distracted. Imaginative exercises involve our hearts and heads, so we can be more fully present when we're doing this kind of visualization exercise.

What methods can I use?

When you call your friend to mind, you might find it helps to see them in your mind's eye. Imagine them happy and smiling.

You might want to remember a time together when you felt particularly close. This will help strengthen your feelings for them. You can recall qualities you really admire and respect in your friend; perhaps the ability to respond well to difficult circumstances, or their ethical sensitivity. Go beyond those qualities from which you personally benefit. If you only feel warmth towards your friend when you think how nice or how generous they are, it's more likely that you're experiencing what's called *pema*, or conditioned affection (which cat lovers know as cupboard love). You might even want to admire and rejoice in positive qualities that sometimes make you feel uncomfortable. It's a rare and precious friend who will point out when we're not living up to our own ethical standards.

You can repeat to yourself, 'May you be well, may you be happy, may you be free from suffering.' Or you can imagine telling your friend what you like about them.

You might invite them into your creative visualization – take them scuba-diving on the Great Barrier Reef, or to a natural hot spring in the Rockies. Or you might want to imagine a light radiating from your heart, touching the heart of your friend and filling them with joy. The point of this is not simply to imagine that you're having a good time, but to feel you are showing your friend love by sharing something precious with them.

"When we're using our imagination in the way I've suggested, we're still aware of our emotional connection with whoever we're cultivating metta towards."

Walking in the forest of your mind

Contacting our emotions requires us to be receptive. We need to open up and just see what's there. Another way of looking at this whole process is to think what it would be like to go charging noisily into a forest full of shy birds and other wild animals. What would we see? Probably not very much. If we go crashing through the undergrowth, when we finally stop and listen and look around, the forest will seem lifeless.

But what if we were to creep very quietly into the forest, and just wait, and watch, and listen? If we were so still that we blended into the background? Our presence might still make some of the shyer creatures elusive, but eventually, with enough patience and stillness, we'll begin to see the deer, and foxes, and birds that were there all the time.

So think of your emotions as very shy creatures that you'll only see if you are patient and quietly receptive. When you meditate, think of creeping very quietly inside yourself, and standing patiently with your ears and eyes (and heart) open. After a little while, you'll see some of the wildlife of your own emotional life.

Metta Bhavana, stage three

In this stage we cultivate metta towards a 'neutral' person.

Stage zero

As always, set up your posture, deepen your awareness of your body, relax, and become aware of your emotions.

Stages one to three

Do the first two stages of the practice (yourself and the good friend), then call to mind someone you don't have any strong feelings for. It doesn't matter if there is some feeling – the main thing is that you neither particularly like nor dislike this person.

Once you've called this person to mind, wish them well, using words or phrases, or your imagination.

Stage omega

Once you've wished the neutral person well for ten minutes or so, let go of the act of well-wishing, and relax back into awareness of your body, your mind, and your emotions. Spend a minute or two assimilating the effects of the practice before returning your awareness to the outside world and opening your eyes.

You can listen to a RealAudio file that will guide you through the first three stages of the Metta Bhavana. You can connect to the RealAudio file by typing the following address into your browser: www.wildmind.org/realaudio/mb_3.html

If you do not have the free RealOne player program that you need to listen to this file, you can download it from www.real.com.

More on the third stage

In some ways, the third stage is the hardest, since we're trying to cultivate metta for someone we feel little if anything for. You'll find some useful reflections on this later in this chapter. But this is almost the archetypal stage of the Metta Bhavana – realizing that even perfect strangers are not perfectly strange, in that we all want to be happy and avoid suffering. That means that we know the most important central fact about any human being before we even know them.

Because this stage is important, it's worth spending some time practising and reflecting upon it. As always, I suggest doing the first three stages (together) for a few days before moving on to the fourth stage.

Why do we have this stage?

We might have lots of friends. We may have a few people we don't get on with. But most of the people in the world are 'neutral' people – that is to say, we don't feel any strongly positive or negative emotions towards them.

Sometimes that neutrality is simply because we don't know someone. At other times (especially in the West) it's more of a cultural habit.

Most of us in the West live in large towns or cities. In the days when most of us lived in villages, we'd know almost everyone we met. We'd probably have liked some and disliked others. If we saw someone we didn't know we might be very interested in them and pleased to see them, or perhaps a bit suspicious – depending on the time and the circumstances.

Nowadays, though, we see hundreds, perhaps thousands, of people in the streets, in cars, in restaurants, on buses, in shops. We can't say 'hi' to every one of them, so we switch our emotions into neutral as a kind of defence mechanism.

That's probably a healthy response to an extreme situation, but have you noticed how we get stuck in neutral?

What happens when we're in a lift or sitting next to someone on a plane? We often try to pretend they don't exist. Even when someone is serving us in a shop (actually helping us!) we can behave towards them as if they were a sort of human vending machine.

What has happened is that we've become stuck in a neutral state. We can become trapped inside ourselves, sometimes even afraid to be human. And that neutrality can easily turn to negativity. We can get frustrated and angry when a queue seems to be moving too slowly. We can end up being rude to the shop assistant even though they're already hassled. That makes things more unpleasant for both of us.

In the third stage of the Metta Bhavana, we're learning to break out of neutral and reclaim our full humanity. We're daring to feel. We're reconnecting with another human being as a feeling being. We're being respectful. We're showing solidarity with other suffering beings.

Ways of working in stage three

Many of the methods we've used in the first two stages can also be used in the third. You can simply call the neutral person to mind, see them in your mind's eye, happy and smiling, and wish them well. You can use words or phrases to do this.

You can use your imagination and share some beautiful experience with the neutral person. You can also use your imagination to visualize meeting them in real life – but this time you're going to imagine behaving in a more friendly fashion than usual. Perhaps you imagine you're giving them a gift, or perhaps you can imagine making eye contact with them and smile with a heartfelt warmth.

Isn't it amazing? Human beings are the most complex life forms on this planet. We have a richer and more multifaceted experience of ourselves and the world than any other known creature. Yet we take each other so much for granted. Think of someone you frequently see but never think much about. This person has a rich, unknown, mysterious life. What makes them tick? What do they do after work? Do they have a family? What was the last book they read? What dreams and ambitions do they have? Do they like their work? You can simply develop a sense of wonder at all of this.

Here's something else you can try: if you have managed to develop an emotional attitude of metta in the first two stages, you can simply extend this to the neutral person. It's as if you've kindled a fire, and can just invite the neutral person to come and warm themselves.

The third stage as rehearsal

I like to think of the third stage as being a sort of rehearsal for life. Say I think of someone that I often see in a lift. Right now, I tend to ignore them. Don't those little lights showing what floor we're on become absolutely fascinating when we want to avoid interacting with another person?

So I call this person to mind, and imagine what might happen the next time we meet. I imagine looking them in the face, smiling, and asking how they're doing. I might imagine introducing myself, shaking their hand, getting to know their name and what they do. If it's a Monday I might ask how their weekend went.

I'm building up a new pattern of behaviour, starting with my imagination. Once you imagine doing something it becomes easier to actually do it.

Of course, the next time I meet them I might not actually do any of the things I imagined. It might not be appropriate, and I prefer to follow my instincts and respond intuitively. When I actually meet them they might have a cold, for example, so I might comment on that, or they might be wearing an attractive new sweater, which gives us a starting point for communication. But having imagined interacting with them in a friendly manner makes it easier for me to be more human with them.

I mentioned following my instincts. I should warn you that one of my students who had just learned the Metta Bhavana decided to practise being friendlier. Unfortunately the first person she chose – a young man who worked in a filling station – took it as a come-on, and then managed to get hold of her email address and started pestering her. It all ended well, but do be careful not to encourage inappropriate behaviour and to use your good judgement.

So this chapter gives you a few ideas about how you can think of the Metta Bhavana as a rehearsal for real-life encounters. As well as wishing the neutral person well, you can build up support for a newer, more creative way of relating to that neutral person; you'll soon find that they're not so neutral after all.

Having trouble feeling much for a neutral person?

Yes, it can be hard to take someone you don't know and wish them well. Because that person doesn't yet exist for us as an emotional being, there's not much to work with. The neutral person can be as elusive as water that slips though our fingers. But the feeling will come with practice. Keep working at it, and you will find ways of working in this stage.

One initial problem can be our expectations: we might expect the Metta Bhavana to be a sort of emotional firework display. The trouble is that in the third stage we discover our matches are damp. So get used to the fact that this stage might take time to develop. Look to accept that change will come at its own rate if you keep working kindly and persistently.

Get used to just sitting with the image of the neutral person, while repeating the phrase, 'May you be well, may you be happy, may you be free from suffering.' From time to time you can take a break from that and try some of the other ideas from the previous page.

You might be tempted to keep changing the neutral person until you find someone who's more interesting (that is, not really neutral). It's probably better to stick with the same neutral person for a good few sessions of meditation to allow yourself time to develop more of a feeling for them.

If you can't find anyone you feel neutral about

Some people are particularly emotionally sensitive to others. If you're one of these people you may find that as soon as you call someone to mind you have some sort of feeling towards them. That's great! It's quite an asset to have such responsiveness. That quality will make it easier for you to practise the Metta Bhavana.

If you're concerned that you can't find a neutral person, that's all right. As long as that person is not a friend or an 'enemy', they'll do. Just choose someone you don't have any particularly strong emotions towards – either positively or negatively. You can choose anyone you don't know well – perhaps an acquaintance or someone who works in a shop that you visit.

Metta bhavana, stage four

In this stage we cultivate metta towards a 'difficult' person.

Stage zero

Set up your posture, relax, deepen your awareness of your body, and then take your awareness into your body.

Once you've grounded your awareness in your body, become aware of the area around your heart.

Stages one to three

Then do the first three stages – developing metta towards yourself, your friend, and a neutral person.

Stage four

Then cultivate metta for someone with whom you don't get on. It might be someone with whom you have long-standing difficulties, or it might be someone who is normally a friend, but you have difficulties with them at the moment.

Call this difficult person to mind, and be honest about what you feel. There may well be feelings of discomfort. Notice any tendency to think badly of that person, or to deepen the conflict you have with them (for example, by getting into an imagined argument with them), and let go of those tendencies and any thoughts of conflict that arise.

Instead, wish them well: 'May you be well, may you be happy, may you be free from suffering.'

You can listen to a RealAudio file that will guide you through the first four stages of the Metta Bhavana. You can connect to the RealAudio file by typing the following address into your browser: www.wildmind.org/realaudio/mb_4.html

If you do not have the free RealOne player program that you need to listen to this file, you can download it from www.real.com.

Ways to work in the fourth stage

The most basic way to work in the fourth stage is to call the difficult person to mind and repeat, 'May you be well, may you be happy, may you be free from suffering.' It's good to imagine the difficult person smiling and happy.

You can also use your imagination in other ways. You can take the difficult person on a guided fantasy you have been using in earlier stages. (Go back and re-read page 245 if you need to refresh your memory.)

You can also imagine that it's years from now, and that the two of you have resolved your difficulties and have now become good friends. (It doesn't only happen in romantic novels.) In so doing you can trick yourself into feeling a sense of friendship for that person.

You can reflect on any good qualities this person might have. We often selectively filter out any good qualities from our perceptions, a bit like the kind of journalist who doesn't let the facts get in the way of a good story. Dwell on the positive qualities of the difficult person.

You can think about what you and this person have in common. Both of you want to be happy and free from suffering. Wouldn't life be better for both of you if you were in greater harmony?

Is there anyone you shouldn't choose?

Ultimately, the aim of this practice is to develop metta for all sentient beings, but there are a few categories of people you should avoid putting in the fourth stage, and some that you should probably avoid putting in this stage while you're first learning the meditation.

Avoid altogether

Don't choose people you don't know personally. It can be tempting to use 'bogeymen' (or 'bogeywomen', I suppose) like Hitler, or Saddam Hussein, or someone like that. It's much more useful to stick to people you actually have contact with. After all, the point of this stage is to help you transform the relationships in your life, so the closer those relationships are to your day-to-day life, the better.

You can put bogeymen in the last stage of the meditation, in which we wish all sentient beings well.

Leave until later

If there is someone you can't bring to mind without getting very upset (sad, angry, or depressed) – perhaps because they've done us a great deal of harm – it's probably a good idea to put them to one side for a while. Doing the Metta Bhavana will eventually help you to develop the confidence to deal with these responses. Let's keep the meditation relatively straightforward for now, though, and return to this person later.

Feeling and emotion in the Metta Bhavana

You may have read elsewhere in this book that meditation relies on the fact that there is a gap between stimulus and response, and that (assuming we're aware) we can make choices in that gap. We can choose how we will respond in any given situation. Buddhist psychology draws an interesting distinction between feeling and emotion, and this distinction throws some light into the gap. This is something we discussed in the section on walking meditation, but it's never harmful to look at old knowledge in a new light.

Feeling

We tend to use the words feeling and emotion pretty much interchangeably, but in Buddhist psychology feeling refers to our basic, gut-level likes and dislikes. Feelings are basically of three kinds: pleasant, unpleasant, and neutral.

These responses are automatic – we have no immediate control over them. There are some things about some people that we simply do not like or feel uncomfortable about at any given moment (though our likes and dislikes can change over time).

Emotion

Emotion, on the other hand, refers to the active responses that arise on the basis of those feelings. On the basis of an unpleasant feeling, we may well generate ill will (which is an emotion). When we're not being mindful, these emotional responses arise automatically – we experience an unpleasant feeling when we see or think about someone, and then we habitually start to experience ill will towards them.

When we *do* have awareness, however, we have more choice over how we respond. When you call to mind someone you don't get on with, you bring into your mind a host of unpleasant associations tied to that person. These give rise to unpleasant feelings of discomfort. Then one of two things happens. If we lose our awareness, the emotion of ill will is likely to arise on the basis of those unpleasant feelings.

However, if we maintain our awareness we have choices. We can choose to experience the unpleasant feelings that arise spontaneously, and we can choose to wish that person well. Wishing someone well is a volitional emotion – it's metta. We might not experience that metta very strongly at first, but as we continue to cultivate it, it will become stronger and more easily perceptible. Even before that happens, our well-wishing will have a subtle effect on our attitudes and on our responses to people.

When we call a friend to mind, we tend to experience pleasant feelings. If we're not aware, then those pleasant feelings can lead to cravings for all sorts of things: sex, food, acknowledgement, and so on. But with awareness we can cultivate deeper love for our friend.

When we think of a neutral person, this usually leads to neutral feelings – feelings that we can't identify as either pleasant or unpleasant. Without awareness, our minds will tend to wander due to lack of interest. With awareness, we can stay with the feeling of neutrality, and wish the neutral person well so that we start to develop a more appreciative attitude towards them.

When we think of a person with whom we don't get on, this usually leads to feelings of displeasure or discomfort. With unawareness this leads to ill will, but with awareness we can avoid ill will and work on wishing the difficult person well.

In these ways, each stage is helping us to retrain our minds so that we don't slip into habitual, reactive emotional states, but instead gravitate towards more creative and positive states.

Anyway, to get back to you and that difficult person, being aware of this distinction between feeling and emotion allows us to become comfortable with the discomfort of unpleasant feelings. If we can appreciate this distinction, we can simply be aware of the unpleasant feelings that arise when we think of the difficult person – without giving rise to ill will.

From time to time our awareness will inevitably slip, and then our minds will follow their habitual patterns of developing negative emotions of ill will on the basis of those unpleasant feelings. When ill will does arise, become aware of that and choose to let go of it. With practice, our mindfulness will grow stronger and our positive emotions cannot but develop and unfold.

Learning to be comfortable with discomfort

One important thing to remember is that unpleasant feelings are not necessarily negative. Take shame, for example. Feeling ashamed is not a pleasant experience. It has an unpleasant feeling associated with it, as I'm sure you know from your own experience, but shame is considered a positive emotion in Buddhism because it's an emotion based on an ethical sensibility.

Sadness and grief are other examples. Sadness and grief are feelings that arise when we experience loss. It would be inhuman to lack this kind of feeling when something precious to us is lost. Sadness is really just the shadow side of love: not the opposite, but the side of love that reminds us when we are separated from something dear to us.

Of course, not everything that feels pleasant is positive. It's possible to take pleasure from being unkind, and unkindness is a negative emotional state. Intoxication (whether due to drink, drugs, or emotion) might feel pleasant, but it often has deeply destructive effects on ourselves and other people.

One of the things we have to learn in meditation is to be comfortable with discomfort – so that we don't react inappropriately and create negative emotional states that will only lead to more suffering in the future.

When you find it hard to call the difficult person to mind

If every time you call this difficult person to mind, it puts you in touch with states such as rage, or sadness, or fear, or depression – emotions that leave you feeling incapacitated or out of control – then perhaps you need to change the way in which you call this person to mind.

If you do have these problems, I suspect that what you're doing is calling the difficult person to mind vividly and in ways that remind you of painful experiences. This is the same kind of way of thinking that I suggested in the second stage, when I said you could clearly recall a time when you felt particularly close to your friend. I suggested that by doing this – by recollecting that time in fine detail – you would recapture the emotions you experienced at that time. And of course this can work with negative emotions as well. If you vividly recall a time when you felt particularly hurt by someone, you'll almost certainly re-experience the hurt.

So how can you call to mind the difficult person without engendering the painful emotions that made them the difficult person in the first place?

There are several things that you can do. First, don't recall this person in a place where you've known them, especially not in a place with bad associations. Places are potent reminders of past emotional states. Instead, imagine them somewhere quite imaginary, or somewhere you've never visited together. Or imagine them in a place that has happy memories for you, in which case make sure you connect with that place and those feelings before you call them to mind. If you do this, those positive associations will change how you feel about that person. If you call to mind the difficult person and the emotions you associate with them, and *then* call to mind a place you like, you'll transfer those unpleasant feelings and emotions to that favourite place, which is not going to help you.

Secondly, rather than imagining yourself physically close to this person, imagine them in the distance, small and far away, to help to put a sense of emotional distance between you. You'll have more of a perspective on your relationship with them, both literally and metaphorically.

Thirdly, try adopting a viewpoint higher than the difficult person, so that you are looking down on them. If you are physically looking down on someone in your imagination you are much less likely to perceive them as a threat on an emotional level.

Doing these three things might well allow you to call the difficult person to mind and feel much less vulnerable. Once you've done this a few times you might find you are able to experiment with bringing the difficult person closer to you, and up to your own level, then you'll be able to meet them with more confidence and strength.

The fourth stage as rehearsal

You can see this stage (like the neutral person stage) as a rehearsal for life outside meditation.

You might want to think about something as simple as how you will greet the difficult person when you next see them. If you can be more friendly than usual it will have a definite effect on your relationship. You can reflect on whatever good qualities the difficult person might have, and think about things on which you might compliment them. Or if you have a habit of maligning this person you might think about speaking well of them.

If you're aware of any unhelpful patterns the two of you have established, you might like to think of a friendly and respectful way in which you can change those patterns – perhaps by giving praise, or apologizing for something. Teresa, one of my online students, reported on the following change in her relationship with a colleague:

'When I encountered the person I had conflict with at work yesterday I felt unusually courteous and sympathetic towards him. And when he engaged me in conversation I listened to him and reciprocated conversation. In the past I would have not really listened to him, just answered him perfunctorily, and got away from a conversation with him as soon as possible.'

Don't be surprised if friendly overtures have the effect of causing suspicion, or even hostility. If there's a bad history between the two of you your well-meaning actions might be misinterpreted as a manipulative trick. But if you persist in being friendly, things will almost certainly start to change for the better.

Why should you develop metta for a bad person?

There are some very bad people in the world. Sometimes evil is not too strong a word for some of the acts they perpetrate, and you might wonder why you should develop metta towards those who commit evil.

Metta is a state of love. It's a state of empathetic awareness that brings about compassion, consideration, and kindness. If those evil people were to experience metta they would not do the things we so deplore. Acts of evil come from a failure of empathy.

It makes sense, then, that if you want the world to be a better place you will want all beings to experience metta – even the very bad ones. In fact especially the bad ones, because if evil people were to experience metta, there would be no evil. I'm not suggesting that we can wish bad people into becoming good people, but simply that it's rational to wish those people freedom from the unwholesome mental states that led to their actions. This implies that we should have compassion even for those who commit evil.

A meditation student of mine who is a psychotherapist pointed out to me that most of the actions we label as evil are committed by people who suffer from what is known as Antisocial Personality Disorder, and that scientific research studies have shown that up to 75% of all those in the US criminal justice system fit the diagnostic criteria for it. This disorder is almost certain to have a genetic component, so that many bad people are born that way and not made that way, although poor environments almost certainly make these genetically based traits worse. Many people, in committing evil, are therefore passing on the results of a sickness they suffer – a sickness that prevents them feeling empathy, remorse, and anxiety. Additionally, they might feel compelled to lie – even when there's no reason to – have difficulty learning from experience, and have trouble controlling their impulses.

There is no reason why we should feel any less sympathetic towards a criminal who, because of a genetic defect, has a lower than normal ability to control his or her impulses, than towards a person with any other genetically-based physical or mental condition. If we can feel sympathy for a person who suffers from, say, Down's Syndrome, then why not towards someone who has a genetic disorder like Antisocial Personality Disorder that ruins the lives not only of its sufferers but also those who are unfortunate enough to be exploited or harmed by them?

> **"It will reduce the amount of intolerance and hatred in the world by reducing the amount of intolerance and hatred in your own heart (which is the only place where you can guarantee to make a difference)."**

As an aside, I hope (although I have no personal experience on which to build this hope) that those suffering from Antisocial Personality Disorder are able to learn to control their impulses. Some mental health professionals have shown that individual and group therapy can help those suffering from this devastating condition to learn to experience and deal with their emotions, and learn more moral concern for others. I don't want to appear to be saying that those who act destructively should be absolved from all responsibility, but simply that not everyone is starting from the same place in learning to take such responsibility, and that it is helpful to them and to us if we have sympathy for those in such an unfortunate position.

You might well ask, though: how is cultivating metta towards a bad person going to have any effect on them? Isn't it just a game you're playing inside your own head?

It's true that your meditation is not likely to have much effect on another person (though you never know – some interesting research has been done which shows that this does happen), but at the very least it will have an effect on you. It will help you to be more truly compassionate. It will reduce the amount of intolerance and hatred in the world by reducing the amount of intolerance and hatred in your own heart (which is the only place where you can guarantee to make a difference).

Metta bhavana, stage five

In this stage we cultivate metta toward all sentient beings.

Stage zero

We start – as always – by developing body awareness and contacting our emotions.

Stages one to four

Then we do the first four stages.

Stage five

Then in the last stage of the meditation we spread our well-wishing in wider and wider circles.

Start with yourself, your friend, the neutral person, and the difficult person. See all four of you together, and wish all four people well. Try to do this equally towards all four of you, and notice any tendency to play favourites by wishing your friend more happiness than the others.

Then spread your well-wishing out in wider and wider circles, until you are wishing that all sentient beings be well and happy.

Stage omega

At the end of the practice, let go of any visualizations or other efforts you are making, and simply relax back into an awareness of yourself. Give yourself time to notice the effects of the meditation, and sit for a few moments enjoying the fruits of the practice and appreciating the positive effort you have been making. Then, when you are ready, bring your awareness back to the outside world.

You can listen to a RealAudio file that will guide you through all the stages of the Metta Bhavana. You can connect to the RealAudio file by typing the following address into your browser: www.wildmind.org/realaudio/mb_5.html

If you do not have the free RealOne player program that you need to listen to this file, you can download it from www.real.com.

Ways of working in the fifth stage

All sentient beings means a lot of people (and not just people – 'sentient beings' includes all life forms capable of experiencing pain and pleasure). How do we develop feelings of metta towards all beings?

In the fifth stage we're working on developing metta as an open attitude of loving. It's as if we are a blazing sun of positive emotion that warms all beings. We're working towards being so radiant that whoever comes into our experience will be received with metta – with friendliness, warmth, and caring. This might sound like a tall order, but think back to those days when, for some reason, you've been in an unshakeably good mood and nothing could annoy you. That's the kind of state we're trying to encourage, except that we want to be like that all the time.

The four directions

Buddhist monks and nuns were traditionally encouraged to walk around radiating metta in the four directions of space. They would do this particularly on their almsround, when they would walk slowly through the streets and have most of their contact with people. They would also radiate metta in this way while sitting in meditation. In the fifth stage you can just imagine you are sending metta out in all directions, or calling to mind each geographical direction and wishing that all beings in that direction be well and happy.

Holding the world in your heart

You can imagine that you hold the world enfolded in your heart, and cherish it along with all the sentient beings that inhabit our world.

Taking a world tour

You can let scenes from around the world come into your mind, and wish the people you see there well.

You don't have to be limited to places you know – you must have seen a lot of the world on television, in magazines, and in movies.

Networking

You can call to mind people you know around the world. You can imagine your metta flowing to them, and through them to all the people that they know, and so on.

They say there are no more than six degrees of separation between any two people in the world. In other words the most distant we can be from any other human being is that we know someone who knows someone who knows someone who knows someone who knows someone who knows them. So you don't have to do much networking to fill the whole world with metta.

"We're working towards being so radiant that whoever comes into our experience will be received with metta – with friendliness, warmth, and caring.**"**

Remembering non-humans

Remember to include animals too. Ideally we should wish that all sentient life be well, happy, and free from suffering.

And there's no need to stop with planet Earth. You can send your metta throughout the universe, to any sentient beings who might be out there.

If all of this business of trying to wish all beings well seems rather overwhelming, I'm not surprised. You don't literally have to wish all beings well. In fact you can't. How could you, if you don't know all sentient beings? All you're looking for is a sense of expansiveness in your well-wishing. If you reach the point where you have a sense of wishing others well, and you can do this for whoever you happen to bring to mind, that's fine.

Think of yourself as a human bonfire, radiating warmth and light in all directions. You don't literally have to warm all beings, but in principle your heat is available to all. Similarly, in the final stage of the Metta Bhavana you don't have to call all sentient beings to mind, just wish that whatever beings do come to mind be free from suffering.

Families and lovers

Remember, way back when we were learning the second stage of the Metta Bhavana, and I said it wasn't a good idea to choose lovers or children or parents as your friend? There were very good reasons for that, but having ruled out those people in the second stage, we may forget about them altogether in our Metta Bhavana, which would be a great shame.

These close, day-to-day relationships are the real working ground for our practice of metta. Our relationships with our parents, children, and spouses or lovers are usually the most important ones in our lives. Those to whom we are closest become, in a way, a part of us. We all realize this when we start to discover (often with a shock) how like our parents we are. The same can be true for our children and partners as well.

And have you noticed how people (I'm talking about you and me here) tend to behave differently towards those closest to them? Because we feel our families are not completely separate from us, we tend to behave towards them in ways we wouldn't consider with people such as colleagues or friends. Lovers will argue and insult each other in public in quite extraordinary ways, and parents will talk to their children in an equally bizarre manner. Of course we realize that often, deep down, this behaviour is a product of the closeness we feel. We let our guard down and drop our social inhibitions with those we are close to. This has its positive side, and its shadow side. It seems to me that the way we relate to people we are close to in some ways mirrors the way we relate to ourselves, that our relationship with our families and partners is a window on how we behave towards ourselves.

For this reason it's vital that we remember to call our family and partners to mind. The fifth stage is the ideal place to do this (unless you have a conflict with someone, in which case you might wish to put them in the fourth stage). Perhaps you could wish your family and partner well immediately after all four people who have been in the practice, and before you start to broaden your metta out to the wider world.

"It seems to me that the way we relate to people we are close to in some ways mirrors the way we relate to ourselves."

Contacting emotions

If we go about trying to contact our emotions in the wrong way, it can actually make it harder to experience them.

When I was once leading a retreat, a young man came to me after a session of the Metta Bhavana looking rather worried, and said, 'I got really upset during that last Metta Bhavana because I couldn't work out how I was feeling. I just couldn't feel any emotion at all.'

I said, 'You felt upset' (which was what he had just told me).

He said, 'So I was!' as if I'd just pointed out something very profound.

It was odd: he told me how he felt, but thought he didn't know how he felt. It was as if he was looking for his emotions in the wrong place. It was odd, but it is common as well.

The British have Christmas stage shows called pantomimes. They're really ritualized (which is part of the entertainment), and one of the rituals is that at some point the bad guy (the Wolf, or the Sheriff of Nottingham, or whoever) is standing menacingly behind the hero. The hero asks something like, 'I wonder where that big, bad wolf is?' and all the kids (and most of the adults, who enjoy these things just as much, but don't want to admit it) shout, 'Behind you! Behind you!'

The hero then turns round really, really slowly, but the baddie moves around behind him at the same time. So the hero turns back to the audience (with the baddie moving round at the same time) and says, 'Where did you say he is?' And this goes on for a while, to everyone's great amusement.

Looking for our emotions is sometimes a bit like that. We make such a heavy-handed effort to find them that we never even catch a glimpse of them. To find emotions requires simply that we be receptive and open. This kind of receptivity starts with body awareness (see the chapter on posture for more details). If we become more aware of our bodies and relax, it's much easier to be aware of those more subtle parts of ourselves like our feelings and emotions.

Metta and 'the divine'

I believe we are all aware of only a tiny part of ourselves. The conscious part of ourselves is the tip of the iceberg, and the bulk of ourselves is beneath the waves. Part of that unconscious is childish and even quite nasty at times. But the deepest parts often have a wisdom at which we can only guess. Our conscious minds rarely pick up on that wisdom, although sometimes we can in dreams or when we're particularly intuitive, that is, when the barrier between the conscious and the unconscious is particularly permeable. There are times when we experience our wiser deep subconscious, but because we don't experience it as 'us', we experience it as 'other'. So we might feel a kind, loving, wise presence, or even have a vision or hear a guiding voice. I think of such experiences as being experiences of 'the 'divine'.

One of my students described such an experience when she said,

'When I was describing the experience I had about a week ago where I felt a strong benevolent presence, you mentioned that the feeling of metta can be external or internal. That really struck me, because at the time I didn't really express how external the feeling was. It really felt as if there was a very strong presence in front of me generating a deep sense of compassion, comfort, and love. To be honest, I thought to myself that I was in the presence of God. I thought that there wouldn't be much place for this sort of experience in Buddhist thought, so I wasn't sure what to make of it, although I certainly didn't want to dismiss it.'

“In this kind of meditation it's very common indeed to feel a sense of metta or other blessings flowing as though from outside oneself.”

This kind of experience is not uncommon in meditation. In fact it forms the basis of some kinds of meditation practice. Buddhist visualization practices are an attempt to integrate qualities of wisdom, compassion, and unobstructed energy through contemplation of symbolic forms that in some way correspond to those qualities (which qualities are already present in us, but are as yet unrealized). So in visualizing the compassionate form of a Buddha image we're really calling to mind our own potential compassion, and thereby creating a channel from the unconscious to the conscious. Eventually, a sort of integration can take place, so that the meditator and the visualized figure merge. So in this kind of meditation it's very common indeed to feel a sense of metta or other blessings flowing as though from outside oneself.

In Buddhism, the distinctions we make between inner and outer have no real validity. That distinction is just a convenient fiction that allows us to make some kind of sense of our lives (although it's not always a very accurate sense). We can see this if we reflect on the common experience of falling in and out of love. When you fall in love with someone, you think they're wonderful. Sometimes it all works out, but other times we discover they weren't the person we thought they were, and then we fall – or even plummet – out of love with them. They no longer seem to have those wonderful qualities that we thought they had.

So where were those qualities? What were we attracted to? Obviously, in such cases, our attraction wasn't entirely for the other person but for some unconscious part of ourselves that we imagined was in them. We'd confused something inside ourselves with something that was outside.

Our inner and outer worlds actually exist in interdependence, not as separate realities. Change one, and you change the other. So the experience of metta might be neither internal nor external, nor both, nor is it something other than internal or external. It's really utterly indefinable. The important thing is that it works. When I think in terms of 'the divine' I don't assume that such experiences of an external source of metta are emanating from a deity; I use this term to suggest a sense of mystery, a sense of the way in which we can experience ourselves as 'other', and the way in which we can connect with those hidden forces that inhabit our depths.

If this kind of experience befalls you, you may well wish to categorize it in terms of your existing belief system. Some people, experiencing an external sense of metta, will assume this is an experience of God, and such descriptions can certainly bring a deeper sense of significance and meaning to your meditation. On the other hand, you may wish just to accept these blessings and reflect on the fact that we really know next to nothing about ourselves and the universe in which we live. You may wish just to experience and accept the mysterious and ineffable nature of these experiences and recognize that you are arriving at a fuller appreciation of the nature of Reality.

The importance of practice

One of the key principles of meditation is that practice makes better – if not perfect. Meditating once in a while will have some effect on you, but to get the full benefits you really have to practise most days, and preferably every day.

It's a bit like going to the gym. If you go once in a while it will have some benefit, but mostly what you're going to notice is how unfit you are, in which case your experience is not very likely to be pleasant. With meditation, if you practise very irregularly you'll notice how scattered your mind is and how distracted you are. Again, that's not going to be very pleasant and you probably won't want to meditate much.

On the other hand, the benefits of training (either at the gym or in meditation) are that you will build on what you achieve. In other words, the effects of regular meditation are cumulative.

To support your regular practice you might want to do a number of things:

❖ Read the suggestions about setting up a regular meditation practice.

❖ Find a local meditation group to sit with regularly (a Zen, Theravadin, or Friends of the Western Buddhist Order group is the most likely to teach meditations similar to those you've learned here). Dharmanet (www.dharmanet.net) has a searchable list of meditation groups, though entries are not always up-to-date.

❖ Watch out for a planned follow-up to this book which will introduce new methods for working to reduce states such as anxiety and anger, and teach skills in developing calmness, energy, contentment, and concentration. It will also introduce insight meditation, which helps to bring more of an existential edge to the meditation practices you already know.

Balancing the Metta Bhavana and the Mindfulness of Breathing

The Mindfulness of Breathing and Metta Bhavana meditations complement each other. We need mindfulness in order to be able to develop metta more effectively, and the emotional positivity we develop in the Metta Bhavana helps us be more engaged and productive in the Mindfulness of Breathing.

Most people like to alternate these meditations, and I think that's a good thing to do. Some of my students practise the Mindfulness of Breathing in the morning and the Metta Bhavana in the evening. That seems to work very well. So does alternating the meditation from day to day.

Of course, you might well go through phases in your life when it's more appropriate to do just one of these practices for a time. If you've been very distracted it might make more sense to do the Mindfulness of Breathing more often, or if you're feeling emotionally vulnerable or you've been getting into bad moods it might be best to concentrate on the Metta Bhavana.

One way to balance the practices is to do more of each, and you can do this by going on a meditation retreat. A retreat is an opportunity to meditate more intensively in a supportive environment. The Internet would be a good place to start looking for a retreat centre, though you should exercise your judgement in choosing a venue.

Places I know or that have been highly recommended to me include:

❖ **Dhanakosa** (www.dhanakosa.com) in Scotland
❖ **Samye Ling** (www.samyeling.org) in Scotland
❖ **Taraloka** (www.taraloka.org.uk), a women's retreat centre in Wales
❖ **Spirit Rock** (www.spiritrock.org) in California
❖ **Aryaloka** (www.aryaloka.org) in New Hampshire
❖ **Upaya Zen Center** (www.upaya.org) in New Mexico

If none of these centres is anywhere near you, visiting their websites and contacting the people who run them may help you to track down somewhere that is more conveniently located and appropriate to your needs.

Many urban Buddhist centres run retreats in hired venues, so if there is a particular tradition you are drawn to you could search the Internet for a local one.

6

metta in daily life

Dimensions of metta

The Metta Bhavana is one of a set of four related meditations that are collectively known as the 'sublime abodes', because they are such fulfilling emotional states and because they have such beneficial effects. Each of these practices helps us to develop a different aspect or dimension of metta, and each of the other three practices deals with metta in contact with a different dimension of experience.

The first dimension of experience we can contact with our metta is the happiness of others. When our metta meets awareness of other people's happiness, it subtly shifts its feeling tone. We call this *mudita*, or empathetic joy. When we are empathetically aware of another's good fortune, we experience a joy that aligns itself with that other joy. We feel happy because another person is happy. This is not the same as the sense that we're going to benefit because someone else has gained something that we want. For example, if a friend has inherited some money, you might think, 'Oh good, now I'm going to benefit because my friend has lots of wealth.' This isn't mudita, but just a selfish greed that attaches to somebody else's good fortune. Genuine mudita is, like metta, unconditional. We're happy not because we might benefit from someone else's good fortune but just because we like others to be happy.

The second dimension of experience we can contact is that of suffering. When our metta meets awareness of suffering, it is subtly transformed into *karuna*, or compassion. Compassion is the meeting of metta with the awareness of suffering. Again, it's a sense of empathy. It's not that we feel anxious or feel pity for the other person. When we feel pity we look down on someone, feel superior to them. Compassion is simply a sense of love and cherishing for the well-being of someone when it meets the fact of their suffering.

The third dimension of experience that our metta can combine with is insight into the conditioned nature of both joy and suffering. When we empathetically sense the joys and sufferings of other people, and also see clearly how those joys and sufferings arise on the basis of their actions, there is a sense of *upekkha*. Upekkha is usually translated as 'equanimity' and that's likely to be as close as we can get in the English language to describing what it is. Upekkha certainly isn't a sense of indifference, nor is it a sense of 'I told you so.' If you experience these attitudes it means your metta has been replaced by something more judgemental and much less positive.

In fact, upekkha is the opposite of those attitudes. Equanimity, in this sense, means that your metta is quite unshakeable, despite an awareness of how all beings bring about much of their joy and suffering themselves. Equanimity is a calm, loving non-judgemental awareness of the way that both joy and suffering flow from our actions. It's a deep penetration into karma, or the way that we construct – for good or ill – our experience through our own actions.

Metta in everyday life

Metta is something that should be cultivated not only on the cushion. We can take our metta out of the meditation and into our lives, and in practising it we can develop it. It's like anything else; practice helps us to become better at what we do. Of course we'll make mistakes, but that's just part of the process of learning any skill.

What we're really talking about here is ethics, but not ethics understood in terms of obeying rules, or in terms of escaping punishments and earning rewards; metta has its rewards, but they are simply the natural consequences of our actions, not something handed out by an external judge.

Our ability to practise metta in everyday life is naturally going to affect our meditation. So the relationship between meditation and daily life is a two-way street; each has effects on the other. If we are trying to cultivate metta in meditation, but we're acting in our daily lives in a way that undermines it, our development is obviously going to get stuck. This may be one of the most common causes of lack of progress – that we are busy undoing the effects of our meditation while at work or with our families. So we need to look at every aspect of our lives and see to what extent it helps or hinders our development of metta.

Metta, diet, and lifestyle

One thing we can do is to look at the effects of our everyday actions. We all tend to see ourselves as consumers these days, but we often don't consider that what and how we consume has truly global effects. If we want to develop the quality of metta, it makes sense to look at the effects of our actions.

Of course, we'd sometimes rather not know the consequences of our actions. Ignorance is bliss, right? (Well, if not exactly blissful, ignorance can be a way of avoiding taking responsibility.) Once we are aware of these consequences, we are faced with choices about how to respond. We have to deal with the discomfort with which our conscience presents us if those actions aren't congruent with our ethical compass. So remember that you have choices here.

Much of our consumerism causes harm. We can't possibly avoid causing any harm at all, but we can become aware of the consequences of our consumerism and make choices that cause less harm. It's not a black and white, either/or set of choices we're working with here, but more a question of worse/better or more harmful/less harmful.

One of the main areas in which we can make a difference is that of food. We're talking meat here. It's undeniable that meat-eating harms the animals that are killed for us. In addition a large amount of ecological damage is done in order to feed those animals. In the West, a hugely disproportionate amount of grain, soya beans, and water goes to feed cattle. This particular use of resources is highly wasteful. It takes a lot of grain and soya beans to make a pound of cow. It would be much more efficient if we cut out the animal and fed ourselves on plant proteins. It's perfectly simple, feasible, and healthy to do this. We might have to buy a recipe book or two to get some ideas about what to cook, but once we've done it we'll end up with a diet that is cheaper, probably more interesting and varied, and almost certainly healthier than one containing meat. (I go into these arguments in more detail in my book, *Vegetarianism*.)

If you don't think you can give up meat altogether, try cutting down. You might find that's a first step towards vegetarianism, or you might just stick there. Even if you go no further than cutting down, you'll have had some effect on reducing the amount of suffering in the world. Eating only organic meat would be another positive step.

> "Once we are aware of these consequences, we are faced with choices about how to respond."

Throughout our lives we're encouraged in many ways to dismiss the sufferings of animals as irrelevant or unimportant, or to think that animals have a pretty nice life on a farm. (The cartoon animals on food packaging are, rather improbably, always smiling.) Life on modern farms is actually stressful and painful. As a student, I worked on pig, dairy, and sheep farms, and saw at first hand how painful an animal's life can be. Its pain is as real as yours, perhaps in some ways worse, since animals do not have the consolations of philosophy.

If you're already a vegetarian you could consider becoming vegan, or just eating fewer eggs and dairy products. The production of milk and eggs also involves suffering. Vegetarianism and veganism are healthy dietry options for humans too. I've been a vegan for several years now and never felt healthier. I hardly ever get a cold (even when everyone else seems to be coming down with them) and any illness I do get passes very quickly.

Another step most of us can take is to eat more organic food (food grown without artificial fertilizers, insecticides, and weed killers). This has beneficial effects for the environment as well as our bodies, since artificial compounds can linger in the food chain for many years. It's more expensive to eat organic, but we can at least buy *some* organic food from time to time. Remember we're not talking black and white here; we're talking about degrees of suffering and harm that can be avoided.

You can look at other purchases you make. Where are your clothes manufactured? Are they produced in sweatshop conditions, or using child labour? If they are, you could write to that company and tell them you disapprove of their employment practices.

And then there is transportation, and the effect of carbon dioxide and other emissions. These are all things that we can think about. Perhaps we can car-share when possible, or take public transport, or cycle, or use a more fuel-efficient vehicle.

These are just a few suggestions of course. We are all different, and we can each look at our own lifestyle to consider the implications of the practice and cultivation of metta.

Metta and generosity

One of the most immediate implications of practising metta in daily life is that we become more generous. You don't need to think about generosity purely in terms of giving material goods or money. In fact, the traditional Buddhist approach is to see material gifts as just part of the picture. As well as material things we can give time and energy, we can give our attention, we can give thanks, we can give encouragement, we can give people the initiative. There is no limit to the ways in which we can be generous. We need to develop a spirit of generosity that expresses itself in many ways, and these are all ways of making ourselves available to help others. Walt Whitman wrote, 'Behold, I do not give lectures or a little charity. When I give, I give myself', and that statement perfectly sums up the spirit of giving through metta.

A greatly respected Tibetan lama called Dhardo Rimpoche, who founded a school in India for the children of Tibetan refugees, was once in the middle of an elaborate devotional ceremony. Tibetan devotional ceremonies can take a long time, and they involve chanting, playing musical instruments, and complex gestures, all of which have to be performed at exactly the right time. In the middle of this particular ceremony a child wandered into the room to ask for help with his homework. Many of us have found ourselves caught up in some task that involves a lot of concentration when we're suddenly interrupted. In such a situation it's hard to respond to the demand that's been put on us, and our response is often to dismiss the other person – perhaps unkindly – as if they're an obstacle to our happiness. But that's not what Dhardo Rimpoche did. Without a second thought, and in a graceful spirit of generosity, he stopped what he was doing, and turned to the child to help him. He didn't do this grudgingly; he gave it his full attention. To Rimpoche, helping a child with his homework was as important as a devotional ceremony. Perhaps we could even say that, for him, helping others *was* a form of devotional ceremony.

Giving our whole attention to someone is one of the highest gifts we can bestow. If you've ever had the experience of talking with someone who really knows how to listen, you'll know what I mean. There's something very affirming about having someone really listen to us. When it happens, we feel valued and consequently take ourselves more seriously. As a result, we're often able to learn a great deal about ourselves. Of course, this is something we can do for others as well; we can learn to become good listeners. The Mindfulness of Breathing meditation helps us to develop the skill of letting go distracting thoughts so that we can be more fully present for another person. The Metta Bhavana meditation helps us to value others more highly so that we want to give them our full attention.

"We have these choices, almost in every moment of every day: to take or to give, to act generously or to act selfishly."

We also need to be aware of the ways in which we tend to negate this kind of generosity. Sometimes we take someone's time and energy without due regard for whether they really want to be with us. We can take people for granted by not giving them praise. We can undermine people and take away their initiative and confidence by carelessly critical comments. We have these choices, almost in every moment of every day: to take or to give, to act generously or to act selfishly. With practice we become able to choose to act more generously.

Of course, our generosity towards others has to be balanced with nourishing ourselves. People sometimes go too far in terms of giving to others and neglect themselves. When we're giving in this way it generally comes out of a sense of guilt or lack of self-worth. In the long term, if we are going to sustain our generosity towards others, we have to make sure we have something to give, so we need to make sure we give ourselves time to reflect, rest, and play.

Over the next few days you might like to notice the ways in which you give (we often give without really thinking about it), and the ways in which you resist giving or perhaps even take unduly, in both the material and the non-material ways I've suggested above. Once you begin to notice a tendency to resist giving, or to take, just be aware there is a choice. You can often create a space in your experience into which a spirit of generosity can emerge, and then you can enjoy that sense of free generosity in which 'the gift is in the giving', where we have a sense that to give is to receive.

What *we* receive when we give in this way is a new sense of ourselves. We can experience the freedom and joy that comes from letting go of a constricting notion of ourselves – a misguided sense that in order to feel secure we have to hold on tightly to our possessions, our energy, and our time.

Honouring the truth

One powerful way of expressing metta towards ourselves and others is to practise truthful speech. There are certainly times when it's best to leave thoughts unspoken – we need to practise not only honesty, but also kindness. But one of the main kinds of truthful speech we need to practise in order to bring more metta into our lives is something very simple: when we've done something hurtful to another person we should be prepared to apologize or confess.

Apology means being honest with another person about something we've done to hurt or disappoint them. And when we're apologizing we're also being honest with ourselves. Have you noticed how we often rehearse lies and half-truths to ourselves? Have you ever done something like this? We're on our way to meet someone and we left a little too late to get there on time. Plus the traffic's heavy so we imagine ourselves saying that we're sorry we're late but, boy, was that traffic bad. Recognize this? We often construct little alternative realities for ourselves to hide our failings. So when we apologize (honestly) for being late we're not just telling the truth, we're also acknowledging to ourselves what the truth is. Some people construct such elaborate systems of alternative realities that they start to lose touch with reality altogether.

Apologizing involves letting go our defences and allowing ourselves to be seen as imperfect. And we're recognizing ourselves as imperfect as well; we're not pretending to be someone else. The act of apology is also profoundly reconciling. Because we've dropped our defences we've allowed the other person to forgive us. Together, apology and forgiveness are means of communication that bring us together with others in a deep way – a way based on a recognition that we are who we are and not actors pretending.

Often we'll avoid apologizing because we think, deep down, that apology makes us look small, whereas in fact it shows that we are big enough to admit to being wrong. And it's all right to apologize even when we haven't meant to do anything wrong, and sometimes even when someone has taken offence quite unreasonably. When we say we are sorry it doesn't necessarily mean we're admitting that we're at fault (though it can of course mean just that). Instead it can mean we are sorrowful the other person is upset, even if they've completely misinterpreted what we said or did. Apologizing in these circumstances can open a door to reconciliation in a way that a defensive 'that's not what I meant' never can. Once the other person has accepted our apology there will be time to explain what we really said or meant or did.

> **"Apology and forgiveness are means of communication that bring us together with others in a deep way."**

Confession is similar to apology, but not necessarily directed to the person we've offended. When we're confessing, we're being honest with a third party (and with ourselves, of course) about who we are and what we've done, but in essence we're standing in front of our ideals in a state of shame and honesty, admitting that we've fallen short of how we would like to behave.

It follows that it's only possible to confess to someone who shares our ideals. If, for example, you confessed you were contemplating an extra-marital affair to someone who actively encouraged you to go ahead and be unfaithful to your spouse, that wouldn't be very helpful for your ethical development. We should consider ourselves very lucky indeed if there is someone to whom we can confess in this way. We can consider ourselves blessed to have a friend in whom we can confide, who can keep confidences, and who shares our ethical perspective and won't let us off the hook.

We should also, in the spirit of metta, be prepared to forgive others when they apologize to us. To withhold forgiveness in order to hurt another person, or out of self-righteous anger, is an abuse of the other person's honesty and ethical sensitivity. We're hardly likely to encourage people to be honest with us if we punish them for it. Of course there may be times when we feel unable to forgive someone instantly. Genuine forgiveness can take time, and false forgiveness is not a virtue. But we should not withhold forgiveness out of anger or mean-spiritedness. We should give forgiveness as freely as we are able.

The power of appreciation

I've said already that speech should be not only honest, but also meant kindly. One of the most effective ways to be kind in our speech and to help others is to express appreciation. This is an excellent practice. We all tend to delete certain perceptions from our consciousness. When we have an enemy, we'll tend not to notice anything positive about them – we just concentrate on what we don't like.

We had a month-long process of ordinations during the four-month retreat on which I was ordained. One person would be ordained each night, and beforehand Suvajra, the retreat leader, would 'rejoice in merits'. This is a Buddhist tradition of celebrating someone's good qualities, so every night Suvajra had the task of finding positive things to say about the man who was about to become ordained.

I found it hard to like one or two people on that retreat. In fact there were things about them I disliked. I found myself wondering what on earth Suvajra would find to say about these people. He never had the slightest difficulty. Every night, without fail, he would spend up to half an hour celebrating the good qualities of the person about to be ordained, even those people in whom I hadn't appreciated such qualities.

The funny thing was that when he rejoiced in the merits of the one or two people I didn't get on with, I recognized that what he was saying was true. He'd say something complimentary and I'd think, yes, that's true, I had noticed that in an almost subliminal way; although I hadn't appreciated those good qualities, I had still dimly perceived them in a not-quite-conscious way. Suvajra's rejoicing in merits allowed me to bring those qualities into a more conscious part of my mind so that I could really see that person without the distorting filters and deletions that had kept them in my mind as a shadow of themselves.

So one of the benefits of appreciation is that it allows us to see others more fully. When we are prepared really to notice another person, we start to notice things about them that we were only dimly aware of before. I know from my own experience that I sometimes underrate myself. Sometimes I delete an awareness of my own positive qualities, and when someone rejoices in my merits, I am forced to see myself in a more positive light, then I can begin to value those positive qualities in myself and begin to nurture them. If I find appreciation so useful, why should I deny it to others?

Having your own positive qualities reflected back at you can, paradoxically, be very painful. Sometimes we find it hard to accept that we are not worthless. It can be hard to be made aware of qualities which we then have to live up to. So notice times when you are resistant to the positive perceptions of others. Beware of false modesty and shrugging off the compliments.

Without appreciation, our positive qualities must struggle to grow, and even to survive. The same is true of other people. The more appreciation we express, the more likely it is that we will create a climate of appreciation in which we will ourselves flourish. But giving appreciation so that we will get some back is not the point. If we're acting from metta we shouldn't be concerned with what we get back. In the same spirit of metta, though, we should not be afraid to ask for appreciation when we feel we need it. We are all worthy of appreciation.

Creating harmony: 'seek to understand ...'

Steven Covey, in his excellent book, *The Seven Habits of Highly Effective People*, highlights the value of seeking to understand others before we seek to make them understand our own point of view.

Have you ever seen two people arguing although they are agreeing with each other? They might have a different emphasis in the way they say things, or express themselves slightly differently, yet they are arguing as if they have completely polarized and irreconcilable differences. What's going on here? They are often so intent on getting the other person to accept their point of view that they are not really listening to them at all. They're often arguing against what they *think* the other person is saying rather than against what they actually *are* saying.

> **"**To have a genuine dialogue with another person, we have to respect them.**"**

Of course, when there is a real difference of opinion it can be even worse; we demonize the other person and their point of view. This happens all the time in the great debates about religion, abortion, divorce, drugs, and so on.

To have a genuine dialogue with another person, we have to respect them. We shouldn't assume they hold a particular point of view because they are stupid or unfortunate enough not to have heard our opinion. They almost certainly have a complete set of reasons for believing and acting as they do. If we want to engage effectively in discussion with them we have to be prepared to listen carefully to what they have to say, and respectfully ask questions that tease out their reasoning. It may well be that their views are self-contradictory on some level, or based on misinformation, but again, these things have to be respectfully pointed out, and with the awareness that there are probably glaring inconsistencies in our own position that they can help *us* to see.

When you find you've become embroiled in an argument, ask, 'Do we want to resolve this, or do we want to win?' The idea of winning derives from an ego-based and highly deluded view that our happiness is best served by getting our own way even at the cost of upsetting others. In fact, we're generally most happy when we get what we want and remain in harmony with others. Winning makes this impossible; winning often means losing.

We should never assume we have all the answers. If instead we start with the assumption that we have a viewpoint which is partly true and partly untrue, we can see those with whom we have disagreements as partners in a joint exploration of the truth, not enemies that have to be bludgeoned by our views.

Of course this is not easy; a lot of the time we'll fail, but anything that is worth doing involves a lot of learning by trial and error. That in itself should remind us to practise humility in our disagreements with others.

Metta and insight

Metta can play a part in the development of wisdom, or insight. I'm quite sure you've already learned some useful things about relating to yourself and others while you've been learning this beautiful meditation. We can learn, for example, that emotions are something we can cultivate. For many people this can be a major insight. We can learn that whether or not somebody is our enemy depends largely on how we relate to them.

But the practice of metta can also fundamentally alter our attitudes and understandings about our relationship with the world. For example, have you ever had an argument with someone entirely in the privacy of your own head? I'm sure you're familiar with that experience, but have you ever wondered who it is you're arguing with? Most of us never get that far in our analysis, but let's do it now. It's obviously not the other person you're arguing with, since they're probably not present, and even if they are it's not the external version of them you're having the argument with. The only conclusion you can reach is that it's yourself you are arguing with. One part of your mind (which you identify as yourself) and another part of your mind (which manifests as an internal representation of your enemy) are locked in a fight. The 'real' enemy isn't involved at all. (It's interesting to ask who, if anyone, wins these arguments, but I'll leave you to figure that out for yourself.)

Let's think about this a bit more. There you are, having an argument with yourself, although you think you're arguing with another person because you're (in a way) hallucinating. In fact we often live in a state of 'hallucination', in which we confuse what's going on in our heads with what is going on in the outside world. Does this kind of internal argument have effects on the outside world and on the enemy? Not directly perhaps, but it certainly does indirectly. After one of these arguments we may well be in a bad mood, and take it out on innocent people like our friends and family. Of course if we meet our enemy we'll almost certainly have a worse relationship with them because of the ill will we've generated. To some extent, the enemy can be another one of those innocent people. They have been away minding their own business, then we inflict the negative mental states we have generated in an argument with ourselves – on them.

So what can we learn from this? We could learn just the simple fact of this dynamic, that we cultivate emotions internally and they have an effect on the outside world. But a more profound reflection is to begin questioning the very nature of the distinction between our inner and outer worlds. What happens inside us affects our perception of the outside world and the people in it. In the example above, I suggested we might develop a bad mood because of internal arguments. As a result of that bad mood we might assume that everyone is out to make our lives difficult. (It's childish, I know, but that's how we act a lot of the time.) And as I've pointed out, our inner argument directly affects how we perceive our enemy – perhaps it even creates the very perception of having an enemy – and then affects how we relate to them.

"The notion of separate internal and external worlds doesn't hold up to scrutiny."

At the same time, we tend to see a sharp distinction between 'inside' and 'outside'. It's a distinction that seems so natural that we rarely, if ever, question it. Yet we've seen that the notion of separate internal and external worlds doesn't hold up to scrutiny. The outside world is really a product of our subjective states meeting the objective pole of our experience. Sometimes when we're sitting in meditation (or even walking in meditation) this distinction between inner and outer begins to blur. We start to have a sense that there is less of a sharp distinction between these two worlds, to see in fact that they are really one world which we unconsciously split in two.

This can happen in the Metta Bhavana. While cultivating metta we are learning to widen our sense of ourselves. We're leaving behind the narrow sense of ourselves that assumes the best way to be happy is to look mainly, or even solely, after our own interests. Yet in the Metta Bhavana we soon learn that we are at our happiest and most fulfilled when we take other people into account by wishing them well. This change in our perspective is just the beginning of what can be a complete transformation in the way we see ourselves.

Most of us have mixed feelings about the term 'selflessness'. We might associate it with an ascetic self-denial, or with self-hatred. But the experience of metta teaches us that there is a loving, joyful, and deeply fulfilling way to experience a dissolving of our narrow sense. Rather than seeing selflessness as a diminution of what we are, we might more accurately see it as a broadening and expansion of ourselves – an expansion that has, in theory, no limit.

The Metta Bhavana is part of the path to complete liberation from limiting assumptions, views, emotions, and behaviours. In Buddhist terms this practice can culminate in the attainment of spiritual awakening, or Enlightenment. This might not be your own personal goal in life, but in the spirit of metta I wish you well on your journey of self-discovery into the rich inner world, and hope you find the happiness and fulfilment that is your inherent and natural potential.

The Buddha's words on metta

This is what ought to be done by one who is skilled in discerning what is good, who has understood the path to peace.

He should be able, upright, and straightforward, of good speech, gentle, and free from pride,

Contented, easily satisfied, having few duties, living simply, of controlled senses, prudent, without pride and attachment to clan.

Let him not do the slightest thing for which the wise might rebuke him, instead thinking, 'May all beings be well and safe. May they be at ease.

'Whatever living beings there may be, whether moving or standing still, without exception, whether large, great, middling, or small, whether tiny or substantial,

'Whether seen or unseen, whether living near or far, born or unborn; may all beings be happy.

'Let none deceive or despise another anywhere. Let none wish harm to another, in anger or in hate.'

Just as a mother would guard her child, her only child, with her own life, even so let him cultivate a boundless mind for all beings in the world.

Let him cultivate a boundless love for all beings in the world, above, below, and across, unhindered, without ill will or enmity.

Standing, walking, seated, or lying down, free from torpor, he should as far as possible fix his attention on this recollection. This, they say, is the divine life, right here.

Not falling into false opinions, virtuous and endowed with vision, having abandoned sensuous greed, he surely is never again reborn.

References

1   Gary Snyder, *The Practice of the Wild*, North Point Press, New York, 1990, p.24

2   Ibid., p.16

3   Ibid., p.10

4   Oliver Goldsmith, *The Good-Natured Man*, BiblioBazaar, Cambridge, Mass., 2009, p.91

5   John Butler Yeats, *J.B.Yeats' Letters to His Son W.B.Yeats and Others 1869–1922*, E.P. Dutton & Co., 1946, p.121

6   Letter from Vincent van Gogh to Theo van Gogh, 22 October 1882, from The Complete Letters of Vincent van Gogh, Bulfinch, 1991

7   G.K. Chesterton, *What's Wrong with the World*, Oxford University Press, 2002

8   David Whyte, *The Heart Aroused*, Doubleday, New York 1996, p.25

9   Yeshe Tsogyal, *The Life and Liberation of Padmasambhava*, Dharma Publishing, Berkeley 1978, p.635

10 Thich Nhat Hanh has written several books on walking meditation. This verse is taken from *The Blooming of a Lotus*, Beacon Press, Boston 1993, p.21.

11 Washington Matthews (tr.), *Navaho Myths, Prayers, and Songs*, Forgotten Books, Berkeley 2008, pp.39–40

12 David Whyte, *The Heart Aroused*, op. cit., p.87

Further Reading

Henepola Gunaratana, *Mindfulness in Plain English*, Wisdom Publications, Somerville MA 2002

Jinananda, *Meditating*, Windhorse Publications, Birmingham 2000

Jon Kabat-Zinn, *Full Catastrophe Living*, Dell Publications, New York 1990

Jon Kabat-Zinn, *Wherever You Go, There You Are*, Hyperion, New York 1994

Kamalashila, *Meditation: The Buddhist Path of Insight and Tranquillity*, Windhorse Publications, Birmingham 1996

Ayya Khema, *Come and See For Yourself*, Windhorse Publications, Birmingham 2002

Ayya Khema, *Who Is Myself?*, Wisdom Books, Boston MA 1997

Paramananda, *Change Your Mind*, Windhorse Publications, Birmingham 1996

Larry Rosenberg, *Breath by Breath*, Shambhala, Boston MA 1999

Sharon Salzberg, *Lovingkindness*, Shambhala, Boston & London 2002

Index

Windhorse Publications is a Buddhist publishing house, staffed by practising Buddhists. We place great emphasis on producing books of high quality which are accessible and relevant to those interested in Buddhism at whatever level. Drawing on the whole range of the Buddhist tradition, our books include translations of traditional texts, commentaries, books that make links with Western culture and ways of life, biographies of Buddhists, and works on meditation.

As a charitable institution we welcome donations to help us continue our work. We also welcome manuscripts on aspects of Buddhism or meditation. To join our mailing list, place an order, or request a catalogue please visit our website at www.windhorsepublications.com or contact:

Windhorse Publications Ltd.
169 Mill Road
Cambridge CB1 3AN
UK

Perseus Distribution
1094 Flex Drive
Jackson TN 38301
USA

Windhorse Books
PO Box 574
Newtown NSW 2042
Australia

Windhorse Publications is an arm of the Triratna Buddhist Community, which has more than sixty centres on five continents. Through these centres, members of the Triratna Buddhist Community offer regular programmes of events for the general public and for more experienced students. These include meditation classes, public talks, study on Buddhist themes and texts, and bodywork classes such as t'ai chi, yoga, and massage. Triratna also run several retreat centres and the Karuna Trust, a fundraising charity that supports social welfare projects in the slums and villages of Southern Asia.

Many Triratna centres have residential spiritual communities and ethical businesses associated with them. Arts activities are encouraged too, as is the development of strong bonds of friendship between people who share the same ideals. In this way Triratna is developing a unique approach to Buddhism, not simply as a set of techniques, but as a creatively directed way of life for people living in the modern world.

If you would like more information about Triratna please visit www.thebuddhistcentre.org or write to:

London Buddhist Centre	Aryaloka	Sydney Buddhist Centre
51 Roman Road	14 Heartwood Circle	24 Enmore Road
London	Newmarket	Sydney
E2 0HU	NH 03857	NSW 2042
UK	USA	Australia

Also by this author

Guided Meditation CD led by Bodhipaksa
This audio CD contains three guided meditations:

❖ The Mindfulness of Breathing (27:12)
❖ The Metta Bhavana (development of loving-kindness) (26:50)
❖ Walking meditation (19:48)

Ideal for newcomers to meditation, the CD will guide you through the most fundamental Buddhist meditation practices.

Available from www.windhorsepublications.com in the UK and from www.wildmind.org/bookstore worldwide.

£13/$14.95

Vegetarianism
by Bodhipaksa
How does what we eat affect us and our world? Is there a connection between vegetarianism and living a spiritual life? Doesn't HH the Dalai Lama eat meat?

A trained vet, respected teacher and happy vegetarian, Bodhipaksa answers all of these questions and more. Tackling issues such as genetically modified vegetables and modern ways of producing food he dispels widespread myths and reflects upon the diets dominant in the contemporary West. In comparison, he considers the diets of wandering monks in Ancient India and the diet of the Buddha himself.

By considering why people eat meat and relating this to Buddhist ethics he explores habits and the possibility of change. He takes a positive view of the benefits of vegetarianism, and shows practically, how to maintain a healthy and balanced vegan or vegetarian lifestyle.

This exploration shows how a meat-free life can not only lighten the body but also the soul.

ISBN 9781 899579 96 9
£7.99/$13.95/€9.95
104 pages

Also from Windhorse Publications

The Art of Reflection
by Ratnaguna
Explaining and exploring the place of reflection in the Buddhist life Ratnaguna offers practical and specific advice on how to go about reflection as a spiritual practice.

With the help of many sources from within and outside the Buddhist tradition, he seeks prove the great value of reflection – not just as a part of life but as a way of reminding oneself of life's true meaning, a 'deepening of the self'.

Ratnaguna's many years of Buddhist practice shine through his words, while his warm, straightforward and encouraging style is sure to engage and inspire any reader, whatever their own level of experience.

ISBN 9781 899579 89 1
£9.99/$16.95/€11.95
160 pages

Buddhism: Tools for Living Your Life
by Vajragupta
Buddhism: Tools for Living Your Life is a guide for those seeking a meaningful spiritual path in busy – and often hectic – lives. An experienced teacher of Buddhism and meditation, Vajragupta provides clear explanations of the main Buddhist teachings, as well as a variety of exercises designed to help readers develop or deepen their practice.

ISBN 9781 899579 74 7
£10.99/$16.95/€16.95
192 pages